Civic Engagements

Civic Engagements

*The Citizenship Practices of Indian
and Vietnamese Immigrants*

Caroline B. Brettell and Deborah Reed-Danahay

Stanford University Press
Stanford, California

Stanford University Press
Stanford, California

©2012 by the Board of Trustees of the Leland Stanford Junior University. All rights reserved.

Printed in the United States of America on acid-free, archival-quality paper

Library of Congress Cataloging-in-Publication Data

Brettell, Caroline, author.
 Civic engagements : the citizenship practices of Indian and Vietnamese immigrants / Caroline B. Brettell and Deborah Reed-Danahay.
    pages cm
 Includes bibliographical references and index.
 ISBN 978-0-8047-7528-1 (cloth : alk. paper)--ISBN 978-0-8047-7529-8 (pbk. : alk. paper)
 1. East Indian Americans--Political activity--Texas. 2. Vietnamese Americans--Political activity--Texas. 3. East Indian Americans--Texas--Societies, etc. 4. Vietnamese Americans--Texas--Societies, etc. 5. Immigrants--Political activity--United States--Case studies. 6. Immigrants--United States--Societies, etc.--Case studies. I. Reed-Danahay, Deborah, author. II. Title.
 F395.E2B74 2012
 323.1191'40764--dc22   2011015777

Typeset by Bruce Lundquist in 10/14 Minion

Contents

Preface and Acknowledgements

This book is the result of a five-year research and writing collaboration that began in 2005. At the time we were both living in the Dallas-Arlington-Fort Worth (DFW) area, before Deborah moved to Buffalo, New York, in the summer of 2006. Before our respective moves to Texas, we had known each other for several years through our mutual interests in the anthropology of Europe and the anthropological study of narrative. When we started this project, Deborah had just published a book on Pierre Bourdieu's work and was completing some other work on education and the European Union and on rural French narratives. Caroline was ending her involvement in a large interdisciplinary collaborative project on immigration in the DFW region that was launched in 2001 with funding from the National Science Foundation (NSF). We were both at the point of deciding what to do next. In some discussions, Caroline expressed interest in doing a more ethnographic study of immigration than her previous one and in addressing, with an anthropological eye, some dimensions of the political incorporation of new immigrants. Together we developed a plan for an ethnographic study of the civic engagement of Asian immigrants in DFW, with Caroline bringing her expertise in studies of immigration in Canada, Europe, and the United States, and Deborah bringing her expertise in political anthropology and anthropology and education, in addition to perspectives from her prior work on internal migration in France. Although Deborah had not previously conducted any work on immigrants in the DFW region, she had supervised thesis work on refugees and was serving on the advisory board of a refugee agency in Fort Worth. Because Caroline had already worked closely with Indians in the broader DFW-area immigration project, she decided to choose that group for her focus. Because of Deborah's background in the anthropology of France and her familiarity with the history of Vietnam through studies of French colonialism, it seemed a good fit for her to work with the Vietnamese population. These two groups were also the largest Asian newcomer groups in this region of Texas.

We developed grant proposals, targeting in particular the Russell Sage Foundation by responding to their call for proposals. We are profoundly grateful for the three years of funding provided by this foundation. Without it we could not have completed the work.

In the introduction to this book, we discuss our research methods. Here we touch on the collaborative dimensions of research and writing, something rare for anthropologists, who are often more comfortable as lone ethnographers in the field. At the end of this preface we speak in our separate voices to acknowledge those who have supported us in this work.

Our collaboration in writing began when we drafted the grant proposals to launch the research. Our technique, which continued as we worked on the book, involved initial discussions on what needed to be done, how we might approach the work conceptually, and what would be the division of labor and the timetable for task completion. As we started to write the book, we met together in Dallas, often at Caroline's house, when Deborah was back in town to finish up her research among the Vietnamese. We had developed the research project jointly and we kept in touch during the work as we went into different phases of it, but essentially we worked on parallel tracks and therefore needed to meet toward the end of each phase and see what our findings had been and how we could develop our comparisons. This was an evolving process, as we both sifted through our notes, interviews, and secondary sources. As is typical in ethnographic studies, much of the substantial information we each collected did not make its way into this book, so we are each also publishing some of the work separately.

In the middle of completing the research and beginning the book, we were invited to present our work at a Russell Sage conference on immigration and civic engagement organized by Karthick Ramakrishnan and Irene Bloemraad. We want to express our gratitude to them for providing us with this early opportunity to begin writing together. Our paper from this conference was published in Ramakrishnan and Bloemraad (2008a) and also became the foundation for Chapter Four of this book. At about the same time, we organized a session for the annual meeting of the American Anthropological Association that focused on processes of political engagement and citizenship among immigrants in Europe and the United States. This session resulted in the book *Citizenship, Political Engagement, and Belonging* (Reed-Danahay and Brettell 2008a). We are grateful to all of the authors who contributed to that book for their excellent work and for the lively exchange of ideas that the project generated.

Once the research was completed and we had decided on an outline of chapters for the current book, we developed a modus operandi for writing. One of us would start a section of whatever we were writing and then pass it to the other for further work—which often included inserting material from her research, adding to the literature review, or further developing a conceptual framework or argument. The chapters in this book have been handed back and forth so many times that we have lost count of all the versions, but there have been at least ten for each chapter! Our original plan for the book was also revised and shaped through this back and forth process. Sometimes, writing together involved compromises between different styles and ways of thinking (when one of us would need to open up to the other's point of view on a particular approach), but many times our exchanges would take the form of appreciation for the other's insights that enriched the growth of the book and the formulation of key arguments. Sometimes one person's way of framing an argument stimulated the other to go back to her data and rethink it, all with the goal of developing the comparisons and producing a better and more unified book.

We spent an entire day at the American Anthropological Association meetings one year working side by side and reviewing a complete draft with critical eyes. The next year we met again to review and edit a second draft. The process took much longer than we had expected because of the challenges of writing with one voice and producing rigorous and balanced comparisons. We are both very grateful to external reviewers of this manuscript for the suggestions and critiques that helped us to produce the final version. We also want to thank Stanford University Press and, in particular, Joa Suorez, for her commitment to this project and for her excellent editorial guidance along the way. It has been a true pleasure to work with her.

Essential to the writing of this book was mutual respect for each other's intellect and ethnographic skills, as well as respect about time and honoring the deadlines to which we had agreed. Our shared commitment to the project sustained us during the months of writing and revision. We are grateful to one another but we each have other people to thank.

Caroline

My previous work with immigration, both ethnographic and historical, has been largely centered on the Portuguese in Canada, France, the United States, and Portugal itself. Only when I undertook the NSF-funded project on new immigration to the DFW area did I begin to learn about India and Indian patterns of emigration. There was, of course, some connection between India and Portugal, centered on the small territory of Goa, which was held as a Portuguese colony until 1961. My early work with Indians in the Dallas area, as well as an invitation to a wedding in Chennai, piqued my interest in traveling to India. In the fall of 2004, I made what became a personally transformative trip to Southern India, a trip that included visits with the family members of a few people I had met in Dallas. I have developed a deep and profound respect for Indian culture and I am humbled by what I still do not know. I am also humbled by those Indians who have left a country they love and family members (especially elderly parents) whom they miss to travel halfway around the world in search of new opportunities for themselves and their children. Therefore, I would first like to acknowledge and profoundly thank all the Indian immigrants I have come to know during the course of this research. They have been so generous with their time, their insights, and their friendship. I cannot list them by name but they know who they are.

I am also grateful to three students at Southern Methodist University (SMU) who helped with various phases of the research for this project, most particularly Faith Nibbs, a graduate student in anthropology who is becoming an excellent young scholar of migration; Rachel Ball, an SMU undergraduate who is currently pursuing a doctorate in Indian history at Boston College; and Marianne Ebrahim, an anthropology major who has taken her passion for the field into her career in medicine. One of the pleasures of being a university professor is working with young people, teaching them as they teach you. In all three cases, this is what has occurred.

My colleagues in the Department of Anthropology at SMU have always provided me with a stimulating environment in which to work. I want to mention in particular Robert Van Kemper and David Meltzer, successive chairs of my department during this project. They were supportive with travel funds to attend meetings where some of this work was presented, and in myriad other ways. Outside my department I would particularly like to thank Steve Lindquist, a member of the SMU Department of Religious Studies and a specialist on Hindu traditions; and Manju Bansal, who for many years taught Hindi on our campus. For two years during this research I served as dean ad interim of the

College of Humanities and Sciences. Juggling those obligations with the obligations of completing the research and launching the writing was challenging. I could not have done it without the support of Lenda Callaway, administrative assistant to the dean, and Cal Jillson, associate dean. I would also like to thank Pamela Hogan, administrative assistant in the Department of Anthropology at SMU, who brightens each and every day and takes care of the many details that are always associated with managing grants and producing manuscripts. Among colleagues around the country I would particularly like to thank Nancy Foner, Donna Gabaccia, and Nina Glick Schiller—fellow scholars of migration whom I have known for a long time, whose work I find continually stimulating, and whose opinions I value.

Finally I would like to thank my husband, Richard Brettell. Rick is an art historian who specializes in nineteenth-century French painting. India is remote for him but he has been a true partner in this research, traveling with me to India in 2004 and attending some of the events in the DFW area just because he wanted to. On one occasion he even lent his pianistic skills to a Christmas celebration at a local Mar Thoma church. He has also decided that Indian kurtas are very sensible clothing in the Dallas heat. Rick may study things, but he loves people and is thus an anthropological spouse par excellence!

Deborah

Conducting this research and writing this book has been a very rewarding experience for me and I am grateful for all that I have learned about the experiences, beliefs, and history of Vietnamese refugees and their children in the United States. It has often been painful to hear of their personal struggles during and after the Vietnam War, but I have taken some comfort in their resilience. My previous ethnographic work has focused on France and Europe, and I had never thought of doing work with Vietnamese refugees before Caroline and I started our discussions, although I had come in contact with their experiences indirectly. My first direct encounter with Vietnamese American experience came just about one year before I started this research, when a student in one of my seminars wrote an autobiographical essay about his identity as a Vietnamese American. This laid the groundwork for my understanding of the conflicting issues of identity that this population faces, and I thank this student for also inviting me to attend an event at a Vietnamese martial arts center during my research.

My acknowledgements are many. I am grateful to my research participants for their generosity of spirit and for sharing their time and experiences with me.

I regret that I cannot name many of them specifically, due to the need to pre-serve their anonymity and privacy, but they will know who they are when they read these words of thanks. My wonderful ethnographic research assistants, Ton Quynh Anh and Le My Linh, helped in innumerable ways. Both Quynh Anh and Linh are now training to be pharmacists, but their ethnographic sensibili-ties and willingness to learn anthropological methods are awesome. They also taught me so much in return. I also thank Serena Do and Kelly Dinh for their help with this project. Marilyn Koble offered superb assistance with the initial research, including the group interviews, and with getting all the research mate-rials organized and the entire project under way; and Bethany Hawkins helped input data from the parent interview materials. More recently, Irene Ketonen has been an invaluable assistant in the final stages of preparing the manuscript, including her help in editing and formatting our bibliography.

My ethnographic research was conducted while I taught at the University of Texas at Arlington and at Buffalo State College (BSC). I particularly want to thank the State University of New York Research Foundation at BSC for their help when I brought the grant to New York. The book was completed after I moved to a position as professor in the Department of Anthropology at the State University of New York at Buffalo, which provides a stimulating intel-lectual climate in which to work and write, and where I have been given the opportunity to present some of this research at forums sponsored by the Asian Studies Program and the Baldy Center for Law and Social Policy, for which I thank Kristin Stapleton and Rebecca French. My work on the Vietnamese benefited from a workshop on citizenship and immigration held in New Delhi, India, and sponsored by the Department of Sociology at the University of Delhi School of Economics, and I thank my dear friend Meenakshi Thapan for inviting me. That presentation has resulted in a book chapter (Reed-Danahay 2010). The working group on sociality in which I have taken part over the past few years and to which I have presented some of my work on Vietnamese Americans and communities of practice has also provided a supportive cli-mate in which to develop my ideas. I thank, in particular, my colleagues Vered Amit, Sally Anderson, John Postill, and Philip Moore for fruitful discussions during the workshop held at the University at Buffalo. I am also grateful to the Department of Anthropology at the University of Rochester, especially Bob Foster and Eleana Kim, for inviting me to speak about my work. In the sum-mer of 2010, as the writing of the book was coming to a close, I was invited to be a Gambrinus Fellow at Dortmund University of Technology in Germany and a visiting scholar at Trinity College Dublin in Ireland, where I was able to further develop my perspective on the research through encounters with new audiences. I thank Juergen Kramer and Daniel Faas for inviting me to their campuses and giving me these opportunities.

Friends and family are important in helping one sustain the momentum of such a large undertaking and I appreciate the support I have received at crucial times from several people very close to me who will know who they are. My children, Emily and Ian, never cease to amaze me and I dedicate my work on this book to them with love.

Caroline B. Brettell, Dallas, Texas
Deborah Reed-Danahay, Buffalo, New York

Civic Engagements

Introduction

ON SUNDAY, JANUARY 2, 2005, two stories relevant to the topic of this book appeared in the *Dallas Morning News*. One, titled "From Saigon to the Texas House," reported on the election of the first Vietnamese American legislator in Texas, Hubert Vo (Graszyk 2005). Vo was elected to the Texas House by a slim margin of only thirty-three votes to represent District 149 in Houston.[1] He had arrived in the United States in 1975 as a refugee and moved from being a busboy, a cook, an assembly-line worker, and a goldsmith to being a computer company owner and real estate developer. The other story, titled "India Group Rallies to Help Its Devastated Homeland," reported on a candlelight vigil sponsored by the India Association of North Texas for the victims of the December 26, 2004, tsunami (Langton 2005). At the event, $20,000 was raised, and plans were laid to collect much more within the coming months. But the story, with its subheading of "charity, culture at core of association aiming to raise $500,000," also reported on a host of other service and cultural activities sponsored by this organization. "Our goal," one official was quoted as saying, "is to keep the community from India involved." These two stories, both of which appeared in the early stages of our research, illustrate the growing presence of new Asian immigrants in the public sphere. This presence is particularly noteworthy in Texas, a state associated most often with Latino immigration.

How do newcomers to the United States learn to become civically engaged? How is this process related to their understandings of what it means to be an American citizen? And where are the sociocultural spaces in which immigrants and their children can begin to participate in the wider public sphere? These questions guide our comparative study of civic engagement among two quite distinct Asian immigrant populations—Indians and Vietnamese.[2] This book is based on ethnographic research done in the Dallas-Arlington-Fort Worth (henceforth DFW) metropolitan area in Texas. Although this region has rapidly become a new gateway for immigrants (Brettell 2008b), it is relatively under-researched compared to cities with a longer history of immigration such as New York and Los Angeles.[3]

Indians and Vietnamese are the two largest Asian immigrant populations in Texas and they rank third and fourth, respectively, among all foreign-born immigrants in DFW. Both groups have experienced growth in north Texas since 1990. It may seem unusual to pair a group from Southeast Asia with one from South Asia.[4] Certainly the differences between Indian and Vietnamese immigrants are striking in terms of their historical and cultural backgrounds, migration patterns, English language skills, socioeconomic status, and connections to homeland politics. We have found much common ground, however, in the ways in which these groups practice forms of civic engagement and learn to "become" American while simultaneously reinforcing a strong sense of their own ethnic identities. Indeed, they share complex and sometimes ambivalent views about becoming and being American and about what it means to be a citizen.

We focus in this book on how these "new" immigrants participate in the public sphere and hence become citizens, not only in the legal sense but also socially and culturally, through various forms of civic engagement.[5] We define *civic engagement* as the process by which individuals enter into and act within civic spaces to address issues of public concern. It involves not only actions but also knowledge about how to participate, and a sense of belonging that motivates people to become engaged. In this book we use the term *civic engagement* interchangeably with *participatory citizenship*.[6] We differentiate between *formal* and *informal* civic engagement in order to distinguish between participation in the political process (such as voting, running for office, and so on) and participation in other spheres (such as voluntary associations and religious institutions).[7] This contrast is illustrated by the stories presented earlier about Hubert Vo, an elected official who participates directly in the formal political system, and the candlelight vigil organized by an Indian immigrant association, which represents a more informal mode of participation. Our emphasis in this book is on the less formal spheres of civic engagement and on the similarities in how Vietnamese and Indian immigrants participate in these spheres.

Civic Engagement and Participatory Citizenship

Civic engagement as a form of participatory citizenship is related to contemporary approaches to citizenship, a concept with multiple dimensions. Citizenship is commonly related to the notion of "belonging" to the polity (Cohen 1982; Castles and Davidson 2000; Fortier 2000) and membership in some civil community (Brubaker 1989), but it is also connected to informal and symbolic processes that are enacted in the *public sphere*—that realm between the private sphere and the sphere of governmental institutions (Habermas 1989). In this book we use *public sphere, civic sphere*, and *civic space* interchangeably to refer to arenas of discursive relationships and collective practice. As our recent edited collection (Reed-Danahay and Brettell 2008a) demonstrates, immigrants to different countries and from different homelands negotiate their own senses of belonging and their own paths to civic engagement and participation.[8]

Many social theorists distinguish between legal citizenship and forms of participatory citizenship. Étienne Balibar (1988: 724), for example, differentiates between citizenship in its "strict sense"—"the full exercise of political rights"—and in its "broad sense"—"cultural initiative or effective presence in the public sphere (the capacity to be 'listened to' there)."[9] Taking this further, Renato Rosaldo and William V. Flores (1997) suggest that immigrants frequently draw on forms of cultural expression to claim recognition and political rights. They label this approach *cultural citizenship,* defining it as "the right to be different (in terms of race, ethnicity, or native language) with respect to the norms of the dominant national community, without compromising one's right to belong, in the sense of participating in the nation-state's democratic processes" (57). Cultural citizenship, as articulated by Rosaldo (1994: 252), takes into account what he terms "vernacular notions of citizenship"—that is, the claiming of distinctive and special rights, representation, and modes of cultural autonomy that are different from official or unitary models of citizenship.[10] The premise of cultural citizenship is that it can accommodate "multicultural conceptions of political belonging" (Baker and Shryock 2009: 11).[11] And as Kathleen Coll (2010: 6) has recently pointed out, it also draws attention to how people experience and practice citizenship in their everyday lives. Cultural citizenship, as a form of participatory citizenship, is critical to any exploration of processes of civic engagement among immigrant newcomers.

The concept of *social citizenship* is another widely discussed dimension of participatory citizenship. T. H. Marshall (1964) originally defined it as full social inclusion in a society—that is, as having the social rights that accompany civil and political rights.[12] Gerard Delanty (2002: 60), who criticized Marshall for neglecting "the substantive dimension" of social citizenship, has suggested (2003: 602) that "citizenship is not entirely about rights or membership of a polity, but is a matter of participation in the political community and begins early in life. It concerns the learning of a capacity for action and for responsibility." Nina Glick Schiller and Ayşe Çağlar (2008: 205), along similar lines, define social citizenship as the process whereby individuals "assert rights to citizenship substantively through social practice rather than through law." In this book, we build on these recent approaches, focusing in particular on how people learn to exercise the responsibilities of citizenship as they define them. Thus our formulation of participatory citizenship, which encompasses ideas about both cultural and social citizenship, implies that citizenship is not simply a matter of rights granted to immigrants by the nation-state, but also entails forms of participation claimed and enacted by immigrants themselves in order to establish belonging.[13]

Legal citizenship, and hence the extension of the right to belong, is not only about inclusion but also involves processes of exclusion based on race and gender. Asian immigrants, along with women and African Americans, have historically not been treated equally with regard to access to citizenship—even though the fourteenth amendment to the U.S. Constitution, ratified in 1868, defines all persons born or naturalized in the United States as citizens of the country as well as of the state wherein they reside, thereby guaranteeing them equal protection under the law. Racial constructions of citizenship became most apparent in the 1920s when several groups of Asian origin, including Japanese, Filipinos, and those of the Hindu faith, were declared by the Supreme Court to be nonwhite and thereby ineligible for citizenship (Kerber 1997: 843).[14] As legal scholar Leti Volpp (2001) has noted, Asian Americans continue to live under a shadow regarding their loyalty to the United States, and racial exclusion therefore continues to shape their experiences as citizens even though they are no longer excluded from legal status (naturalization) as citizens.[15] Noting that "citizenship has served as a proxy for race" (66), particularly for Chinese and Japanese Americans, Volpp, who underscores the notion of citizenship as identity and solidarity, suggests that discourse about the citizenship of Asian Americans "refers to people's collective experience of themselves, their affective ties to identification and solidarity" (58). Despite recent attempts to tease out the relationship between forms of identity and notions of citizenship, we find it analytically useful to emphasize that citizenship is an aspect of identity and not easily separable from it.[16] We therefore devote the second chapter of this book to a discussion of how Vietnamese and Indian immigrants in DFW perceive their own identities, including as Americans, or hyphenated Americans, as well as how they respond to how they may be identified by others. We view these identities as critical to an understanding of how immigrants enter the public sphere and become civically engaged.

Becoming a naturalized citizen does not necessarily obviate participation in the sending society, and immigrants often develop a dual sense of belonging.[17] Wong and Pantoja (2009: 266) have explored the relationship between civic engagement and naturalization among Asians in the United States and have hypothesized that "Asian immigrants who are civically engaged are more likely to become U.S. citizens *ceteris paribus.*"[18] However, they conclude from their survey research that "being active in politics of the home country is associated negatively with naturalization" (268). We did not find this to be the case among the Vietnamese and Indians in the DFW region, and we suggest that ethnographic research can help illuminate more nuanced understandings of naturalization and its relationship to civic engagement. Recent studies of citizenship, often informed by ethnographic research, take into account a changing terrain of geographic mobility and mass communication that enhances immigrant groups' continued attachment to their homelands. They describe simultaneous participation in citizenship practices both within and across the borders of nation-states—practices that constitute expressions of transnational identity. Ties to the homeland can enhance immigrant political participation, as has been demonstrated by research on a number of immigrant populations both in the United States and abroad.[19] Although the main focus of our research is not these transnational aspects of civic engagement but rather the practice of citizenship in the United States, we take seriously the role of what anthropologist Lok C. D. Siu (2005) calls the "third space" of diaspora, that is, the space between the past and life in the homeland, and the present and life in the new country.

Refugees and Immigrants, Displacement and Emplacement

Scholars have generally accepted the division between immigrants (such as Indians) as economic migrants seeking a higher standard of living, and refugees (such as the Vietnamese) as those who migrate for political reasons and are compelled to exit their homeland rather than being motivated primarily by the attractions of the new country (Hein 1993). Sociologist Rubén Rumbaut (2006: 277) has noted that "a distinction is often made between refugees and other classes of immigrants [that] revolves around their different motives for migration and the traumatic nature of their flight experiences." Although we agree with his further point (2006: 279) that the distinction between immigrants and refugees along these lines can be simplistic, we also believe it is helpful to remember the very different "exit motives" to which he refers in his work and that apply to our research participants. There is, moreover, a legal basis for this distinction. According to the U.S. Department of State, a refugee is "a person who has been forced from his or her home and crossed an international border for safety. He or she must have a well-founded fear of persecution in his or her native country, on account of race, religion, nationality, membership in a particular social group, or political opinion."[20] Under U.S. law, refugees are a particular type of immigrant—with *immigrant* defined as someone granted "legal permanent residency," usually for the purposes of reuniting with family, seeking work, or avoiding persecution. Although different exit motives for migration may exist, both immigrants and refugees experience forms of displacement and the need to establish modes of belonging in the new land. Although in this book we refer to both first-generation Indians and Vietnamese as "immigrants" for the sake of comparison, we recognize the unique and painful experiences of Vietnamese refugees.[21]

The forms of civic engagement and modes of belonging of the Vietnamese Americans in our study are affected by the historical relationship of the Vietnamese to the United States, including the Vietnam War. The first-generation Vietnamese in the DFW region came as refugees as a direct result of the Vietnam War, which escalated during the 1960s and finally ended in 1975, when the South Vietnamese government collapsed and surrendered to the North. The United States had officially ended its involvement in 1973 by withdrawing all troops, although American personnel remained in South Vietnam until the fall of Saigon in 1975. The war had immediate antecedents in 1954, when the Indochinese War between the French and the Viet Minh ended with the defeat of the French and the demise of French colonial rule in Vietnam. Vietnam was then divided into North Vietnam and South Vietnam, with the north heavily influenced by China and communism, and the South influenced by the United States and operating with a democratic government. Many Vietnamese families moved to the South at this time, especially if they had ties to the former colonial rulers and were Catholic. From the perspective of South Vietnam and the United States and its allies, the Vietnam War was fought primarily to prohibit unification of the country under communist rule. Following the Vietnam War, a political unification resulted in the establishment in 1976 of the Socialist Republic of Vietnam, which still rules the country. This government is not recognized as legitimate by former Vietnamese refugees who fled the country and now live in the United States and elsewhere. The United States and other countries accepted political refugees from South Vietnam starting in 1975 and, as we describe in more detail in Chapter 1, Vietnamese refugees continued to arrive in significant numbers until the end of the 1990s; the rate has declined to a trickle since then.

No similar geopolitical context or legacy of war defines the relationship between Indian immigrants and the United States. The first immigrants from India were primarily men who came to the United States in the late nineteenth century, largely from the Punjab region in the northwest area of the subcontinent. They had farming backgrounds and found employment in agriculture in California. As did other immigrants of Asian origin in California, they experienced discrimination. Some married Mexican Americans, and their wives and children came to be known as "Mexican Hindus" (Leonard 1997: 39, 42). These early Punjabi immigrants were part of a dispersion of native-born Indians to places as far afield as South Africa, Fiji, and Trinidad during the nineteenth and early twentieth centuries, often in connection with the expansion of the British Empire and the need for manual labor. Although a small number of Indians ventured to the United States after World War II, a true second wave of Indian immigration to the United States began only after 1965, roughly coinciding with the beginnings of Vietnamese immigration.

In this book, we compare two groups that are referred to in much of the literature as being part of a contemporary global "diaspora"—one created as a result of French colonialism and, more recently, by the Vietnam War; the other created by former colonial subjects who now migrate to pursue economic and educational goals. Both groups are reflected in Stéphane Dufoix's observation that "dispersion implies distance, so maintaining or creating connections becomes a major goal in reducing or at least dealing with that distance" (2008: 3). We see the Indians and the Vietnamese as similarly displaced in their new surroundings (even though the forced nature of migration for the Vietnamese is a cogent fact) but also as working toward *emplacement* (a sense of belonging) by constructing complex and fluid identities, forging multiple connections, learning how to become engaged citizens, and hence claiming civic and political presence. In their work on Asian diasporas, Wanni Anderson and Robert G. Lee (2005), inspired by Angelika Bammer's earlier work (1994), suggest that the notion of displacement may be "a productive paradigm for understanding the Asian experience in the Americas" (10). These authors argue that Asian immigrants rely on identity categories that tie them to their homelands, thus expressing an ongoing tension inherent in "the contradiction between laying claim to America and the claims of diaspora" (9). We also see this tension in the ways in which the Indian and Vietnamese participants in this research project talk about their identities.[22]

We must be careful in our assumptions about displacement, exile, and di-aspora, however, as Liisa Malkki has pointed out (1995: 511). She suggests (515-516) that modes of emplacement should be considered alongside displacements. Kirin Narayan (2002: 425), writing about South Asian immigrants, observes that emplacement occurs not only through the creation of physical spaces, but also in the imagination—"the orienting of self within multiple frameworks of mean-ing." In her work on former Yugoslavian refugees in Amsterdam and Rome, Maja Korac (2009) argues that the concept of emplacement helps us understand the experiences of migrants with transnational locations, loyalties, and senses of "home"—experiences that cannot be captured by the idea of assimilation to or integration within one particular nation-state. These ideas about emplacement, applied to the study of both refugees and economic migrants, are, we suggest, fundamental to any consideration of the process by which immigrant newcom-ers develop a sense of belonging and become engaged citizens.[23]

Communities of Practice, Social Capital, and the Mainstream

Among immigrants, emplacement goes hand in hand with participation in the public sphere. We argue in this book that as social actors with both agency and intention, immigrants are involved in the "cultural production" of the citizen.[24] They actively learn to be civically involved through varying levels of social practice in a wide range of associative contexts. To understand how im-migrants develop a sense of belonging and learn forms of civic engagement in their new host country, we employ Jean Lave and Etienne Wenger's concept (1991) of the "community of practice"—a group with shared ways of doing things and mutual understandings of behavior (including modes of commu-nication). Although *community of practice* is not a new concept and has been applied to various other spheres, we suggest that its implications for the study of immigrants have not yet been sufficiently appreciated.[25]

In developing their analytical model, Lave and Wenger sought to "draw at-tention to the point that learners inevitably participate in communities of prac-titioners and that the mastery of knowledge and skill requires newcomers to move toward full participation in the sociocultural practices of a community" (1991: 29). The emphasis in this approach is on *situated learning*, a process akin to apprenticeship—learning by doing and observing. Stephen Billett (2007) has observed that much of the more recent communities-of-practice literature ne-glects social agency, despite its central place in Lave and Wenger's book *Situated Learning* (1991). Billett points out that Lave and Wenger stress the relational as-pect of communities of practice and that "rather than the individual being posterior to the social practice in which they engage, the relationship is agentic on both sides" (56). This perspective is essential to our own focus on immigrants as social actors in the process of becoming engaged citizens.

Along with the concept of situated learning, Lave and Wenger (1991) also identify the process of "legitimate peripheral participation" (39). Newcomers, they argue, start from a position of peripherality and then move toward full participation. Access is a crucial element in the process through which one becomes a "full member" of a community of practice, and membership requires "access to a wide range of ongoing activity, old-timers, and other members of the community; and to information, resources, and opportunities for participation" (101) By adopting this framework for the study of immigrants and civic engagement, we posit that American civic life itself can be viewed as composed of various localized communities of practice, some composed of immigrants themselves, which may or may not be receptive to newcomers.

Communities of practice related to civic engagement may be located at various levels of sociality, ranging from informal forms of mutual aid to organizations and associations and to more formal political parties. Each individual participates in multiple, and sometimes overlapping or interconnected, communities of practice, which are "homes for identities" (Wenger 1998, 2006). Each community of practice "needs to develop various resources such as tools, documents, routines, vocabulary and symbols that in some way carry the accumulated knowledge of the community" (Smith 2003: 3). However, a community of practice does not necessarily require "co-presence, a well-defined identifiable group, or socially visible boundaries," to be identified as such (Lave and Wenger 1991: 98). Rather, the emphasis (for full participants) is placed on shared understandings about the meaning of activities in which members engage.

We suggest that conceptualizing the civic sphere in terms of communities of practice allows for a more dynamic approach to the processes by which newcomers become participatory citizens than does the social capital approach to civic engagement that is commonly associated with the work of Robert D. Putnam.[26] Putnam's work inspired a number of studies that look at immigrant participation in religious assemblies and ethnic organizations, as well as research on the implications of different forms of social capital for political participation.[27] For example, on the basis of their research in Amsterdam, political scientists Meindert Fennema and Jean Tillie (1999) have argued that ethnic voluntary associations create social trust and that this in turn establishes political trust and high rates of participation in the political sphere.[28] The social capital approach (Portes 1998, 2000) tends to focus attention on individual resources and relationships that are accrued (that is, on having high or low social capital, civic skills, and so on) and that assist in achieving specific ends. We suggest that an emphasis on social capital alone tends to overlook the role of social agency and process in civic and political engagement among immigrants. The emphasis on social capital and its relationship to democracy has, moreover, been criticized by those who offer caution about the "dark side" of civic engagement.[29] We argue that although there are certainly cases in which associational life can have a "dark side," and that homogeneous groups can exclude others and thereby work against democracy,[30] voluntary associations are important spheres in which immigrants learn and develop practices of civic participation. An emphasis on social capital neglects questions about how immigrants acquire a sense of "belonging" and the knowledge of how to participate in American civic life that helps them work together to express their presence in the civic sphere. A community-of-practice framework directs attention to these processes of learning and collaboration.

Our attention to the relationship between civic engagement and emplacement is related to questions about what constitutes immigrant political incorporation and what constitutes "the mainstream" in relation to which immigrants are often positioned (and sometimes describe themselves) as "marginal." The idea of moving toward the center of civic life through communities of practice prompts the question, What are immigrants moving toward? Is it the mainstream? In a discussion of what they call "Arab Detroit," Nabeel Abraham and Andrew Shryock (2000: 16) write that the Arab population in Detroit exists within both the margins and the mainstream, suggesting that these terms reflect "overlapping imaginative zones." These authors argue that Arabs "enter the American mainstream whenever they represent or think of themselves in relation to a larger, non-Arab society" (16). Richard Alba and Victor Nee (2003: 12) take a somewhat different approach, one that seeks to describe the mainstream not as an imaginative zone but rather as "that part of the society within which ethnic and racial origins have at most minor impacts on life chances or opportunities." These authors propose that the mainstream has changed in recent years, and that it is no longer to be viewed primarily as "middle class" but instead also "contains a working class and even some who are poor" (12). Despite their efforts, and despite their new view of assimilation as a workable concept that can now include a group's "visible point of reference on the social landscape, embodied in an ethnic culture, neighborhood, and institutional structures" (11), the concept of mainstream remains shrouded in normative views of a Euro-American middle class that are used by the general public, so we do not wish to use it analytically here.[31]

We do not therefore argue that Indians and Vietnamese are moving toward the mainstream, but we *are* interested in the ways in which they talk about doing so. In fact, our Indian research participants evoked this concept quite often during conversations and interviews. In our view, the important research question is not whether people are entering a mainstream, but what they think the mainstream might be and how they feel they can (or cannot) belong to it. We believe that Abraham and Shryock's casting of margin and mainstream as "imaginative zones" is a highly productive way of looking at how immigrants might see their emplacements and displacements. Learning to talk about American society in terms of having a mainstream signals participation in the community of practice that is civic life, and learning the modes of discourse available within it. Becoming civically engaged is not about "assimilation" in order to move from the margins to a mainstream, but rather is a movement from peripheries to centers in various communities of practice that make up the civic sphere.[32]

Formal Political Participation

Although the major focus of this book is on less formal modes of civic participation, we argue that it is also through participation in communities of practice that immigrants enter the public sphere as political actors. In other words, there is a link between informal and formal participation, and both of these modes constitute civic engagement. The community-of-practice model captures the transition from a peripheral to a more central position through processes of situated learning. We argue that people can acquire civic skills through participation in communities of practice such as ethnic associations and then transfer those skills to more formal political spheres. Here we outline some of the major contours of the growing formal political participation of Indians and Vietnamese in the United States, a topic to which we return in our concluding chapter.

Among South Asians there is certainly evidence of early forms of political mobilization in order to respond to specific cases of discrimination or violence—for example, against "dotbuster" gangs in New Jersey (Leonard 1997). Padma Rangaswamy (2000: 291) has identified three types of politically inclined immigrants active in the Indian community in Chicago in the 1990s: those who promoted greater involvement in homeland politics, those who promoted more involvement in local U.S. politics and becoming part of mainstream America, and those who supported both kinds of activities. None of these groups, she suggests, had the support, or for that matter the attention, of the entire community, and few Indians were involved in local politics during the 1990s. She attributes what she calls "disunity and apathy toward political issues" to the small impact they would have, given their numbers locally and the difficulties of building pan-Asian coalitions (Rangaswamy 2000: 293), but she also acknowledges that with the growth of this community, and as job discrimination, restrictive immigration laws, and more racial attacks have emerged, they have begun to "wake up." A similar disinterest in American political life was reported for New York City Indian immigrants until the late 1990s, when they began to participate more in presidential elections. At that time, *India Abroad,* a New York-based national newspaper for Indians in the United States, founded the India Abroad Center for Political Awareness and opened a Washington, D.C., office (Khandelwal 2002). But Indian involvement in local politics was minimal and offered a striking contrast to other Asian groups (such as Chinese and Koreans) whose levels of local participation were greater.

Although these early studies of Indian communities in different U.S. cities stress a low or barely emerging political profile, it is safe to say that during the first decade of the twenty-first century, while our research was being conducted, this situation had begun to change.[33] At the 2008 Democratic Convention, the Indian American Leadership Initiative, a Washington-based organization, sponsored a cocktail reception to which it invited leading Indian lawmakers from around the country, including six individuals (some first and some second generation) who were serving in state legislatures (Raj Goyle of Kansas, Updendra Chivukula of New Jersey, Jay Goyal of Ohio, Kumar Barve of Maryland, Satveer Chaudhary of Minnesota, and Swati Dandekar of Iowa). On the Republican side, Bobby Jindal, governor of Louisiana, was on John McCain's short list for vice president. Indians in the United States were active in fundraising during the 2007 and 2008 primaries and continued into the fall 2008 election season; and on November 4, 2008, nine of the fifteen Indian Americans who ran for various state and local offices won their races ("Indian Americans Score" 2008). Pollsters reported the largest Indian American turnout ever for a U.S. election (Sohrabji and Springer 2008). Several Indian Americans were involved in the Obama transition team, including Nick Rathod, who was appointed director of the Office of Intergovernmental Affairs, and Parag Mehta, who was selected to oversee the affairs of minority groups as deputy director of the same office.[34] Traditionally, Indians in the United States have been affiliated with the Democratic Party, but with their increasing success there has been some gravitation to the Republican side. Some of this, observers note, has resulted from the positive policies toward India fostered by the Bush administration, including the proposed nuclear arms deal. The importance of both parties is evident in South Carolina state legislator and Republican Nikki Randhawa Haley's election as governor of that state in 2010, and Democratic state representative and majority whip Jay Goyal's identification as a serious candidate for lieutenant governor of Ohio. In June of 2010, the Associated Press ran an article with the headline "Record Number of Indian Americans Seeking Office" (Washington 2010). In the summer of 2010 there were six Indian Americans from across the country running for the U.S. Congress. One of these was Ami Bera, a second-generation Indian whose parents came to the United States in the 1950s and who had a career as a physician and educator before entering politics to run against Republican Dan Lungren in the third congressional district in California.

In comparison with Indians, Vietnamese have participated less in formal spheres of domestic politics in the United States. This difference has generally been attributed to their recent arrival and their ongoing engagement with homeland politics.[35] There has, however, been increased participation among the younger generations. Divisions within the Vietnamese population, such as conflicts between the more "traditional" political activists who are focused on homeland politics and anticommunism and those who are more "Americanized" and focused on domestic issues (Hein 1995), also play a role. Among the arenas identified by Jeremy Hein (1995) as those in which Vietnamese American leaders have became politically engaged after arriving in the United States are mutual assistance associations (MAAs); grassroots, mainstream, and international political arenas; and legal disputes and courts. Examples of Vietnamese political activity cited by Hein range from protests against political repression in Vietnam to activism aimed at establishing a separate Vietnamese Catholic parish in San Jose, to court challenges and housing discrimination. Vietnamese student organizations at universities and colleges have served as other significant arenas for the development of political engagement (Do 1999).[36] As early as 1987, Esther Ngan-Lin Chow (1987: 290) reported that there was a "Vietnamese Women Association" in the United States that worked to "maximize the participation of Asian American women in the larger society." These earlier studies draw attention to the growing political participation of the Vietnamese not only in homeland politics but also in domestic politics. Recent survey research in Orange County, California, suggests that a "protest to politics" model is useful in understanding Vietnamese American civic participation. Collet and Furuya (2005: 1) report that "taking part in a protest increases the likelihood of voting and that interest in, and active engagement with, the homeland contributes to both modes of participation." Their work suggests that the first generation's interest in homeland politics can help it and subsequent generations become more civically engaged overall.

Vietnamese Americans have started to participate at high levels in the U.S. government. Most notably, Viet Dinh, who served as an assistant attorney general in the Bush administration, was the primary author of the Patriot Act. A former refugee, H. B. Le is now serving as the first Vietnamese American naval commander.[37] Vietnamese American Linh Nguyen, who served as a team leader in government operations, was among several Asian Americans on the Obama transition team.[38] The growing political clout of Vietnamese Americans is particularly evident in California, where the largest concentration of this population resides. For example, in Orange County there are now ten Vietnamese American elected officials, and 40 percent of all registered voters in the city of Westminster are Vietnamese Americans. Tony Lam became the first Vietnamese American elected official in the United States when he was elected to the Westminster City Council in 1992 (Tran 2008). Vietnamese in Louisiana and Texas are also demonstrating new political participation in a wider arena. In 2008, a Vietnamese American born in Vietnam and raised in Louisiana, Republican Anh (Joseph) Cao, was elected to the U.S. House of Representatives.[39] And Democrat Hubert Vo, mentioned earlier and also born in Vietnam, serves in the Texas House of Representatives. Vietnamese Americans are frequently affiliated with the Republican Party because of their strong anticommunist stance, but this can vary.[40] In California, there are significant regional differences, with more Vietnamese registered Republican in southern California and more registered Democrat in San Francisco (Ong and Lee 2001: 162). In a recent survey, 22 percent of Vietnamese claimed Democratic affiliation—the lowest percentage among Asian ethnic groups surveyed (Junn et al. 2008). However, many (49 percent) claimed independent or nonpartisan status.

Within both the Indian and Vietnamese immigrant populations there is evidence that the second generation in particular is beginning to participate more directly in the political process. In some cases, political candidacies have energized local communities (including those outside the relevant state), and if they have not generated monetary support, they have at least generated pride. Such pride can in turn enhance the forms of participatory citizenship that we explore in this book in the context of local communities of practice. As we demonstrate in Chapters 5 and 6, those who have succeeded in the more formal public political sphere are sometimes showcased in the activities of organizations that emphasize the practice of citizenship in a more informal civic sphere.

Research Methods

We employed three types of ethnographic research in this project: (1) contextual research on the cultural landscapes of the two immigrant groups, (2) participant-observation research, and (3) semi-structured interviews. Our contextual research included demographic and historical background research on Vietnamese and Indians in the United States and the DFW region. We also mapped the commercial centers, religious institutions, and other public places where our two populations tended to gather. In addition, we documented the breadth of media outlets and their role in the community.

Over the three years of our research, between 2005 and 2008, we conducted many hours of participant observation at a variety of community events (voluntary association meetings, fundraising and other banquets, ethnic festivals, religious ceremonies, youth group meetings, political protests, and so on). Informal discussions with members of voluntary associations, including religious assemblies, occurred throughout the duration of the research project. Such discussions often took place at people's homes before and after more formal interviews, or because we were included in some family or community event. Our involvement with young adults of the second generation of each of these groups on university campuses also meant that we interacted with these individuals in more informal contexts—in coffee shops and before and after events in which they were involved.

Doing fieldwork in regions characterized by suburban sprawl is challenging and often required us to be in many locations during the course of any given week. DFW is replete with highways connecting scattered cities, and our research involved a great deal of driving, or "car fieldwork," as we traveled across the region to attend events or meet with interviewees. Our commitment to participant observation required this approach but also offered a wealth of opportunities to engage in informal ways with members of the research populations. We certainly also took advantage of the unexpected as it occurred—for example, Reed-Danahay tracked a controversy involving the display of the Vietnamese flag on a university campus, and attended a press conference organized by the Vietnamese community regarding a racially charged incident involving a Vietnamese police recruit in one inner-ring suburb; and Brettell participated in two fundraisers for political candidates held at the homes of local Indian families. Much of what we observed during the course of our fieldwork could not make it into the book, but it informed our understanding of the issues we discuss.

We conducted three types of semi-structured interviews but did not begin these until we had done preliminary fieldwork and established contacts within the two immigrant populations. We also wanted to make sure that we were formulating questions that would make sense to our two groups. Different sets of questions were developed for (1) one-on-one interviews with community leaders and media professionals, (2) group interviews with college students, and

(3) one-on-one interviews with parents of high school- and college-age children. We conducted these interviews in phases. We began interviewing community leaders early in our research, and continued this throughout the project as we identified research participants. We met with and interviewed not only various leaders in the Indian and Vietnamese communities, but also community leaders from other ethnic groups who interacted with at least one of our groups. In these interviews, we sought to elicit details on the mechanisms by which people learned the skills necessary for leadership, their attitudes toward civic participation in the United States (including pan-Asian activities), and their senses of ethnic identity. We also asked background questions about religious participation, education, migration history, and so on. A range of professionals involved in ethnic media were also interviewed (including publishers, editors, and journalists, in print media as well as radio and TV).

Our group interviews on two university campuses (one public and one private) were conducted in spring 2006. We solicited participants for these interviews both through broad campus networks we had established among these groups during initial fieldwork, and through the Asian, Vietnamese, and Indian student associations on these campuses. Each group interview was composed of between five and ten students, both male and female. In these interviews, our questions were intended to elicit college students' views on and experiences with civic engagement and ethnic identity. All the interviews were tape-recorded and anonymous (each participant chose a pseudonym). Three group interviews (two with Vietnamese, one with Indians) were conducted at a major public university in the area, and four (three with Indians, one with Vietnamese) were conducted at a major private institution. Each of these interviews was conducted by one of us, using a script of questions that we developed together and with the help of a research assistant who took notes and managed the tape recorder. In addition, at the private institution, two additional interviews were conducted with the leaders of the Indian Student Association. At the public institution, a short questionnaire that probed similar issues was distributed to members of the Vietnamese Student Association. The student leaders of the Vietnamese and Asian student associations at the public institution were interviewed separately and not in a group format, and issues similar to those addressed in other leader interviews were explored.

A third set of interviews was conducted among parents of high school- and college-age youth who were in midlife and raising families. We did not begin the parent interviews until spring 2007, permitting a long period of ethnographic research before we formulated the questions for those interviews. We conducted them with thirty-four first-generation Indian parents and thirty-three first-generation Vietnamese parents.[41] We attempted to select a broad and representative range of individuals through networking and multiple-entry techniques. Because we waited to get a better sense of the overall demographic characteristics of our two research populations before we began to solicit interview participants, we were mindful of creating a balanced group, including both males and females across the range of religious backgrounds that characterize the Indian and Vietnamese immigrant populations. These interviews elicited general demographic details about the families and their migration histories. We also asked questions about political behavior, civic engagement, citizenship, education, and religious participation. In addition, we explored questions of ethnic identity. The questions were translated into Vietnamese for use when those interviewed did not speak English or were not fluent in English.

In our interviews with parents, as well as in those with community leaders and college students, we were particularly sensitive to personal narratives or life stories that touched on ethnic identity and civic engagement, and many of these narratives are incorporated into the chapters of this book. Our interviews complement the materials we collected through participant observation and background research, providing the voices of our participants and a sense of their agency in learning forms of civic engagement as immigrants or as the children of immigrants living in the United States. Where we have included these narratives and other references to particular individuals, we use pseudonyms rather than real names. We do this to protect the privacy and anonymity of our research participants. Some minor details of personal characteristics were also altered. None of these changes affect information about the socioeconomic status of the person, and no changes were made to directly quoted material. When we refer to public figures from our two populations, we use their real names.

Organization of the Book

In this book we juxtapose details and observations about Indians and Vietnamese in order to bring into focus the commonalities that cut across these two populations. We weave personal stories of individual immigrants into our observations in order to convey their experiences. In Chapter 1 we set the stage for the chapters to follow by providing an overview of Indians and Vietnamese in the DFW region—the circumstances under which they arrived and settled there, and the cultural landscapes they have created and in which they dwell. In Chapter 2 we explore the fluid and situational aspects of ethnic identity as well as what they mean for understanding the cultural dimensions of civic engagement.

We draw on our interviews with parents and with college students in order to unpack the meaning of citizenship and the expressions of identity articulated by those of the first and second generations.

Starting with Chapter 3, we draw increasingly on our participant-observation research and turn to the specific communities of practice in which immigrants learn about and engage in participatory forms of citizenship in the United States. We begin by focusing on the religious assemblies—temples, mosques, and churches—that are attended by our two populations, and on the modes of engagement fostered by these institutions. In Chapter 4 we turn to Indian and Vietnamese ethnic associations in order to discuss the ways they form important communities of practice and the ways in which they may differ from one another according to their emphases on local, national, or transnational engagement and mobilization. We highlight the personal narratives of men and women in both groups who have taken leadership roles in these ethnic associations.

In Chapter 5 we turn to a realm that has received scant attention in the literature on contemporary immigration. Here we draw on ethnographic research conducted at festivals and banquets in order to address how each of these contexts provides opportunities for immigrants to acquire civic knowledge and civic skills, as well as opportunities for them to claim a place as participatory citizens in the public sphere. These claims are often implicit but sometimes explicit. In these contexts, Indians and Vietnamese, young people and adults, express their sense of belonging and their desire to participate as members of American society. Although we begin to address pan-Asian contexts for civic engagement in Chapter 5, these are explored more fully in Chapter 6, which also addresses broader arenas of sociality and more formal contexts in which leadership skills are learned as part of teaching curricula. We also share the stories of four immigrants who became civically engaged on a pathway from ethnic to pan-ethnic or through involvement that extends beyond ethnic affiliation.

In our concluding chapter we review the importance of the community-of-practice model to an understanding of processes of civic and political incorporation, as well as the various dimensions of civic engagement that inform our analysis and extend the understanding of participatory citizenship beyond formal naturalization and electoral participation. We end the book with a look toward the future. We consider the implications of our research for scholarship on these two groups and for understanding their modes of belonging and of becoming "American."

1

Arrival, Settlement, and the Construction of Cultural Landscapes

MAI P., A MOTHER OF TWO in her early forties who was born in Vietnam, arrived in DFW in the 1980s, but this was not her first destination in the United States. Mai first came to America as a young child, as part of what she calls "the first wave" of refugees after the fall of Saigon in 1975. "My Mom and Dad wanted to escape, so Dad had a plan. He knew that a U.S. warship was in the harbor waiting so he chartered a boat to take us out to it." Her family spent a few months in Guam to be processed as refugees, and then were sent to a refugee camp in the Unites States, at Indian Town Gap in Pennsylvania. A Baptist family sponsored them and they moved to a small town in the southeast where they spent two years. The sponsors were pleasant and helpful, but the town had no other Vietnamese living in it. Mai's family eventually made contact with relatives who had already settled in New Orleans. "My parents saw that there was a strong Vietnamese Catholic community down there, and we had a large extended family already there, so we moved down." She and her two brothers attended Catholic schools and went to college. Her older brother had become an engineer and moved to the Dallas area, and in the 1980s her family relocated again to be near him. "My Dad had passed away and so my brother became the head of the family." Mai finished her college education at a university in the DFW region and settled in Tarrant County. She married another former Vietnamese refugee and now works as a computer professional. Mai feels that the most important issue for Vietnamese parents is to raise their children so they can adapt to living in the United States. Her own children do well in school, but she bemoans the fact that neither of her children can fluently speak Vietnamese.

Salim K., a native of India, also arrived in DFW in the 1980s and, like Mai, had spent time elsewhere in the United States first. After completing both bachelor's and master's degrees at the Bombay branch of the Indian Institute of Technology,[1] Salim decided to pursue a doctorate in nuclear engineering in the United States. He chose to enroll at Midwestern University (a pseudonym) because it offered him a scholarship and because his wife's uncle had been a Midwestern student and had told him about it. When Salim and his wife arrived on the Midwestern campus in the fall of 1969, they were met by a host family who were kind to them and sympathetic to the fact that they had never experienced such cold weather before. This family helped them obtain winter clothes and transportation, and invited them to talk about India and their religion (Islam) at their church. "America was not as diverse then as it is now," Salim commented. "Indians were a novelty." In 1973, Salim and his wife had a baby girl, and a year later they moved to the Boston area, where their son was born. They were the first Muslim family in the community where they lived, but other families moved in and eventually several families worked together to start a mosque. In 1986, Salim was offered a position at a major nuclear facility. The family moved to Texas and settled in Plano, a northern suburb of the city of Dallas. Shortly afterward, Salim and his wife became American citizens. They had decided they were going to make their lives in the United States. Salim noted that in those early years it was difficult for his children at school because there were few Indians in their classes and often no other Muslims. "Now it is different for Indian children because the Indian community and the Muslim community are both bigger."

The experiences of Salim and Mai underscore the differences between refugees and educational and economic migrants. A first-generation immigrant who came to the United States as a young man, Salim earned an advanced degree and achieved a high income within years of arrival. Mai is a 1.5 generation immigrant, and her refugee parents struggled and worked hard so that their children could gain economic and social power. In contrast to other Indians, like Salim, for whom education and work opportunities stand out as major reasons for coming to the United States, very few of the Vietnamese interviewed for this book gave these as major reasons. Instead, they emphasized "political" motives and forced migration.

Although these two migration stories are unique in many respects, they also illustrate some common themes in the immigrant experience. Along with their respective families, Mai and Salim initially arrived in another part of the United States before moving to Texas. Although both families were attracted to this region by a growing economy, each articulated the important role of the extended family in their migration. Salim's wife's uncle paved the way for him at Midwestern, and Mai's relatives drew her first to New Orleans and later to DFW. These stories also demonstrate the feeling of "otherness" experienced by the two families after their initial settlement. Mai spoke of her family's isolation from other Vietnamese when they were settled in a small southern town where, as Catholics, they were also quite different from the majority, who were Protestant. Salim describes being the first Muslim family in his Boston-area community. Both Salim and Mai acquired an education and sought a professional occupation after arriving in the United States.

To better understand the reasons that immigrants move to the DFW metropolitan area, and its unique qualities as a receiving context, in this chapter we describe this setting. We briefly discuss overall immigration trends before turning to the ways in which Vietnamese and Indians in particular have claimed space in DFW through the construction of cultural landscapes. We use the term *cultural landscape* to refer to ethnic commercial centers, cultural institutions, and the virtual and imagined spaces of ethnic media. Establishing such spaces for forms of sociality based on shared national origins that transcend family or religious institutions is often an initial step in the process of emplacement by which newcomers enter the public sphere and establish their local social and civic presence.

The DFW Context

The DFW metropolitan area lies "outside of the large urban agglomerations at the eastern and western flanks of the country" (Jones 2008: 4) that have been most associated with immigrant incorporation and, as such, provides a new context for immigrant settlement. It has, however, particular features that not only attract immigrants, such as Salim and Mai, but also shape their experiences once they arrive. This region is complex in that it includes two major cities—Fort Worth and Dallas—as well as several large suburban cities, such as Arlington and Plano; it is therefore fragmented and quite diverse in terms of settlement patterns (see Map 1.1). Fort Worth and Dallas were both established as cities in the mid-1800s and at first grew primarily due to their roles as transportation hubs with major railroad stations.[2] Cattle, farming, and later oil were the major bases of the economy. There is a rivalry between the two cities and each is viewed and promotes itself differently.[3] Fort Worth is seen as a western city, and its Stockyards neighborhood attests to the strong cattle industry there, whereas Dallas is seen as more eastern and was able to develop into a larger city with a more vibrant economy (at the expense of Fort Worth, in the minds of some in Tarrant County). Separated by suburbs like Irving and Arlington, the two major cities each support a newspaper (the *Fort Worth Star-Telegram* and the *Dallas Morning News*), major museums and performance centers, and universities. Both cities have significant populations of Latinos and African Americans whose histories are intertwined with those of the white-dominated power bases that long reigned in each city.[4] Although Fort Worth has its share of elites and philanthropists, the majority of DFW's wealth is concentrated in the northern sector of Dallas and in its northern suburbs.

The strong economy of DFW, despite its ups and downs during previous recessions and the post-9/11 crisis, is a major factor in its ability to attract immigrants. Its growth, however, has been relatively recent compared to cities in other regions of the United States. Economic and demographic expansion in Tarrant County and Fort Worth began in the 1950s with the post–World War II

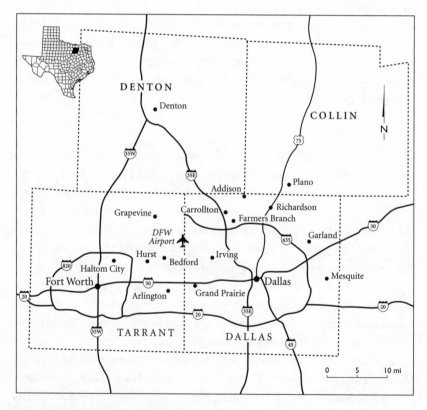

Map 1.1 Dallas–Fort Worth metropolitan area

defense industry, when what are now Lockheed Martin and Bell Helicopter established bases in Fort Worth. A General Motors plant that opened in Arlington in 1954 caused that city to grow from a few thousand inhabitants to almost 45,000 by 1960. Fort Worth's growth was slower; it gained only about 80,000 inhabitants (to reach a total of 356,268) during that decade. Between 1950 and 1960 the population of Dallas grew by just over 245,000 (to more than 680,000) and the city limits expanded from 40.6 square miles in 1940 to 279.9 square miles by 1960. Dresser Industries, an oil and gas firm, relocated to the Dallas area in 1950, and Texas Instruments, a local company founded in the 1930s, expanded into the electronics business during the 1950s, developing the integrated circuit in 1958. Continued expansion of the regional economy in the 1970s was spurred by the completion of DFW International Airport, which again made the area an important transportation hub.[5] By the mid-1980s, DFW was ranked "third behind New York and Chicago as headquarters for companies with more than $1 million in assets" (Payne 2000: 423). In the 1990s, the area ranked first in the nation in employment growth.[6] The economy was also becoming more diversified. The health care industry and higher education institutions are now major employers in the region; there are eighteen four-year and graduate-level colleges and universities. Recent drilling for natural gas, especially in the Barnett Shale in Fort Worth and Arlington, is currently providing revenue windfalls for local governments and individuals.[7] Corporations based in the region include defense contractors, such as Raytheon; retailers, such as RadioShack, Pier 1 Imports, and JCPenney; and Nokia, Exxon Mobil, and American Airlines.[8] By 2008, DFW had twenty-four companies on the Fortune 500 list—the "fourth-highest concentration among U.S. metro areas."[9] There is an entrepreneurial spirit in this region, and it is particularly marked in Dallas, where being a can-do city for business is part of its self-image.[10]

The civic environment and political climate that provide the context for the development of forms of civic engagement among immigrants in DFW shape and are shaped by the region's location in Texas, home of former president George W. Bush and now classified as a "red state" that has had a Republican in the governor's office since 1995.[11] Tarrant County tends to vote Democratic more often than areas closer to Dallas, and at the time of this study the mayor of Fort Worth, Mike Moncrief, was a Democrat.[12] Arlington, however, is now considered the "Republican stronghold" in Tarrant County, even though its former mayor was a Democrat.[13] It is also worth noting that in the 2008 election, Dallas County voted Democratic, which was attributed in part to the high proportion of Hispanics in the county. During our research, both Texas senators were Republican, and although the majority of congressmen from the area are also Republican, some state legislators, such as Lon Burnam from Fort Worth and Rafael Anchia from Dallas, are highly visible Democrats. As we illustrate in subsequent chapters, those members of our research populations who interacted with politicians frequently did so with members of both parties.

There is one other dimension of the "culture" of Texas and of the DFW region that is best illuminated by drawing a comparison with California—another high-immigration state. Although California has been more strongly committed to big government and safety nets,[14] and has a high tax rate to support these commitments, Texas has no state income tax and emphasizes laissez-faire markets and individual responsibility. This approach transmits a message to immigrants arriving in Texas that they are essentially on their own in terms of governmental support, although at the local level a few nonprofit organizations offer services to newcomers. In Texas no sweeping anti-immigrant legislation that is equivalent to California's Proposition 187 has been passed, but a number of bills designed to deal with illegal immigration have been proposed at the state level, and some DFW-area communities—specifically Farmers Branch—have garnered national attention for passing local ordinances to regulate illegal immigration (Brettell and Nibbs 2011).

At the local level, various forms of urban governance operate in the suburban communities that surround Dallas and Fort Worth and together comprise the DFW region. It is worth noting, however, that only in the early 1990s did the city of Dallas become politically inclusionary and hence more representative of and responsive to the area's growing diversity. Dallas moved from a citywide election process to council district elections, with each district electing one of the city's fourteen councilors. In 2010, the suburban community of Irving wrestled with a similar change that would establish a more inclusive and representative system. Since 1996, Arlington's system of government includes eight city council members, five of whom are elected by and to represent a single district, and three of whom, like the mayor, represent and are elected by the city at large. In Fort Worth, the mayor is elected at large, but each city council member is elected by his or her district. The counties in the region are all members of a broader board, the North Central Texas Council of Governments (NCTCOG).

Religion plays an important role in this region and is closely connected to the economic and political climate. Considered to be in the so-called Bible Belt, DFW has a heavily Protestant slant—mirrored in the names of two large private universities that stand at the eastern (Southern Methodist University) and western (Texas Christian University) ends of the region. There is also a Catholic institution of higher education in Irving (University of Dallas), and equal numbers of Southern Baptists and Catholics, the two largest groups, reside in the area.[15] The region has had a substantial Jewish population since the late nineteenth century, and there are several prominent synagogues. The conservative political climate is linked to right-wing religious institutions, and there are several "mega-churches," such as The Potter's House, that increasingly use technology to reach members.[16] The religious context of the area however, is quite diverse and includes a wide range of institutions, including those that are more liberal. It is difficult to gauge the influence of these trends on the religious participation of Indian and Vietnamese immigrants (which we address in Chapter 3), but certainly the overall climate of religiosity means that the religious participation of immigrants is viewed positively, even if their religions (especially Hinduism, Buddhism, and Islam) are "new" to the area. There is reinforcement for being affiliated with a church or temple, although attitudes toward mosques have been shifting since 9/11.

Immigration in the DFW Region

Not surprisingly, given the economic growth described in the preceding pages, since the 1970s the DFW region—the largest metropolitan area in Texas—has been an increasingly important destination for immigrants.[17] The economy has attracted both highly skilled and well-educated immigrants, such as those from India, who are drawn to the area by the telecommunications, health, educational, and financial industries, as well as immigrants who have less education or insufficient English language skills (as is the case for many Vietnamese refugees) but have nevertheless found employment in construction or manufacturing, or in the low- or unskilled service sector. In 1975, when Vietnamese refugees first arrived, the economy was growing fast and they were able to find jobs relatively easily. The economic crisis at the end of the first decade of the twenty-first century, however, has made it increasingly difficult for newer groups of refugees to find such jobs (Meyers 2009).

The growth of the foreign-born population in Texas as a whole has been dramatic. It increased from 2.8 percent of the total population of the state in 1970 to 16 percent or an estimated 3.7 million by 2008. Seventy-six percent of these foreign born are from Latin America and close to 17 percent are from Asia (Table 1.1). In DFW, Mexicans are the largest foreign-born population; their numbers remained small, however, until the 1970s and grew dramatically only after 1980.[18] The next largest foreign-born populations are Salvadorans, Indians, and Vietnamese, in that order.

Table 1.1 Characteristics of the foreign-born population in Texas (2006–2008) (as percentage of total foreign born in Texas)

Total Foreign-Born Population	3,787,550
Year of Entry	
Pre 1980	19.1%
During 1980s	20.1%
During 1990s	31.6%
After 2000	29.1%
Regional Place of Origin	
Latin America	76%
	(53.4% nationwide)*
Asia	16.6%
	(26.9% nationwide)
Top Four Sending Countries	
Mexico	62.3%
El Salvador	4.2%
Vietnam	3.5%
India	3.2%
Proportion of Foreign Born Who Were Citizens	30.9%
	(42.5% nationwide)
Proportion of Foreign Born Who Were Citizens Who Entered:	
Before 1980	66.4%
	(78.5% nationwide)
During 1980s	46.7%
	(58.8% nationwide)
During 1990s	22.4%
	(35.2% nationwide)
After 2000	6.0%
	(8.8% nationwide)

* Nationwide figures are percentage of total foreign born in the United States.
SOURCE: U.S. Census Bureau, American Community Survey, 2006–2008. Three-year estimates.

The 2000 census counted 34,128 foreign-born Vietnamese and 36,910 foreign-born Indians in the four central counties (Collin, Dallas, Denton, and Tarrant) of DFW. The numbers were higher (47,090 foreign-born Vietnamese and 49,669 foreign-born Indians) for the broader Dallas-Fort Worth-Arlington Consolidated Metropolitan Statistical Area (CMSA). The Vietnamese population increased by 132 percent between 1990 and 2000, and the Indian population increased by 190 percent. Even after 9/11 the foreign-born population continued to grow. By the middle of the first decade of the twenty-first century, when this research project got under way, an estimated 73,013 foreign-born Indians and 56,851 foreign-born Vietnamese were counted.[19]

Many newcomers to the area arrive as refugees. Texas resettled approximately 4,500 refugees each year during the first half-decade of the twenty-first century, and in 2007 it ranked third (after Florida and California) as a receiving state for refugees.[20] Agencies in Dallas and Fort Worth that have contracts with the U.S. Department of State to provide refugee services, coordinated through the Texas Office of Immigration and Refugee Affairs, include Catholic Charities, Refugee Services of North Texas, International Rescue Committee, and World Relief. Although Southeast Asian refugees continue to be among the most numerous overall, Vietnamese refugees have dwindled in number since the earlier peak, and only 1,500 were granted this status in 2007 in the entire United States (Office of Refugee Resettlement 2007). However, newer refugee groups are arriving in the region, most recently from various African nations, including Somalia and Liberia, as well as from Iraq, Bhutan, and Myanmar (Burma).

The Vietnamese and Indian immigrants in our study live within an ethnically diverse region that has not only large numbers of Latinos (immigrant and native born) and African Americans, in addition to newer groups arriving from Africa, but also a substantial Asian population (see Table 1.2). Political scientist Michael Jones-Correa (1996: 184) noted more than a decade ago that most research on immigrants retains a focus on the "urban core," so immigrants in suburbs remain "an unknown quantity."[21] This effect is particularly

Table 1.2 Place of birth of selected foreign-born Asian populations in Dallas–Fort Worth–Arlington metropolitan area and in three selected counties, 2006–2008

	DFW Metro	Collin County	Dallas County	Tarrant County
Total Population	6,150,823	730,176	2,383,735	1,707,185
Total Foreign Born	1,090,385	125,744	568,626	267,104
Total Asian Foreign Born	230,041	58,282	83,495	56,897
China	27,655	13,258	7,487	3,944
Korea	21,546	3,685	9,137	3,697
India	50,595	17,168	18,990	7,831
Pakistan	12,461	2,539	4,738	2,674
Cambodia	3,527	313	1,500	353
Laos	6,090	308	2,266	3,336
Philippines	14,376	3,334	5,398	4,253
Thailand	5,310	1,067	2,015	1,370
Vietnam	47,882	5.579	19,180	18,597

SOURCE: U.S. Census Bureau, 2006–2008 American Community Survey. Three-year estimates.

salient in the case of Asian immigrants, because more than half of them live in suburbs (184), and our two populations reflect this trend. Within the four central counties of DFW, the Indian and Vietnamese populations are dispersed across a number of local suburban communities, as well as the cities of Dallas and Fort Worth proper (Table 1.3). Although far fewer Vietnamese live in Collin County, which is more affluent than either Dallas or Tarrant Counties, those who live there have high levels of education and income. As indicated in Table 1.4, a higher percentage of Vietnamese than Indians own their homes, but the value of the houses owned by Indians is drastically higher, and in two of the three counties profiled, per capita income and household incomes are lower for the Vietnamese overall. In the next two sections of this chapter we treat in more detail the patterns of arrival and settlement for Indians and Vietnamese, drawing on the life stories of first-generation immigrants, as well as on census data and our parent interviews.

Table 1.3 Indians and Vietnamese in selected cities of DFW area, 2000

	Total Population	Total Foreign Born and % of Total Population	Indians	Vietnamese
Dallas (Dallas County)	1,188,204	290,436 (24.4%)	5,339	6,325
Irving (Dallas County)	191,611	50,696 (26.4%)	4,295	1,394
Garland (Dallas County)	215,991	45,588 (21.1%)	1,959	5,420
Richardson (Dallas and Collin Counties)	91,635	17,274 (18.8%)	1,684	1,415
Plano (Collin County)	222,301	37,923 (17%)	3,524	1,481
Carrollton (Denton County)	109,215	21,796 (19.9%)	2,176	1,876
Fort Worth (Tarrant County)	535,420	87,120 (16.3%)	1,417	4,195
Arlington (Tarrant County)	332,695	50,911 (15.3%)	1,636	7,274
Haltom City (Tarrant County)	39,229	5,539 (14.1%)	230	1,135
Grand Prairie (Dallas, Ellis, and Tarrant Counties)	127,049	20,841 (16.4%)	440	1,738

SOURCE: U.S. Census Bureau, Census 2000, Summary File 3.

Table 1.4 Selected demographic characteristics in three counties of the DFW region for those identifying as Indian and Vietnamese alone ancestry (2000)

	Dallas County		Collin County		Tarrant County	
	Indians	Vietnamese	Indians	Vietnamese	Indians	Vietnamese
Total Population	23,736	19,878	8,746	3,493	9,474	19,171
Median Age	29	30	30	31	30	29
Average Household Size	2.91	3.38	2.85	3.27	2.86	3.79
Average Family Size	3.43	3.75	3.20	3.59	3.41	4.16
% of Owner-Occupied Housing Units	35.8%	48.0%	55.5%	78.0%	37.9%	61.6%
% of Population 25+ Years of Age with BA or Higher	60.8%	19.6%	83.3%	52.4%	65.2%	16.0%
% Foreign Born	78%	78%	77%	72%	77%	75%
% of Population 5+ Years of Age Speaking Language Other Than English at Home	85.7%	88.1%	76.7%	97.6%	82.4%	94.5%
Median Household Income in 1999 (Dollars)	56,759	46,061	80,446	85,269	59,167	49,337
Per Capita Income in 1999 (Dollars)	24,880	16,534	34,466	27,758	25,506	14,921
Median Value of Single-Family Owner-Occupied Homes (Dollars)	123,500	93,400	199,800	173,800	143,900	86,700

NOTE: This table is based on respondents identifying as Indian alone or Vietnamese alone; figures would differ somewhat if Indian alone or in combination or Vietnamese alone or in combination were chosen.
SOURCE: U.S. Census, 2000, Summary File 4.

Indian Immigrant Arrival and Settlement

Indians have been one of the fastest-growing immigrant populations in the United States, and by 2006 they were the fourth-largest immigrant group after Mexicans, Filipinos, and Chinese. The largest communities of Indian immigrants can be found in California, New Jersey, and New York. They have been settling in the DFW region in measurable numbers since 1965, when the Immigration Act of 1924 was repealed.[22] As Salim's story at the outset of this chapter indicates, Indians largely come voluntarily to the United States from the most populous democratic country in the world, in pursuit of higher education or employment or both. They have entered on student visas, as skilled workers on H1-B (nonimmigrant) visas, with "green cards" (for example, women recruited for nursing), or as dependents or sponsored relatives.[23]

Nationwide, Indian immigrants are characterized by high levels of education and income, and they often have the advantage of already speaking English when they arrive, although they may use a native language at home.[24] As indicated in Table 1.4, high levels of education and household income are characteristic of Indians in DFW, including our research participants (Table 1.5). Ninety-three percent of Indian men and 72 percent of Indian women in our parent interview cohort had completed a bachelor's or higher degree. Almost three quarters of the Indian men and one-third of the women interviewed were in either managerial or professional occupations, also reflecting nationwide trends.[25]

Table 1.5 Educational level and occupation (parent interview cohort)

| | MALES | | FEMALES | |
	Indian (N = 16)	Vietnamese (N = 12)	Indian (N = 18)	Vietnamese (N = 20)
Highest Education Level Attained				
6th grade or less	0%	0%	0%	20%
Some high school	6%	17%	0%	25%
Completed high school	0%	42%	11%	10%
Some college or technical school	0%	33%	11%	25%
BA or BS degree	31%	8%	17%	15%
MA or MS degree	12%	0%	33%	5%
PhD or professional degree	50%	0%	22%	0%
Education Acquired After Arrival				
Completed high school	0%	0%	0%	5%
Some college or technical school	6%	17%	17%	30%
Completed college	12%	0%	0%	5%
MA or MS degree	6%	0%	22%	5%
PhD or professional degree	44%	0%	17%	0%
Current Occupation				
Managerial	37%	0%	0%	10%
Professional and related	37%	0%	33%	20%
Service	6%	33%	33%	20%
Office/maintenance/production	0%	50%	0%	30%
Sales and related	12%	0%	11%	0%
Office/administration	0%	0%	11%	0%
Unemployed/housewife/retired	0%	17%	0%	10%

SOURCE: Parent interviews

Table 1.6 Reasons for emigration to the United States and for settlement in the DFW area (parent interview cohort)

	Indian Respondents (N = 34)	Vietnamese Respondents (N = 33)
Reason for Coming to U.S.		
Education	38%	0%
Work/opportunity/money	21%	6%
To join family or accompanied parents	18%	9%
Marriage/love	23%	0%
Political reasons/refugee	0%	64%
Freedom/better future	0%	21%
Reason for Coming to DFW		
Education	12%	0%
Job/work opportunity	65%	13%
To join family	15%	39%
Had acquaintances there	3%	3%
Settled by refugee agency or sponsored by a church or charity organization	0%	42%
Other	5%	3%

SOURCE: Parent interviews

Among the first-generation Indians who participated in our parent interviews, all of the men had arrived prior to 1990, as had close to 80 percent of the women. As indicated in Table 1.6, 38 percent of respondents (half of the Indian men and slightly more than a quarter of the Indian women) said they came to the United States for education. Table 1.6 also shows that just under a quarter—and these were mostly female respondents—came for "marriage/love," that is, they were generally following or joining a spouse. Twenty-one percent came to the United States to pursue work opportunities and it was work opportunities that drew almost two-thirds of our parent interview respondents to the DFW area. When women gave this response they often indicated that it was their husband's job that caused the move.

Indians first settled in the inner-ring suburb of Richardson, north of Dallas, where the public school system was strong and some of the early high-tech companies had set up offices. Another important early but continuous locus of settlement is Mesquite, an inner-ring suburb to the southeast of Dallas. Many of the Indians in this community are Christians from the state of Kerala in southwest India, and many of them work as nurses or technicians in the health care sector of the local economy.[26] Since 1980, the Indian immigrant population has doubled during each decade, expanding north into the cities of Collin County, especially Plano, where Indians were 9.3 percent of the foreign-born population in 2000; west into the community of Irving; and most recently northwest into communities such as Carrollton and Lewisville in Denton County (see Table 1.3). This is a very suburban immigrant population; many Indian families bought homes in newly developed suburbs that were growing rapidly during the 1990s.

One of the earliest Indians to arrive was Kamal S., a Sikh from Punjab who said his interest in migrating to the United States was piqued by watching American movies that were shown in the local cinema in his village. Born in 1929 in an India that was very different from the India of today and where his father worked for the Maharaja of Patiala, Kamal applied to a university in Fresno, California. He entered the United States in May of 1954 and took a bus across the country to the West Coast. In 1956 he moved with an Indian friend to Dallas to work at a local steak house; later he took a position as maître d' at a popular restaurant in the area. In 1958 he married an American woman who was originally from a small town in east Texas, and in the mid-1960s he opened his own clothing store.

Soon after his arrival in Dallas, Kamal enrolled at a local private university and there found a handful of other Indian students. He began to be invited to speak around town on Indian culture and society. In 1962, together with other students on his campus, he founded the India Committee Against Chinese Aggression—which a year later adopted the name India Association of North Texas (IANT)—to "make a statement and raise money for India's defense when China attacked." Among the early members of this organization were a couple of professors from Kamal's university who were of Indian origin, and four or five who were on the faculty at another college in the area. This organization, which celebrated its fortieth anniversary in 2002, remains active.

In 1966, Kamal became a U.S. citizen, and in the fall of 1966 he cast his first vote. By that time, more Indians were arriving in DFW to take jobs in technical and scientific fields at local universities, with companies such as Texas Instruments, and in the growing health care sector. As some of the first wave of post-1965 Indians became citizens, they began to sponsor relatives, some of whom did not have the same level of education as they did.

Bashir L. was one of these Indian immigrants who entered the United States after 1965 and then helped other members of his family to emigrate. Bashir arrived in 1971 on a student visa to study mechanical engineering at a technical university in the northeast. After graduating, and with a training visa, he took a position with a boiler manufacturing company in Providence, Rhode Island. Four years later he had his green card. In 1978, after returning to India to be married, he moved to Michigan to work for a utility company. In 1981 he moved his family to Texas to take a position with another major utilities company. As soon as Bashir became a U.S. citizen, he began to sponsor other family members to come to the United States. A Hindu originally from the state of Gujarat in northern India, Bashir said that the obligation to help extends to fellow villagers. "You cannot sponsor them to come to the U.S., but if people from your village show up here you treat them as a brother or sister, you help them out, you pick them up at the airport, you let them stay with you, you help to find them a job, you call up people you know here so that they can get started."

Bashir sponsored his immediately younger brother to come to the United States to study at a DFW-area University. This brother completed a degree in electrical engineering and eventually moved to Houston to work for a computer company. Bashir also sponsored his eldest brother and his youngest brother, although his initial plan was for his youngest brother, a banker, to remain in India to take care of his parents. The eldest brother, who had worked in the hardware store with his father and had no advanced education, found little opportunity in the United States and elected to return to India, leaving his children in Bashir's care. Bashir's youngest brother also decided to return to India, to the bank job he had there, but he too left his son in the United States. Bashir and his wife thus raised not only their own two daughters but also his elder brother's two children and his youngest brother's son, as well as the son of his wife's sister. "We had six children in the household, and three graduated in the same year." All have remained. Eventually his eldest brother returned and took a job working at the toll booths at the DFW airport. Bashir described him as happy. "He is not an ambitious man but he makes more money here than he ever did in India and he enjoys his life. So in the end the plan worked out—the banking brother is back in India taking care of the parents."

Bashir's story of sponsorship of his kin and of helping out others from his home region offers an excellent illustration of patterns of chain migration using U.S. immigration law, and of the significance of social networks in the migration process. It also demonstrates how a second wave of post-1980 Indians settled in the area. These individuals, many of whom did not have or pursue advanced degrees, often found employment as small business owners who provided a range of services to other businesses, from restaurants to motels, from grocery and convenience stores to jewelry and sari shops. This wave also included immigrants of Indian ancestry who had been expelled from Africa (Uganda and Zambia, for example) and are now among the more successful small business owners in the area. Finally, the 1980s wave included individuals like Salim who moved to the Dallas area from other parts of the United States, attracted by a local economy with lots of opportunity.

In the 1990s, the new boom in technology and the expansion of the H1B highly skilled worker visa category resulted in a new wave of immigration—largely composed of young, well-educated Indians, many of them software engineers. They have contributed both to the overall growth of the Indian population since 1990 and to the pattern of suburban settlement, particularly as they have married and begun to establish families.

Vietnamese Refugee Arrival and Settlement

Large numbers of Vietnamese refugees began to arrive in the United States after the fall of Saigon in 1975.[27] By 2006, according to American Community Survey data, the number of Vietnamese immigrants in the United States was 1.1 million, placing them in fifth place after the Mexican, Filipino, Chinese, and Indian foreign-born populations.[28] The largest numbers of Vietnamese immigrants in the United States reside in California and Texas. Only a handful of people born in Vietnam lived in the DFW region before 1975, and most of them were university students. Like Mai and her family, the refugees who arrived after 1975 were frequently sponsored by local families recruited through church groups. Refugee agencies also helped many of these newcomers settle and find work.

There is much variation within the Vietnamese population, which is related to their refugee experience and such factors as timing and circumstances of arrival, educational background, and generation.[29] The visa status of those who have migrated more recently is often still tied to the aftermath of the Vietnam War—related either to former military imprisonment, Amerasian status,[30] or sponsorship by relatives who were able to gain refugee status and subsequently become citizens.[31] A growing number of Vietnamese continue to arrive as international students but in many cases plan to return home after finishing their education. A large portion of the Vietnamese immigrants who have arrived in the DFW region since the 1990s—a period during which the number of foreign-born Vietnamese doubled—came to the United States through the Orderly Departure Program (ODP), particularly under the HO visa subcategory, which pertains to former reeducation camp detainees. Many families that arrived through these programs either started out in Vietnam in a lower social class than those of the first wave of immigration, or fell into poverty during the years after the Vietnam War. Many adults who arrived more recently struggle with language barriers and often must take low-skilled jobs despite their educational backgrounds in Vietnam.

Among the parents who were interviewed, the differences in education levels and occupations between Indians and Vietnamese are apparent (see Table 1.5). The percentage of Vietnamese in our study who had a bachelor's degree is close to the averages in Texas and the United States across all populations, but first-generation Vietnamese had lower income and educational levels than Indians.[32] Further, the percentage of Vietnamese immigrants holding an undergraduate or graduate degree was lower than the national average (only 8 percent of men and 20 percent of women). There were significant gender differences in education among the Vietnamese we interviewed. More women had college degrees, but almost half (45 percent) of the Vietnamese women lacked a high school degree. Although the Vietnamese men had lower rates of college education than the women, more of them (four-fifths) had completed high school in Vietnam. Several of the males interviewed mentioned that their educational aspirations had been thwarted by the war because they were conscripted into military service. It is also significant for this study that the Vietnamese adults we interviewed live primarily in Tarrant County, where, as shown in Table 1.4, larger numbers of Vietnamese live than in Collin County, where education and income levels are higher.

When asked about their reasons for coming to the United States (Table 1.6), our Vietnamese research participants cited politics (which pushed people out of Vietnam) or the desire for freedom and democracy (which pulled people to the United States). The vast majority of those interviewed indicated that they came for political reasons, with some (more recent immigrants) coming for economic reasons or to join family members. And although there has been secondary migration to the DFW region among the Vietnamese, almost half of those interviewed were settled in the area by a refugee agency or sponsored by a local church group.

There are two significant nodes of residential settlement for Vietnamese Americans. When the Vietnamese first arrived in the area as refugees, they were initially settled in Fort Worth or Dallas, but due to secondary migration from other areas of the United States and to residential movement within the region, substantial numbers of Vietnamese now live in places like Arlington or Garland (see Map 1.1 and Table 1.3). According to many of the research participants, the more wealthy and elite Vietnamese live in the suburbs near Dallas, whereas more recent and less well-off migrants tend to settle in Tarrant County.

Among the first to arrive was Hong C., who is among the wealthy elite of the Vietnamese population in Tarrant County. Born in 1944, he had been a businessman in Vietnam and served in the Air Force during the Vietnam War. He owned a hotel in Saigon at the time of the fall of Saigon in April 1975. Unlike many more recent Vietnamese immigrants, Hong already spoke English before he arrived in the United States. He had studied English in high school, and later used it on the Air Force base in Saigon, where many Americans were stationed. He arrived in the United States in California at Camp Pendleton but soon moved to Texas. "I heard that it was larger and easier to find a job than in California, and that the weather was like the weather in Vietnam." He worked at various low-skilled jobs while also attending college. After accumulating some capital and experience in Texas, he moved back to California to run a used-car business but returned to Fort Worth shortly thereafter to purchase a small grocery store. Starting in 1991, he purchased large tracts of commercial real estate and now owns several Vietnamese shopping plazas across the DFW region. His five sons are all also successful businessmen, and his daughter works in the nail salon business.

Hong has been active in his Catholic parish, in Vietnamese veterans associations, in the Asian American Chamber of Commerce, and in the Vietnamese American Community (VAC) of Tarrant County. He was one of the first officers (as vice president) of the VAC, which, he reported, began with a group of people who helped to settle the arriving refugees. These early members were former military servicemen. As the group grew, they developed a more formal structure for the organization. Later, he said, people left Fort Worth for smaller cities like Arlington. But they did not spread out much because, as Hong put it, "we like living together." He describes his generation thus: "When we came here, we worked every day, we saved money, and we helped each other." Hong now lives in a large, beautiful custom-built home, with its own pool and tennis courts, in an affluent neighborhood in the Mid-Cities area. He has achieved much since arriving and is proud of his service to his community and of his hard work.

In stark contrast to the experience of Hong and his family is that of a Vietnamese family that arrived more recently, in the mid-1990s. Their lives are more typical of the majority of Vietnamese refugee families in Tarrant County. Thuy and Minh B. arrived on an HO visa. This was possible because Minh had spent six years in a reeducation camp after the Vietnam War; although he was released in the early 1980s, it took a decade for them to get this visa status and leave Vietnam. Minh is in his early sixties and Thuy is in her fifties, and both said they aspired to better lives as young adults. Minh was in law school when he was conscripted into the army and never had the chance to continue his education after that. Thuy hoped to be a nurse and although she had started college and had worked as a biology teacher she never finished her training. Minh now works as a janitor, and Thuy has not worked outside of the home since they arrived in the United States, though she earns some money babysitting children in her home. They have four children of their own, all born in Vietnam after Minh was released from prison. Due to the circumstances of the war, they had their children later in life than many other families. The oldest was eight years old when they arrived in the United States, so their children have been educated here and speak fluent English. Two are now in college and two are in high school, and all do well academically. The older two attend a nearby major public university, live at home, and work to help pay for their education. Minh explained, "My education was disrupted in Vietnam, so I want my kids to have a good education. I am sad because I wanted more education myself, to set an example for my children." Despite their low level of income and job status in the United States, these parents value education and are literate (in Vietnamese) and knowledgeable themselves, but they lack the language skills necessary to communicate this knowledge in English. Because neither parent has good English skills, they depend on their children to translate for them in many cases.

The hardships experienced by this couple both in Vietnam and in the United States are striking. The husband and wife are both from rural backgrounds and their parents were farmers. Thuy remained in the village while Minh was in the war and during his imprisonment. She would travel a long distance to visit him while he was in the prison camp. She said, "We first filed for a visa to leave in 1990. We were afraid to file, since we lived in a small village and had to be careful to avoid communist retaliation for trying to leave. At first we tried to get ODP status, and needed to get an ID number to do this, but that was not easy. Then we later filed for HO status. We first had the idea to go to California, but later found out that this was not a good place to raise a family. We had relatives already living in California. Eventually, my husband's uncle, who lives in [a city in DFW region], sponsored us and we came to Texas. At first we lived in that city, but then when my husband got the job here, we moved closer to his job." Minh added, "But our neighbors at that house complained that we had too much company, too many cars parked there at times, and made too much noise, so we recently moved to the house we have now." He said he felt the complaint by the non-Vietnamese neighbors was racially motivated. Rather than make trouble or be subject to more complaints, they moved.

The stories of these two types of Vietnamese refugees—the ones who came earlier, such as Hong, and have had a chance to establish themselves economically and socially; and others, such as Thuy and Minh, who came more recently after many years of struggle and poverty in Vietnam after the war—show the diversity of this population. Their social class positions in the United States, despite the original educational aspirations of Minh and Thuy, are quite different and have implications for their ability to participate effectively in the public sphere. Coming from a more elite, wealthy background in Saigon and already having a command of English when he arrived in the United States, due to his connections to Americans in Saigon during the war, Hong was able to accumulate both wealth and social status in the United States. Minh and Thuy, more typical of the Vietnamese families in DFW, work hard to support their children and devote most of their energies to ensuring that their children will receive an education; these parents hope that their children, the next generation, will attain a higher social position and greater participation in the civic sphere. Mai, whose story was related at the beginning of the chapter, presents another, middle position between these two extremes. The migration and settlement stories of the Vietnamese refugees differ in significant ways from those of the Indian immigrants who came to the United States on student visas, profiled earlier. Both populations, however, are actively creating cultural landscapes within which to establish their presence and participate in the civic sphere.

Cultural Landscapes:
Commercial Centers, Cultural Institutions, and the Ethnic Media

When individuals and families arrived in the United States, they experienced feelings of displacement associated with immigration but also sought modes of emplacement and ways to connect with both co-ethnics and the wider American society. The patterns of Indian and Vietnamese settlement in DFW offer good examples of what geographers Wilbur Zelinsky and Barrett Lee (1998) have labeled *heterolocalism*. These authors argue that in the absence of residential propinquity, immigrant groups use other mechanisms—ethnic churches, business associations, athletic leagues, social and service clubs, bars and cultural centers, and festivals—to, as they put it, "make place" and hence build centers for community activity. These mechanisms are all part of a cultural landscape, "the ordinary or commonplace visual elements of a community that residents create to satisfy their needs, wants, and desires" (Airriess 2002: 228), and they have expanded as the Vietnamese and Indian populations have grown. We view these manifestations of the cultural landscape as spaces of cultural citizenship where Indians or Vietnamese can come together to express their ethnic identity and their ties to their respective homelands through the shared consumption of food, music, entertainment, and ritual practices. Emotional attachment is a significant facet of this landscape. These sites are not unique to the DFW area, but they may take on particular importance for groups that are otherwise spatially dispersed and suburban in their residence patterns.

Our analysis of cultural landscapes includes the virtual spaces of interaction that are fostered through *ethnic media* and less formal modes of communication. The ethnic media have long been a part of the cultural landscape of immigrant populations in the United States, and they are particularly important for the first generation as "places where ethnic communities constitute themselves and their cultures" (Gerstle 1999: 285).[33] Although a large portion of print space and airtime in ethnic media is used for cultural entertainment and advertising, these media also keep immigrants connected and informed about their homelands. In addition, ethnic media play an important role in educating newcomers about their host society and culture.[34] The spaces created by ethnic media therefore offer a facet of the cultural landscape that is vital to the construction of participatory citizens.[35]

Vietnamese Cultural Landscapes

Cultural geographer Joseph Wood (1997: 58) has written that "Vietnamese Americans are imbuing suburbs with their own novel meanings. Passersby may notice a cluster of Vietnamese stores in a shopping plaza, a zone of Southeast Asian cuisine, a Buddhist temple or Vietnamese Catholic church announced with a distinctive script. . . . Vietnamese Americans see a vibrant community center, economic enterprise, reflections of tradition, contested interests, and complex social and economic geographies." This description of the area around Washington, D.C., also applies to the DFW region. Although there are significant concentrations of Vietnamese in a few cities and suburbs across the region, there are no clearly defined ethnic enclave settlements, in contrast to other urban areas with large named neighborhoods and commercial districts, such as Little Saigon in Orange County, California; or Versailles Village in New Orleans.[36] There is a Little Saigon in Houston, but no place in DFW has that label. Because of this residential dispersion—more of a suburban than an urban pattern—activities and spaces for the building of ethnic networks or for engagement with the wider civic sphere take place across a broad geographic space. The spatial presence of Vietnamese Americans in Tarrant County is most evident in Asian commercial centers and restaurants in such places as Arlington and Haltom City.

The civic presence of Vietnamese in Arlington was underscored in a recent attempt to add new "sign toppers" to existing street signs in neighborhoods where Latino, African American, Muslim, and Vietnamese populations had a residential or commercial presence or both. *Saigon* was the topper proposed to be added to Arkansas Lane, a street with two large Vietnamese shopping areas. The other toppers were to be *Cesar Chavez, Martin Luther King, Jr.*, and *Al-Salam* (an Arabic greeting). Although there was support for this proposal during initial discussions in the city council, the mayor of Arlington opposed it, and opposition grew. The proposal was ultimately defeated and none of the sign toppers was approved. Although the initiative did not pass, the inclusion of the Vietnamese shows the growing recognition that they are part of the social fabric of Arlington.[37] Their inclusion, however, is a racialized one that puts them in the "minority" category along with several other groups in a way that distinguishes a particular type of ethnicity and brings into relief some differences between newer Asian immigration and older European immigration.

The most significant spatial markers of the Vietnamese presence in Tarrant County are shopping centers that cater to the Vietnamese population and host events, even if they do not all have Vietnamese labels. One grocery chain is called Saigon Market, and another large market associated with the Vietnamese population is called Hong Kong Market (established in 1985). This anchor store for a strip shopping mall in Arlington recently built another store along the same road, at a new mall called Asia Times Square, built on the site of a former Wal-Mart Supercenter. Whereas the earliest malls were built near the residential neighborhoods first settled by Vietnamese refugees, the development of Asia Times Square in a newer location demonstrates the growing residential dispersion. This new mall also combines American and Vietnamese symbolism, with its name, Times Square, echoing New York City, and its clock tower echoing the major shopping center in the former Saigon. It is American, Asian, and Vietnamese.[38]

Although the Vietnamese Buddhist temples and Catholic churches, discussed in greater detail in Chapter 3, also signify the presence of this population in the region, these large shopping malls are the most visible signs of a growing Vietnamese social space. In these malls, people can find an array of services, from insurance companies to hair and nail salons. Consumers can purchase religious symbols (both Catholic and Buddhist), ceremonial foods, and everyday items—such as just the right fish sauce or a special brand of noodles, and DVDs of popular films or variety shows such as *Paris by Night*. There are both larger and smaller Vietnamese shopping plazas in Arlington. Several large Vietnamese restaurants associated with shopping strips also provide key stages for the performance of activities ranging from weddings to commemorations, organization meetings, banquets, and awards ceremonies. There are more than twenty smaller Vietnamese restaurants in the city of Arlington alone. Some cater to a younger, "hipper" crowd, while some are aimed at the older generation. There are also several nightclubs in the suburbs of Dallas that are frequented by Vietnamese American young adults.

Even if some younger and more affluent professional families do not shop on a regular basis at the Asian malls, they take their children there when these malls are the sponsoring locations for events such as the Mid-Autumn Moon Festival, or when it is time to buy special foods for such occasions as the Tet (Lunar New Year) Festival, analyzed in Chapter 5. These younger families and young adults do frequent Vietnamese restaurants, either for casual get-togethers or to attend ceremonies and meetings. The Vietnamese markets display posters about upcoming musical events and performances at larger venues.

In addition to the fixed locations of stores and restaurants, there are social spaces in this cultural landscape that shift geographic location depending on the event. The population's stable visual anchors—the restaurants, shops, religious institutions, and community centers (one in Arlington and one in Garland)—are not the only locations for group events. Although these physical places help constitute the "imagined community" (Anderson 1991) of the Vietnamese American population, other sites also exist for the expression of Vietnamese identity and articulation with the wider civic sphere. The flag of South Vietnam (1948–1975)—the so-called freedom and heritage flag with a yellow background and three horizontal red stripes—has become a significant marker for Vietnamese activities and helps demarcate spaces used for events. This flag differs from the flag with a red background with a gold star in the middle that represents the current Vietnamese government, the Socialist Republic of Vietnam. The latter flag is not accepted as legitimate by many Vietnamese Americans who fled that government as refugees. The freedom and heritage flag is placed at the entrance to parking lots or along routes to help visitors and participants find a location and recognize that it is a "Viet" event. The flag is an enduring rallying point among the Vietnamese population and provides a potent and multivocal symbol for their diaspora community, even if its meaning is not obvious to the general population, most of whom are unfamiliar with this flag. Although there are disagreements among the Vietnamese regarding the anticommunist sentiment associated with many uses of the flag, it is part of the "cultural intimacy" (Herzfeld 2005) that creates bonds across the many divisions among Vietnamese Americans in the United States. This flag is displayed at a variety of events, including political rallies associated with homeland politics, cultural festivals, and activities related to children. Vietnamese Buddhist temples and Catholic churches also display this flag along with the American flag.

In addition to the ethnically charged physical spaces just described, Vietnamese speakers have access to a wide array of print media, television stations, and radio programs, as well as Internet sites. Although not all of the members of the first generation of Vietnamese are literate in English, they are a very literate population in general, and they read widely to learn about international, national, and local news. Many homes visited during our research were filled with treasured books (some were among the small number of possessions that refugees took with them when they left) and other print material. At least twenty newspapers and magazines published in the Vietnamese language are available in the DFW region. Most are relatively new, with the oldest going back about fifteen years. Before these regional ethnic newspapers were started, Vietnamese immigrants relied on publications from California and Houston.

Three of the major newspapers are *But Viet News* (published twice a week), *A Chau Thoi Bao Weekly Newspaper*, and *Vietnam Weekly News*. According to its publisher, when he started publishing it once a month in 1982, *But Viet* was the first Vietnamese newspaper in the region. It has a staff of seventeen, including eleven full-time and six part-time employees. Some of its staff members were prominent journalists in Vietnam. Such local publications cover local, national, and international news, and share some columns and stories with Vietnamese media in other regions of the country. In addition to the newspapers there are several locally published and widely read magazines, most of which have glossy covers and are printed in color. These include *Tre Magazine, Ca Dao, Kien Thuc, Pho Thong, Cam Nang, Little Saigon News*, and *The Gioi Moi*. In addition to publishing news stories, they offer serial stories, poems, advice columns, horoscopes, and other features of interest to their readers. Most of the Vietnamese-language magazines are free and depend heavily on advertising; they have many ads for Vietnamese restaurants, stores, businesses, goods (such as furniture and nail salon supplies), lawyers, and doctors. The locally published print media available to Vietnamese living in the area are important sources of information not only about homeland politics and national events in the United States, but also about local news that affects the Vietnamese population and local events of interest. The advertisements are an important means for informing the population about goods and services that are available to them, often from co-ethnics, and they help Vietnamese businesses and professional legal and medical practices to grow.

Before the on-air debut of two Vietnamese AM radio stations (Radio Saigon Dallas and Vietnamese American Broadcasting, or VAB) in the middle of the first decade of the twenty-first, those who wanted to listen to Vietnamese language radio had to purchase a special set for the frequency that was transmitted. Many still listen to the older stations such as Dallas Vietnamese Radio, which has its offices in Arlington. The newer AM stations try to appeal both to the younger generation and to the elders, and they have programming in both Vietnamese and English. VAB, which broadcasts from both Dallas and Houston, calls itself "the voice of the new generation." Both Radio Saigon Dallas and VAB have Web sites in English. Vietnamese Americans in Tarrant County also have access to satellite radio stations that are broadcast from outside the region. Some research participants reported that they listen to the Vietnamese version of BBC and to VOA (Voice of America). There is one major television station for the Vietnamese population in the United States, Saigon Broadcasting Television Network, which has offices in several cities and is available through satellite. It also has a Dallas office and a few local correspondents based in Dallas. Representatives of Vietnamese American media are present at most activities that take place in the region, such as festivals, camps, political meetings, and protests. There are several Vietnamese American professional media organizations, including the Vietnamese American Press Club (founded in 2005) and the Texas Vietnamese American Media Association.

In addition to using these older forms of media, Vietnamese Americans participate in chat rooms such as Paltalk.com and, for the younger generations, Facebook and MySpace groups based on Vietnamese American ethnicity. There are also Yahoo groups and Web sites associated with various organizations and interest groups. The Vietnamese mobilize to attend political demonstrations and to express support for such efforts through Web pages, cyber networks, and cell phones. Most major ethnic associations have Web pages, frequently in both English and Vietnamese, but primarily in the Vietnamese language. These new forms of media provide sources of pleasure during leisure time but also help share information about both domestic and homeland politics. They create a Vietnamese American public space for communication that interacts with the wider civic sphere.

Indian Cultural Landscapes

Indian immigrants have made their mark in the cities and suburbs of America where they have settled by building temples and mosques and by reinvigorating older strip shopping malls by opening grocery stores, sari shops, restaurants, and travel agencies.[39] Like the Vietnamese, Indians are residentially dispersed, although they have largely settled in the suburbs to the northwest, north, and northeast of Dallas. At the center of this semicircular pattern of settlement is Taj Mahal Imports, a grocery store in the Richardson Heights shopping center, a strip mall that has been taken over, for the most part, by Indian stores and that is a physical and social mecca for the Indian community.[40] Members of local Indian organizations often gather at Taj Mahal Imports for informal meetings, to sell tickets for upcoming events, or to raise funds to help victims of major disasters—such as the earthquake in Gujarat, the 2004 tsunami, or the Mumbai attacks of 2008. Indian businesses can post information about their services on a bulletin board inside—a common practice in India and hence something that Indian immigrants in the United States are used to seeing. In addition, it is at Taj Mahal Imports that the goods and materials necessary for cultural and religious observances are also available—candles for Diwali (the Hindu Festival of Lights), small images of Ganesh (a Hindu deity with an elephant head) used in the observance of his festival, or colored powders for Holi (a Hindu spring festival). Each year, in a room at the back of the store, a large *rangoli* (a painting made of colored sand) is installed as part of the Diwali celebration.[41] Indian families in the area who are unable to create a rangoli on their own doorstep, as they might do in India, make a special trip to Taj Mahal Imports just to see this painting.

As the Indian population has grown, other visible examples of cultural placemaking have developed. These include other, smaller strip malls; the host of religious institutions that are discussed in Chapter 3; and FunAsia, a 32,000-square-foot community center located in the inner-ring suburb of Richardson. Here Bollywood films are shown in three theaters, the annual banquets of various organizations are held, and members of the community hold private parties and receptions, either in a big hall or in the disco club.[42] During movie intermissions, Indian snacks are sold at the concession stand, and a later addition to the facility is a disc jockey booth perched above the crowd. From this booth, radio programming directed at a South Asian audience is now broadcast 24/7. The first FunAsia was opened in 2002 and became so successful that a second facility (6,500 square feet) was opened in the northern suburb of Carrollton in 2005, and later a third facility, with a 15,000-square-foot theater and a 4,500-square-foot banquet hall and meeting room, was opened in a shopping center in Irving. Both Carrollton and Irving were areas of growing Indian settlement during the 1990s and the first decade of the current century. As the Bollywood star has risen, Indian movies have begun to attract a small non-South Asian audience that can on occasion be found among the weekend audiences at FunAsia. Further, about 15 percent of the banquet business at the original FunAsia is now Hispanic. The facility has become a popular place for *quinceañera* (a girl's fifteenth birthday) celebrations. In October of 2007, FunAsia became a subsidiary of Pyramid Saimira Theatre Ltd. (a company based in Chennai, India) and was thus launched as a multimedia entertainment enterprise across North America. FunAsia thus offers a good example not only of the business acumen of Indian immigrants but also of their civic presence. Indeed, the facilities of the original FunAsia have been used for meetings and events sponsored by DFW International Community Alliance, an umbrella organization for the region's immigrant communities, and once for the screening of a series on immigration produced by the local public television station.

Beyond opening strip shopping malls and various business enterprises (such as jewelry stores, sari shops, and video stores), Indians, like the Vietnamese, have also established their presence with a host of restaurants that have cropped up across the metropolitan area. The DFW Indian Lions Club has its monthly meetings at one of these restaurants, and the members of one of the myriad regional associations meets at another. Sometimes a restaurant owner offers the space for a fundraiser—for example, when someone of Indian ancestry who is running for political office somewhere in the country passes through town to rally support. These restaurants, and other businesses, are also vital to the success of Indian cultural events in the city. They make monetary or in-kind donations of food or other items that can be auctioned off to raise funds. In return they are able to advertise in printed event programs or in the high-tech visual presentations that are often part of Indian charity or cultural events.

Another important place in the Indian cultural landscape is the office of the IANT, whose location in Richardson (and not far from Taj Mahal Imports) is well known largely because, until recently, it was here that Indians in the area could go once a month (when Indian consular officials visited from Houston) to renew an Indian passport, file papers for dual citizenship, or apply for a visa for their American-born children or for themselves, if they were naturalized U.S. citizens without dual citizenship, to travel to India.[43] The IANT also operates a monthly health clinic run by volunteer physicians, and a host of special interest forums (for women, for senior citizens, for youth).[44]

Finally, IANT sponsors two annual events for the local Indian community, one of which—India Nite—is discussed in Chapter 5. The second event is the Anand Bazaar, a celebration of India's Independence Day (August 15) that includes a large bazaar of booths where one can buy clothing and other items, pick up promotional literature from organizations and businesses, and even register to vote. There is also a stage with musical entertainment, and a host of food stalls. Each year thousands of Indians attend the Anand Bazaar, which takes place at Lone Star Park in Grand Prairie, a town between Dallas and Fort Worth. They transform a horse racing track into a bustling and noisy Indian public space for an afternoon and evening.

Like the Vietnamese, Indians also claim virtual space and engage the public sphere through media organizations. Because their command of English and their level of education are generally high, they do not rely solely on the ethnic media, but South Asian radio programming flourishes in the area. The oldest is Radio Bharati, a program launched by the IANT that originally played for two hours on Saturday mornings but is now on the air 24–7 playing Indian music, welcoming guests, and promoting Indian activities in the area. The Radio Bharati operation has moved from a small room within the IANT's office in Richardson to the large Richardson FunAsia complex mentioned earlier. DFW-area Indian nationals and their offspring can also listen to Desi Masala, a station originally founded in Houston that moved into the Dallas market after 2000 and quickly set up 24/7 programming. Even more recently, Salaam Namasté, a radio station that attempts to cater to the South Asian (broadly defined) community of North Texas, has entered the Dallas market. The station employs both Indian and Pakistani individuals.

Although music programming dominates the airwaves, these radio stations also provide Indian news, announce community events, air advertisements for local businesses, and host interviews with visiting dignitaries. In advance of major activities in the region, sponsors are invited to discuss the activity on the air. There are also opportunities for listeners to call in to ask questions and voice their opinions. Experts in various fields may address particular issues— such as domestic violence or immigration laws. A staff member at one of these stations said the station's mission was "to keep the community informed and together," but this person also noted the brokerage role that the ethnic media can play. "The mainstream sees us as the representative of the community and the community sees us as the representative to the mainstream media." This brokerage role establishes the civic presence of Indian media in the DFW area.

The local Indian media also play a role in civic education, bringing their listeners into the public sphere. For example, after 9/11 an FBI agent was invited onto one show to talk about security, and on occasion politicians running for local office are interviewed. However, a staff member at one radio station emphasized that, in general, religious and political topics are off limits because they are volatile in India. "Anything about India and Pakistan or Muslims and Hindus we try to avoid. But then we are also criticized by people who say that there are serious things going on in India between Muslims and Hindus and we do not talk about it. We do carry a prayer direct from the mosque on Friday afternoons because we have a large Muslim community of listeners, but that is the extent of it."

In contrast to the Vietnamese community, there are no local newspapers serving the Indian community. As immigrants with a good command of English, they read the U.S. national press, and the *Hindu Times* on the Internet, and they subscribe to one or more of the U.S. national Indian newspapers—for example, *India Abroad* out of New York or the *India Tribune* out of Chicago, both of which are published in English. These newspapers keep DFW-area Indians informed about local and national politics, about Indian politics, and about Indian cultural events locally, nationally, and globally. Stories about the role of Indians at the Democratic National Convention may run alongside stories about the celebration of a Ganesh festival or India's Independence Day in some part of the United States, about Kashmir, or about a wealthy U.S. billionaire who supports programs for the underprivileged in India. From time to time, events sponsored by the various local Indian organizations are covered.

The primary local print source of information for Indians is the monthly magazine *Bharati*, which is distributed to members of the IANT. While full of advertising for local businesses and organizations, this magazine also contains regular columns on immigration issues written by a local Indian-born immigration attorney, as well as articles on health issues written by local physicians. There are also articles directed at civic education—about school issues, about what to do with a traffic ticket, about how to handle conflicts that might arise at work.

Many households subscribe to Zee TV or some other satellite service that brings them Indian television programming. Finally, one of the most powerful means of communication serving the Indian population is an electronic community bulletin board, or "Internet neighborhood" (Appadurai 1996), called ekNazar.com (the word means "a glimpse"). Founded in 1998 by an Indian studying at the University of Texas at Dallas, ekNazar has several sections—one for business advertising, another for classified ads (it facilitates cyber neighborhood yard sales), a discursive space for the exchange of ideas and opinions, and information on community events.[45]

Claiming Space in the Public Sphere

Our research indicates that despite their significant differences—which are rooted in the distinct historical and geopolitical relationships between the United States on the one hand and the nations of India and Vietnam on the other—Indian and Vietnamese immigrants in DFW have much in common: their settlement and resettlement through secondary migrations within the United States, their ability to reconnect with family members who have either preceded or followed them in the migration process, their challenges in raising children in a new environment, and their ongoing ties to their respective homelands. Further, we have found that, once settled, both populations begin to construct cultural landscapes through which they both experience and impact the region. The cultural landscapes we have described in this chapter are spaces not only of commerce and pleasure but also for civic learning, civic engagement, and cultural citizenship—the latter in the sense of social spaces where newcomers can "express themselves and feel at home" (Flores 2003: 88). It is through the attractions of the commercial and pleasurable aspects of these spaces that newcomers are drawn into the communities of practice that, as we argue in this book, provide both avenues and venues for participation in the public sphere.

The Vietnamese and Indian immigrant populations are effectively making their presence known at the local level. They are reinforcing bonds among themselves as co-ethnics, creating ties to other groups, and constructing important venues for communication and the dissemination of information. For immigrants and their children, participation in the public sphere is connected to felt identities, a sense of belonging, and the meaning of citizenship that they construct for themselves in the context of the cultural landscapes we have discussed in this chapter. As we explore various communities of practice, sites for civic learning, and the stories of individuals from both groups in the following chapters, we point out differences as well as similarities in their modes of civic integration. In Chapter 2 we draw on a series of interviews with people of different generations to reflect on the "situated nature" of ethnic identity and belonging, and to explore what this means for understanding the social and cultural dimensions of participatory citizenship.

2 Immigrant Identities and the Meanings of Citizenship

"**WHEN I THINK OF MY IDENTITY,** I feel that my soul, values are Muslim; my intellect, [my] confidence and freedom to reason are American; my heart, emotions are Indian, and my work ethic is Asian. I'm one person, but in me are all these identities operating at the same time." This is how one Muslim Indian responded to a question about his identity as a first-generation immigrant in the United States. A Hindu father told a somewhat different story about his six-year-old son. His little boy had come across the term *American Indian* in a storybook. He went in to his mother, who was working in the kitchen of their home in north Dallas, and asked her if he was American Indian. His mother tried to explain that this was a term applied to Native Americans, who were the original people in the land that is now the United States. She then told her son that he was Indian American—whereupon the little boy replied, "No, I am American Indian because I am American first and Indian second."

These generational differences were also expressed, if in a slightly different register, by our Vietnamese research participants. One first-generation former refugee observed, "I still keep my Vietnamese traditions and at the same time I'm learning new things from American people and their traditions. If I see something that's worth learning, then I will learn it, but no matter what, I will always feel Vietnamese." Another first-generation Vietnamese American parent told a story that she perceived to be humorous about her young daughter, born in the United States. Although still a preschooler who does not yet speak English, this little girl is aware that she is different from her much older siblings, who were born in Vietnam and moved to the United States with the family in the 1990s. She tells her parents that, in contrast to her siblings, "I am an American girl, an American 'white' girl."

These stories demonstrate the complexities of identity among the most recent Asian immigrants to America, and the differences between immigrants and their U.S.-born children. They also raise the sensitive issues of race, ethnicity, and identity. In this chapter, we explore the meanings of "feeling" Vietnamese or Indian, and "being" American as perceived by adult immigrants of the first generation and youth who either arrived as children or were born in the United States. An important question for anyone seeking to understand civic engagement and political incorporation is to what extent do immigrants consider becoming a legal American citizen to mean "being" or "feeling" American, and how does this attitude shape the practices of participatory citizenship? If becoming a citizen and becoming American are kept distinct in people's minds, as we frequently found them to be among the first-generation adults we interviewed, does this distinction then provide the foundation for forms of cultural citizenship—that is, for entering the civic sphere from a position of difference?

In the United States, a self-defined "nation of immigrants," belonging has frequently been defined through the prism of ethnic group affiliation.[1] This approach is particularly complicated, however, for immigrants from the countries that make up South Asia, Southeast Asia, and North Asia, all of whom are categorized as Asian or Pacific Islander on the most recent U.S. census forms, and viewed as simply Asian by many people they encounter. What do these populations really have in common as Asians? And is *Asian* a meaningful category in which to build effective communities of practice for civic learning and civic engagement? All of the questions we pose here, which form the basis for this chapter, are of great interest not only to us but also to our research participants, who were very articulate about issues of identity and belonging.

In our discussion here, we follow anthropologist Fredrik Barth's seminal work on ethnic boundaries and the situated nature of identity. According to Barth (1969: 33), minority populations in "poly-ethnic" societies (such as the United States) may choose "to emphasize ethnic identity, using it to develop new positions and patterns to organize activities in those sectors formerly not found in their society. . . . " He also stresses processes of inclusion and exclusion, noting that "categorical ethnic distinctions do not depend on an absence of mobility, contact and information, but do entail social processes of exclusion and incorporation whereby discrete categories are maintained despite changing participation and membership in the course of individual life histories" (9–10). This conceptualization of ethnic identity is compatible with viewing a community of practice as a potential "sector" of inclusion or exclusion relative to civic participation and membership.

The ways in which ethnic identity is constructed and employed among our two populations has a lot to do with boundaries. People who identified themselves in one way in their homeland come to think of themselves in another way in the United States; social divisions at home may recede as new categories come into play. In our research we found that whether or not Indian or Vietnamese immigrants became U.S. citizens in the legal sense, they still confronted often troubling questions about what it means to be American (rather than Indian or Vietnamese), Indian or Vietnamese American (rather than, for example, Mexican American), Asian (rather than, for example, white Texan or Latino), or Asian American (in contrast to, for example, African American). These constructions of identity across boundaries and in relation to others also have important implications for how members of these two populations define meaningful citizenship practice and become civically engaged.

Although we also explored the topics of citizenship and identity throughout our research with community leaders and in informal ethnographic contexts, this chapter draws primarily on the two sets of formal interviews we conducted: individual interviews with sixty-seven first-generation Indian and Vietnamese parents (many of whom were naturalized U.S. citizens) and group interviews with Indian and Vietnamese college students (in their early to mid-twenties) who were the children of immigrants and either were born in the United States or arrived as young children. In these interviews, which yielded exceedingly rich insights, we asked questions about identity, citizenship, and participation in the political, religious, and civic spheres. We asked what it means to be Indian or Vietnamese, American, and Asian. Not surprisingly, we found significant generational differences in many aspects of identity among our two populations. In the following pages, we first describe the ways in which first-generation immigrant and refugee parents spoke about becoming naturalized or legal American citizens, and what it means to be or become "American." We then discuss the significance of the categories *Asian* and *Asian American* for adults of the first generation. Finally, we contrast their attitudes and values with those of college-age youth.

The First Generation:
Becoming a Citizen, Becoming American?

Every immigrant comes to the U.S. with one foot in America and one foot remaining in their old country. That was me. For years I had the intention of returning to India to live. But slowly you start putting more and more weight on that foot in the new country as you become acculturated. Finally I went back to India for a visit, still with the intention of returning to live. But when I got there I experienced this great culture shock. I noticed how different I had become, and that I was a stranger in my own land. It was at that moment that I realized that I no longer had a foot in India. I had become American. So with no reason to remain politically tied to India, I decided I would make legal what already was—I became a U.S. citizen.

This was the way one Indian male immigrant, fifty-five years old at the time he was interviewed, described his decision to become an American citizen. Most of the first-generation Indian participants in this research had been naturalized.[2] They explained that they had pursued naturalization because their lives and the lives of their children were now in the United States, because they wanted to sponsor relatives or to travel more easily, or so they would not have to worry about immigration status. One woman used the metaphor of a bridge— that becoming a legal American citizen is a bridge you cross that in turn creates a bridge to a new life. A male participant used a different metaphor, describing how many Indians, for a time, buy dual-voltage appliances so that when they returned to India they can take these appliances with them and they will work there. "Then I decided that I did not want to be 110/220—that I had to choose." It was then, he said, that he and his wife decided to become American citizens.

Although some respondents, particularly women, felt that taking U.S. citizenship was a betrayal of their heritage, most noted the pragmatic and advantageous aspects of making the decision to be naturalized. One man offered the following as his narrative of the path to citizenship:

I was working here in the petroleum business and I was sent on a job somewhere overseas once, as I often am, and I got ill and needed a shot. I went to the U.S. Army clinic, and even though I lived and worked in America and had my green card, they wouldn't touch me because I wasn't an American citizen. I had to go to this bad Indonesian clinic. I thought, if I'm going to work in this industry I better get my citizenship for protection. So I filed for citizenship right away.

A female participant said that for some time she and her husband did not consider becoming naturalized citizens because they both had elderly parents in India. If something had happened to their parents and they were U.S. citizens, it would have taken some time to get the visas to return to India. But eventually they shifted their focus to concern about being separated from their America-born children. After twenty years, this woman became a naturalized citizen. Another male participant asserted, "You cannot refute the fact that the U.S. is home for us. We are here. We are Indian, but we are here." For him and for many others, it was living in America that made one both Indian and American, rather than any particular behaviors. These locational claims, driven by ideas about emplacement, are offered as reasons for becoming an American citizen, and they help first-generation immigrants to distinguish their sense of cultural belonging (as Indian) from their sense of political belonging (as American).

Several Indians interviewed for this research did suggest that in the United States their Indian identity is situational—that is, it pertains to particular contexts—while others said their desire to return to India—that is, to maintain a transnational outlook—is what sustained their "Indianness" during the early years of immigration. However, for the majority, *Indianness* is a cultural category and they express an enormous amount of pride in their rich heritage, their traditions (including food, clothing, religious practices, cultural festivals, classical dance and music, and so on), and their values. The most critical values are those rooted in respect for family and the institution of marriage, hospitality, and a general concern for others. Here is the way one adult female, an Indian Christian, put it:

> I still commonly identify myself as Indian because we believe in our culture
> and believe it is the best. I was born in India and not America. I also do not
> like many aspects of American culture. Americans give their children too much
> freedom and this is not necessarily good. . . . Also, Americans do not take care
> of their elders, they just dump them in a nursing home. I work in a nursing
> home, and I truly feel bad for the elders there, and I hope to never be like them.[3]

Among first-generation Indians there was more variation in attitudes toward the concept of being Indian American than in attitudes toward being Indian, although almost twice as many men as women who participated in the parent interviews said they used the former descriptor. One woman, who said she used the term rarely, suggested that it was a label applied by outsiders and that it never occurred to her to use it when talking about herself. A male respondent who had a more positive assessment of the term (yet still defined it as an external label) said that if he were to be categorized by Americans, this is the category he would prefer. He went on to note, however, that the second generation was exploring the idea of Hindu American, parallel to Jewish American.[4] A woman who said she used it "on occasion" made the following observation:

> This is the answer that I gave my kids when they asked me what they were. I said it was like choosing between two parents. Can you be just your Mom's or your Dad's? No, you are equally from both parents. They both make up who you are. We are equally Indian and American, we are Indian American.

Those who were more favorably disposed to the term *Indian American* to describe themselves noted that the longer one is in the United States, the more one feels comfortable with a descriptor that encompasses a dual identity.

When we talked with first-generation Indian participants in this research about whether they identify themselves as American, we found that 81 percent of the male respondents in the parent interviews replied "at least somewhat commonly" compared with 44 percent of the women. Further, whereas close to a third of the men replied "commonly" to this question, only 18 percent of the women gave this answer. Conversely, whereas 12.5 percent of the men replied "rarely" to this question, 28 percent of the women chose "rarely." These gendered differences are significant and reflect different positionalities in relation to identity, that is, being American at work and Indian at home. More Indian men than Indian women are out in the workforce and, like the Muslim man quoted at the outset of this chapter, they "feel American" in relation to the culture of the workplace. One male respondent in fact distinguished between the identities he had in his personal life and those he had in his professional life, characterizing this as "having two lives." Another male respondent noted that his whole working life has been in the United States and hence he had developed the American work ethic. He observed that if he had to work in India he would feel like a foreigner and get impatient. Others talked about feeling more American when they return to India because they realize when they are there that they are not truly Indian anymore, that they have changed as a result of their experience in the United States. "We feel different," said one female respondent, "and others draw the difference. They treat us differently."

Beyond naming the workplace and being back in India as important contexts within which many of them feel most American, several of our first-generation Indian respondents, both men and women, said they feel American when they are engaged in politics or when commenting on the state of the economy—that is, when they enter the civic sphere. Additionally, a few answered that they feel American when engaged in American sports, or when traveling, because they carry a U.S. passport—the document of legal citizenship. By contrast, it is in relation to friends and family that they feel most Indian and, secondarily, at religious or Indian community events and activities.

Another theme that emerged in these discussions of identity in relation to the label *American* was sensitivity to phenotypical characteristics in the context of a country where "race matters." An adult male respondent with self-acknowledged political ambitions commented, "It would be more beneficial to my political career to identify myself as American, but with my name and my physical features I cannot escape the Indian identification. Whether I want it or not it is with me." A female respondent who at first said she "commonly" thought of herself as American quickly changed it to "somewhat commonly" and explained:

> Well, when an Indian refers to an American, they think of a white American. So when I say I am American my kids always correct me, saying, "Mom, you are not white." So I guess I cannot say "commonly"; that is reserved for "real" Americans.[5]

These remarks substantiate previous observations about Asians being "forever foreign no matter how much they think or act like Americans. 'Being American' is equated with being white. And as a result, Asian ethnics, despite being longtime Americans, lack the option to cast aside their racial and ethnic affinities as European ethnics, who by birthright are part of the American mainstream, freely do" (Tuan 1998: 40). A female research participant reflected on the matter in the following way: "People will ask you what nationality you are and when you reply that you are American they respond, but where are you originally from? They draw a difference."[6] The implication of her comment was that people should not make this distinction if someone feels American and it is part of their personal sense of belonging in the United States.

With regard to being American, first-generation Indians are clearly operating within complex, multiple, situational, and gendered spheres of identity. They can choose these identities for themselves, but their choices are often influenced by context and by the extent to which others define them as similar or different (and hence include or exclude them) according to their phenotypical appearance, their accented English, or their behaviors (for example, when they are identified as American upon returning to India for a visit). Becoming a legal U.S. citizen does not necessarily mean being American in a cultural sense, although there is a very strong claim to that identity in a political and legal sense. America has nurtured them, it is where they live and where they have spent much of their adult lives. This emplaced sense of belonging—which anthropologist Kirin Narayan (2002: 425) has described as the process by which people who have left old homes create new ones and come to belong somewhere—should not be underestimated as a parameter for how Indians in the United States define not only their rights but also their responsibilities as participatory citizens, and hence how they engage the civic sphere. The various identities with which Indian immigrants wrestle and that have been discussed here constitute these multiple frameworks of meaning. It is an embodied presence in the United States, or in particular spheres of activity, that undergirds an American identity for first-generation Indians.

Like the Indian parents interviewed, Vietnamese parents distinguished between the cultural sense of being American and the legal aspects (rights and duties) of being an American citizen. In contrast to Indians, for first-generation Vietnamese, issues of emplacement and belonging are influenced by their experiences as political refugees who fled persecution "at home" in Vietnam and feel a sense of displacement both in Vietnam and in the United States. Because of their forced exile from Vietnam, they have less of a sense of freely choosing to be in America, although they strongly assert that they have chosen freedom and democracy over communism, and this affects their sense of identity in the United States. The Vietnam War continues to shape identity among the first generation, and Vietnamese American identity. Their experiences as refugees from the war are expressed in an anticommunism stance that reinforces their feelings of shared history as well as their sense of forced displacement.[7] Also because of the war, Vietnamese refugee identities are shaped not only in relationship to "American" identity, as is the case for Indians, but also in relationship to (and especially against) Vietnamese communists and the current government of the Socialist Republic of Vietnam. The experience of the war has led to ambivalence about America for many of the older refugees. Although America represents freedom and escape from the communist regime, for which all are grateful, it is also the country that abandoned them by pulling out of the war and leaving South Vietnam, and Saigon, to fall to the communists. Also as a result of the war, however, many Vietnamese refugees were acquainted with America and Americans even before they arrived in the United States, through the occupation of Vietnam by American soldiers during the war and sometimes through their direct contact with them as fellow soldiers or government workers. Many among the first wave of refugees arrived in the United States already speaking English and being acquainted with American institutions of government. Their refugee status also permitted them to gain relatively easy access to permanent residency, and accounts for the high rates of citizenship among Vietnamese who settled in the United States.

More than three-fourths of the Vietnamese adults in the parent interview cohort had become naturalized citizens, a figure comparable to the overall population of Vietnamese in national studies.[8] The rest were in the process of working toward naturalization and intended to become citizens. The Vietnamese parents who were interviewed said frequently that they became citizens primarily in order to enhance their rights, such as the right to vote, the right to a passport and the ability to travel freely, and the right to social security and health care in old age. The right to vote in a democracy was considered to be of paramount importance. Here is how one sixty-seven-year-old Vietnamese refugee expressed his reasons for becoming a naturalized American citizen:

> I'm not yet a U.S. citizen, but I will get my interview in two or three months. I just got my fingerprint today. I took the citizenship test before, back in 2002, but I had difficulty in understanding the questions they asked me so I didn't pass. I asked them if they could write the questions down and I'll give them the answers; they said it's against the regulations. This time the test will be in Vietnamese. The reason I want to become a U.S. citizen is because I want to have a passport to go to other countries (but I'm not much into that), but the main reason is to vote. I feel angry for not being able to vote against someone I don't like.

One woman explained the important protections she gained with citizenship as follows: "The advantage of citizenship is that when I get old, I will get SSI and people with low income can live in public housing. That is an advantage over a green card." Although the Vietnamese parents may have placed more emphasis on the rights of citizenship than the Indians did, they shared with the Indian parents the idea that an important reason for becoming a legal citizen is that you have settled permanently in this new country and are raising children here. One person said, "I've been living here for a long time, so it only makes sense to become a citizen of this country," while another expressed her reasons as "so my children could become citizens, because they will spend the rest of their lives here."

Even though the term *Vietnamese American* is commonly used by former refugees to refer to themselves, the parents interviewed were conscious of a distinction between being a legal citizen of the United States (one connotation of the word *American*) and being American in a cultural sense. The term *Vietnamese American* is rarely spelled with a hyphen (as can be seen in the ethnic organizations called Vietnamese American Community that are discussed in Chapter 4), reflecting perhaps a subtle difference between being Vietnamese in America and being a Vietnamese American. There are contrasts in attitudes between those who are receptive to the label *American* and those who are not. One woman commented, "Ever since we got U.S. citizenship, we see ourselves as American"; another one woman put it this way:

> I'm not forgetting my Vietnamese background. I am Vietnamese. I respect the Americans. We (Vietnamese and Americans) are all the same underneath our skin colors. We are two [races] but underneath the skin color, we are just one. We are one family.

But for others, such as one man who suffered in a reeducation camp after the Vietnam War and had to wait until 2001 to gain refugee status and come to the United States, it is harder to adjust. As he expressed it, "I will always be Vietnamese. I had to leave my country. I will try to go back and be buried there." In still other cases, racial phenotype was a barrier to feeling American. One middle-aged Vietnamese man who is a U.S. citizen nonetheless said, "I don't look American. How can I be American?" A woman who arrived in the United States in the mid-1990s also expressed her identity in physical terms: "Look at this yellow skin and only yellow. Nobody will ever see us as American." She is also reminded of her Vietnameseness, she joked, when she goes shopping and has trouble finding clothes in her small size.

In spite of some ambivalence when asked whether they identified as American, two-thirds of the Vietnamese men and one-half of the women in the parent interviews stated that they identified as American at least "somewhat commonly." However, it is also significant that 27 percent of Vietnamese men and 36 percent of Vietnamese women reported that they "rarely" felt or identified as American. Given that 76 percent of the Vietnamese parents interviewed had become U.S. citizens, there is a disparity between the high level of naturalization among them and the fact that almost one-third of the men and more than a third of the women do *not* identify as American. Among those Vietnamese who had become citizens, 24 percent reported that they "rarely" saw themselves as American (in contrast to 63 percent of those who had not become citizens).

Although both Indian and Vietnamese men were more apt than women to "commonly" identify as American, more Vietnamese women than Indian women identified "commonly" as American. There are several reasons for this. First-generation Indian women in this study were mostly middle class and often—particularly if they had school-age children—did not work outside the home. Further, through food, dress, and the maintenance of religious rituals, they are the ones charged with sustaining Indian cultural practices. Vietnamese refugee women, by contrast, tend to work outside the home and need to do so to help support their families. They are thus exposed to Americans and American culture through work, as are both the Indian and Vietnamese men. The fact that one-third of the Vietnamese American men who had been naturalized "rarely" feel American (compared with only 12.5 percent of the Indian men) is also striking, and related to the adjustment problem and, for the first-generation members who served as soldiers and often later as prisoners of war, to the lingering trauma of the war. As a Vietnamese American psychiatrist explained, many Vietnamese men suffer post-traumatic stress disorder as well as guilt over their loss of the war and their escape to America and leaving behind their countrymen. Although women also suffer psychological trauma from the war, many of the men were in the military and had more direct dealings with the violence. This background leads to less ease in taking on a new identity than Indian men experienced.

Vietnamese of the first generation were, like the Indians interviewed, aware of how their sense of identity was connected to situation or context. Vietnamese identity continues to be expressed and experienced among the first generation through a constellation of factors, including language; strong family values and respect for elders (including ancestors, parents, and teachers); ways of moving the body and other forms of materiality connected to the body, such as skin color and notions of shared blood; traditional ceremonial dress; food and cooking methods; gardening of traditional plants and vegetables; and so on. These aspects of identity are most often expressed at home, but also in Vietnamese public spaces, such as festivals and the cultural landscapes described in the last chapter. People spoke quite explicitly about the situational nature of identity. One husband said, "We cannot say we are exactly Americans, but this is our second country. We still think of our country, but now we sleep here; it is our second country and where our kids live." His wife added, "In our home, we keep the culture. We remember where we came from. We are American on the outside, but inside we are Vietnamese." She described her home as the "inside" place of Vietnamese culture, protected from the "outside." Another man said about his sense of identity, "It depends on the context. When I interact with people in American society, I feel American." Like the first generation of Indians, many Vietnamese adults reported that it was at work that they felt most American, although eating American food was also a prominent theme. One man said, "When do I feel most American? When I'm in McDonald's eating a hamburger or eating a big steak. Thanksgiving and eating turkey with my family."[9]

The situational nature of identity was articulated in this way by an Amerasian woman whose experiences differed from others': "Now I feel very Vietnamese, now that I am in the U.S., but before in Vietnam I did not. When I was younger, my face, my hair, and my eyes were not Vietnamese." Because of the discrimination against Amerasians in Vietnam, she was made to feel other "at home," but after coming to the United States and joining other Vietnamese with whom she shared a language and culture, she felt more comfortable expressing her Vietnamese identity. Due to the rejection she felt from her father, however, she does not feel American. For this woman, paradoxically, coming to the United States caused her to feel more Vietnamese, and this is something she values. The Amerasian case presents another contrast with the Indians interviewed in that this type of mixed-race identity, the result of a war, does not exist among the generation of Indians who have settled in Dallas.[10]

In addition to revealing their situational understanding of identity, the Vietnamese parents we interviewed articulated their sense of identity in terms of percentages, indicating an embodied aspect to this issue that was not exclusively tied to racial phenotype but pointed toward more internalized bodily changes as well as to changes in outlook.[11] For example, one elderly woman told us, "I am Vietnamese, and I am not 100 percent American. I understand their culture, their traditions. Maybe I adopt some of them. Maybe I am American in some way." A middle-aged man said, "I am not yet a U.S. citizen, and even if I become a U.S. citizen, I think I will feel about 10 percent American." These responses show that identity is considered somewhat mutable and can change with the situation and also alter over time.

Vietnamese Americans are subject to various situations of exclusion and inclusion because of their identities, and their ability to "choose" to highlight or minimize ethnic identity is constrained by their perceptions of racial and political factors in identity. They perceive that American identity is associated with certain phenotypical characteristics that they lack and that exclude them; for Amerasians, this experience can be even more painful. At the same time, many in the first generation, especially males, cling to the South Vietnamese identity because of the trauma of the war, and sometimes at the expense of adopting newer forms of identity in America. U.S. citizenship and the freedoms of democracy are strongly appreciated and embraced by these former refugees, however, despite shifting attitudes toward being American. For former Vietnamese refugees, to be American is a highly complex matter with historical and gendered dimensions. We see in the contrasts between Indians and Vietnamese that even though both groups are becoming U.S. citizens and, as we show in subsequent chapters, participating in American civic life, they do so from very different positions and experiences of identity. Both groups, however, share ambivalence toward the labels *Asian* and *Asian American.*

Being Asian or Becoming Asian-American?
First-Generation Ambivalence

Little attention has been paid to how individuals from North, South, and Southeast Asia experience, understand, and respond to the designation *Asian American* (Kibria 2002: 17); nor have scholars paid much attention to how this designation might guide social and political behavior. The differences among Asian immigrant populations call into question the meaningfulness of a pan-Asian category in the context of a "politics of recognition" (Ong 2003: 256).[12] One Indian participant in the parent interviews made the following comment about being Asian:

> To the American public, anything Asian means oriental; it does not encompass India or Indianness. To the American public, Indians and Pakistanis are not Asians. The Chinese and Vietnamese do not even like that the Asian world is being hijacked, so I will stick with Indian American.

His comment is indicative of the kinds of answers that were given by first-generation Indian participants to questions about such identity labels as *Asian, South Asian,* and *Asian American.* These identifiers did not resonate particularly well with them, for a variety of reasons. Most intriguing was the absence of any real identification with the term *South Asian,* which, according to some literature, seems to have greater, though by no means universal, appeal among Indian youth, along with the term *desi,* which also has a South Asian meaning.[13] The history of India and its political divisions clearly makes the differences among South Asian countries (Pakistan, Bangladesh, Nepal, Sri Lanka) seem greater to those born in those countries who have emigrated than to their offspring born in America, who emphasize the shared culture (food, clothing, music, entertainment) that brings them together.[14] For example, one male respondent said this about the term *South Asian:* "This is a meaningless term used only be geographers. There is no unification in South Asia that we can relate to." Another observed, "I don't see things like this, that is, spatially, so I guess I can't identify with it. At least I never thought of myself in those terms." A woman who claimed that she rarely identified herself as South Asian nevertheless said she had started to use the term in connection with her work with a charitable organization that offers nutritional services to the elderly whose culture includes a vegetarian diet.

> I don't want this service to be just to Hindus, or Indians, because there are other South Asian cultures that share this diet. So I am billing it as elderly dietary services to South Asians who have lived a vegetarian lifestyle.

These observations convey that *South Asian* is a cultural identity that has been embraced by some members of the second generation but only rarely among the first generation, for whom it carries only a vague geographical reference and seems to be an attempt to equate them with Pakistanis, with whom they do not want to be equated.

For several first-generation Indian research participants, *Asian* was also a geographical term: "Asia is too big a place and encompasses too many countries to be anything but a label." The implication of this comment is that labels that are assigned are different from identities in which people themselves find meaning. Among the more subtle responses was this one: "If it's just someone wanting to know value systems or practices, along the lines of 'Asians do this,' that is not me."

The difference between *identity* and *identification* (Gans 2007) is further illustrated in attitudes toward the label *Asian American*. Several first-generation Indian research participants suggested that it also is too broad a label and that they use it only on forms that ask for some kind of ethnic identification. "I check Asian American because I think this is our classification now. I don't know. It keeps changing. It's hard to keep up with, you know." Some participants raised the classification *Asian American or Pacific Islander* with amusement, indicating that any affinity with those who are considered Pacific Islanders is a stretch. Prior to 1980, Asian Indians were not a separate category in the U.S. census, and racially they were included in the "white" category along with peoples of Europe, the Middle East, and North Africa.[15] In 1974, the Association of Indians in America lobbied to have Asian Indians reclassified from the "other/white" category, where they had been allocated in the 1970 census, to Asian American (Kibria 2007: 620). At the time, this effort was hotly debated in the pages of the national newspaper *India Abroad* (Bhalla 2006).[16] The Asian and Pacific Islander category emerged, and along with it, minority status. Today the large number of Indians in the United States, as well as the development of India itself, makes the umbrella term *Asian American* both less meaningful and less useful to U.S. residents of Indian origin. It is a category that encompasses significant diversity and, as Nazli Kibria (2007: 620) observes, homogenizes what is not homologous. It is important to note, however, that first-generation Indians understand that their children may think and operate differently than they do. Here is how one respondent put it:

> I don't think of my dual identities in a melded sense. I see them as different, coexisting but still separate. I think maybe because I wasn't born here, there is this feeling of being an external visitor in America, like I haven't earned the right to identify myself equally in terms of Indian and American. Our children, I think, they are born here and have been raised here; they are the ones who probably identify themselves in these conglomerate terms, but not us.

When asked if Asians of various backgrounds could work together politically, most first-generation respondents were doubtful. One Hindu woman, a professional in her late thirties, commented, "I don't think we get along that well. We don't think of ourselves collectively like that. It's like the U.S., Mexico, and Canada—I don't see that you all identify yourselves as a collectivity. It's the same for us." Several respondents in the parent interviews pointed to different agendas, to political differences at home, to the absence of a shared language (unlike Latinos), to vast cultural differences, and to competition among Asian groups as major barriers to collective Asian political action. "It won't happen," asserted one Indian male respondent. "We do not have any solidarity in Asia; the Indians and the Pakistanis don't even see eye to eye; we even see some of the countries as our opponents." Another noted that even Indians themselves cannot get together on anything. "Each state within our own country is a separate block and that is seen even here, where Indian associations are organized by state—Kerala, Bengali, etc. To include all of Asia and their factions into the mix [is] . . . [he laughed] impossible." Again, however, the first generation recognizes that things might be different for their children, who, as one Hindu housewife put it, "have some things in common because they are all Americans and grew up here."

Despite the pride that many Indian immigrants across the United States have taken in the election of Bobby Jindal, the born-in-America son of India-born parents, to the U.S. Congress and subsequently as governor of Louisiana, some respondents suggested that making political choices on the basis of ethnic identity did not seem particularly important. They stressed instead the importance of issues. One Indian respondent offered that quotas in education (that is, limiting high-achieving Asians' access to top universities), might be the kind of issue that would mobilize Asians across different groups. In other words, collective action would be a political strategy rather than a reflection of collective identity (Visweswaran 1997), a form of *strategic essentialism*—to borrow a term from literary theorist Gyatri Spivak (1987)—invoked for political purposes.

Vietnamese Americans are also conscious that people in the United States frequently use the generic *Asian* label to identify them. Although some of the first-generation parents we interviewed had adapted to this term and did use it to refer to themselves during interviews, the vast majority of them claimed that *Asian* was not a meaningful term. One person said, "There are so many differences." An astute comment about Asian identity came from a woman in her sixties who had arrived as a refugee in 1975: "That is a place for nobody. Americans make up that word. I'm Vietnamese. Nobody refers to themselves as Asian. But there are categories in the U.S. for black, white, Asian."

In the United States, prejudice against Asians in general was felt by many of our Vietnamese informants. A woman said she felt Asian at work because "people make fun of me and other Asians. I am treated differently." Another woman, who said she does not feel Asian, told us nevertheless that "people ask me if I am Korean or Chinese sometimes. I cannot look American, but I go to work and I am just like everyone else." This woman tried to be tolerant toward American prejudices against Asians, explaining that in Vietnam the tribal people are looked down on, even though "some of them are really smart." She said, in an effort to be tolerant, "it is natural in societies to do that, it is always like that."

Historical legacies play a large role in Vietnamese attitudes toward Asian or Asian American identity. The distance between various groups of Asians was expressed by a person who, appealing to historical tensions over the imperialist occupations experienced by Vietnam, explained that

> Asians are different from Americans. They live individually in their own ethnic groups and do not work together. We do not see Chinese or Japanese all together. We were ruled by the Chinese for a thousand years. The Japanese killed millions of our people. So we don't get along very well.

The issue of whether or not Asians would work together politically prompted other types of responses in our interviews. One Vietnamese woman said, "Asia is just a group of countries. It is not about individual identity. We are not close to each other." One woman felt that Asians do not necessarily support one another politically, citing as her example, "when Hubert Vo was running, he was supported mainly by the Vietnamese community, but not by other Asians."

As one Vietnamese research participant pointed out, there is an Asian American Chamber of Commerce. It is in the realm of economic cooperation that an Asian American consciousness seems to be most prominent, but it touches mainly those businesspeople who are engaged in their local chamber. One non-Vietnamese leader in the Fort Worth Asian American Chamber of Commerce echoed the perspectives of the Vietnamese respondents when he observed that it was difficult to get the first generation of Asians working together. He said that lack of trust between the different Asian groups kept them from working across ethnic lines. Although he was born outside the United States, this college-educated professional had taken a college course in Asian American studies after immigrating to America. He realized that *Asian* was a socially constructed identity in the United States, but he felt that Asian American unity, which he strongly advocated, was a "political choice."

Our research thus suggests that categories of identification such as *Asian*, *South Asian*, *Southeast Asian*, and *Asian American* do not resonate strongly with the first-generation parents we interviewed. Instead, both Indian and Vietnamese research participants emphasized that these are official or geographic labels applied by outsiders and do not have much influence on their own constructions of self. This distinction is important to understand because the identities that immigrants embrace or reject often shape how they engage with the public sphere through forms of participatory citizenship. But first-generation Vietnamese and Indians recognize that the second generation may have different perspectives on identity and citizenship, and that pan-Asian categories might be more meaningful to their lives because they were born in or spent most of their childhood in the United States. In our group interviews with college students, to which we now turn, we observed that youth are learning to negotiate their identities in ways that help them move between their parents and their peers.[17]

"Viet Pride" and "The Indian Side": 1.5- and Second-Generation Youth

Like the first generation of immigrants who arrived as adults, Vietnamese and Indian youth who either arrived in the United States as children or were born here to immigrant parents distinguish between legal U.S. citizenship and American ethnic (or cultural or racial) identity. Vietnamese and Indian college students express their discomfort with being between two worlds: the world of the first-generation immigrants—their parents—and the world of their new home—the United States—a world that includes contact with other youth (both those of the same and those of other ethnic identities). They are conscious of experiencing what Bourdieu (2004: 130) called a "split habitus," and they engage in complex negotiations of identity as they move across social situations.[18] At the same time, they are more receptive than their parents are to the idea of a pan-Asian identity.

Some of the Vietnamese American college students who participated in our group interviews were born in the United States, and some arrived as children. Their ideas about citizenship and identity are shaped by their exposure to the American educational system and other institutions, and by the attitudes they learned at home. One young woman recounted her experiences in an American high school where, as the child of Vietnamese refugees, she was in the minority.

> I went to a school where the majority was Caucasian so I hang out with more white people. I was more influenced around them and so whenever I'm at home or something like that, when I'm by myself I can still feel that they have some kind of influence over me because, like the music I listen to, it's totally like their kind of music. I don't listen to my own country and heritage music really. So I kind of noticed that sometime I'm very much influenced by the people I hang out with. But now that I'm in college I hang out more with, a little bit, interact more with Asian people. I noticed that I kind of picked up some of their traits.

These Vietnamese American youth mentioned the concept of "Viet pride," which is being proud to be Vietnamese while living in the United States. It is a way to avoid becoming too "Americanized," a topic of conversation and debate in the Vietnamese population.[19] In the last quote, this idea was expressed in terms of racial categories (Caucasian versus Asian) and indicated the speaker's sensitivity to the situational nature of identity.

The Vietnamese American students also expressed their attitudes toward citizenship in terms of rights and benefits. One student remarked that citizenship implies "freedom of speech and rights"; another commented that "it means to be recognized by law that you are now a part of whatever country you have citizenship for, that you have the same rights if you were born here [even] if you weren't . . . here." A third response was, "Citizenship is when you become an American and get benefits of being American. That's when you can vote. You can travel to any countries you want without being constricted." Becoming or being a legal U.S. citizen was less fraught than the issue of patriotism, which was emotionally charged and reflected the continuing influence of history and homeland politics on these children of former political refugees.

Vietnamese American college students have been exposed to their parents' strong feelings of patriotism for a regime that fell (South Vietnam), and this exposure affects their views on patriotism in the United States. One student summarized the differences between citizenship and patriotism in a way that clearly reflects the perspectives of his parents:

> Patriotism [is] you're gonna have love and loyalty for your country that you're living in. And with citizenship you're just trying to find a better place to live. You don't have to love the country that you're living in 'cause you just want to find a better place to live . . . versus where you were living in the past. And you want to have a better future for the next generation, which is your children.

Vietnamese refugees and their children frequently report that they love their *country* (South Vietnam), even though they left it, and they distinguish their country from its communist regime.[20] One student voiced this as, "A lot of people don't have citizenship in Vietnam but we're still patriotic [toward South Vietnam]."

Disagreements arose among students in one group interview about whether or not patriotism and citizenship go hand in hand, with some students following the lead of their parents and separating the two, and others seeing them as inseparable. As one student who espoused the latter view said, "I'm an American citizen and so I was thinking, you know, if there's a war and stuff, I'm going to fight for America. And so I think they go together." Another said, "You can't just get the benefit of the country and not give something back to them. To get your citizenship is to get the benefit of the rights of the country provided, so you have to give to get, you have to give something back in return."

Like those we interviewed from the first generation, these Vietnamese American youth distinguished between U.S. citizenship and American identity. Among the youth, however, racial metaphors were more commonly used to express identity; for example, "banana" was sometimes used to describe someone who had internalized Americanness ("yellow on the outside but white on the inside"), or "whitewashed" was used for someone who identified too much with whites or Caucasians. At the other extreme, the initials FOB ("fresh off the boat") are used to characterize those who are "too traditional" or "too Vietnamese." One college student spontaneously outlined this folk typology of identities as follows: *Viet-Viet, Vietnamese American, American American.* Another student added the category *American Vietnamese* to the mix. She said she was American Vietnamese but labeled another student Vietnamese American because "he knows the language more than I do, he gets more involved [with the Vietnamese community] than I do."

One male student, who arrived in the United States as a child, explored the complexities and ambivalences of identity when he observed the following:

> I find, like, I have a hard time communicating with American people because I communicate in a different way and when I'm doing that with Vietnamese people or Asian people they understand what I mean. They understand my facial expressions and they can understand me.... And, uh, there's just a lot of stuff that I have to go through with this, this differentiation between the Vietnamese culture and American culture. And growing up in between, I can't identity myself with either one. So really, I, um, when it comes to, especially when it comes to elections and stuff and talking about freedom and stuff, all these American values and loyalty and all these qualities, I just have a hard time identifying with them. Because I'm not really American, you know, and this isn't really my country and I just don't feel that sense of belonging . . . and it's pretty much the same with wherever I am trying to identify myself with Vietnamese culture. Because there is really no Vietnamese country and there's no place that I can call home. And so, I'm like in the middle of nowhere, no man's land.

In contrast to this perspective is that of a young woman born in the United States who criticized those who are "like, 'Oh, I don't want to associate with this person' because they're not going to be able to relate to me or whatever . . . or, 'this person is too American and they think they're arrogant and everything like that so I'm not going to associate with them.' And I don't know, I don't like how that affects friendships and how that affects people's interactions."

These youth were conscious of "acting" Vietnamese or American rather than having any fixed identity. They expressed a "fuzziness," which their parents noticed and that can cause conflict between the generations. Some expressed the need to separate how they acted at home and how they acted outside, echoing some of the comments made by Vietnamese parents. Students articulated that being reserved and polite, and respecting elders, is a way of being and acting Vietnamese. For example, one young woman said, "I think a lot more about what I am going to say whenever I'm being Vietnamese." When these students were in high school, having Vietnamese parents caused many of them to feel conscious of difference, despite their desire to participate more in activities. Friendships with non-Vietnamese students could be difficult. One young woman commented:

> My friends would sleep over at everyone else's house but I wasn't ever allowed to. And it's mostly because, I'm not sure if it's because they didn't trust anybody

or because they were American. I think it was more because they didn't trust anybody, 'cause I couldn't spend the night at family members' houses if they lived too far away either. . . . I felt awkward inviting friends over to my house because . . . that would be too formal, I thought. Because, like, 'Mom these are my friends,' 'My friends, this is my Mom,' and then there would be this awkward silence. And they would have to take off their shoes. And there's so much . . . there's this big culture gap. . . . So it's better just to keep them all separate.

Vietnamese American youth see Asian identity as an inevitable category in their lives, and this marks a striking departure from the reticence to identify as Asian that is prevalent among the first generation. The category *Asian* or *Asian American* is very familiar to Vietnamese American youth and is often applied to them in everyday life. In Arlington, where a relatively high percentage of children are of Chinese and Vietnamese ancestry, most high school students, whatever their own ethnicity, categorize such students (as well as Koreans, Thai, and so on) as *Asian* (in contrast to the other frequently used labels—*black, Mexican,* or *white*). Among the general population, *Asian* is a catch-all term used to refer mainly to East and Southeast Asians. One Vietnamese university international student even remarked on this, citing her amazement when an Anglo high school student asked her, "Are you Vietnamese or are you Asian?"[21]

Vietnamese American youth expressed a common experience of being the children of immigrants from Asia. One young woman said, "I noticed whenever I am around Asian friends, those that are Vietnamese or just Asian in particular, I feel more comfortable and I'm able to communicate with them better, whereas with my non-Asian group I'm more conscious of what I say around them because of my non-Asian friends, their beliefs are way different from mine." Several Vietnamese American students remarked that Asians in general are less individualistic than Americans, and as one male put it, "I think that with Vietnamese students or just with Asians in general, they have a very collective mental attitude. It's always about a greater purpose. . . . It's less about the individual." The youth we interviewed said that identifying as Asian depended on the prevalence of Asian students at their high schools and on how an Asian identity was constructed there. One young man referred to Asian identity as a "style" adopted by the second generation. He remarked, "I remember back in high school there's a term [for the] stereotypical Asian. You have the spiky hair, the bangs, your hair has to be either yellow or white at the ends. If you don't meet those requirements, then you are not Asian. And you have to wear pants that, like, don't show your shoes, and a shirt that's too large. . . . " In other words, if you adopt a more conservative or traditional Vietnamese style, you cannot be Asian. This attitude illustrates the role of American popular culture in the development of new ethnic identities—a factor related to what sociologists Rubén Rumbaut and Alejandro Portes (2001: 7) refer to as the transition of the children of "new immigrants" from immigrant to ethnic.

For Indian youth in the United States, this transition to being an "ethnic," to "being Indian," is equally fraught with complications. One male college student articulated these complexities well by describing how he moves back and forth between what he referred to as his Indian side and his American side.

> I would say my Indian side came out, like, once a month. Like if it was a special holiday, or we were going to my relatives' house for dinner, or going to temple. When I came to college I met a lot more Indian friends, and I think it was a complete reversal. My Indian side came out 90 percent of the time and the American 10 percent—at least for the first two years of college. Now I am more blended. I feel like my American side got lost, so I'm actively trying to get in touch with it now.

This young man's use of the word *blended* suggests something else: that his two sides come together in one person in the form of a hybrid identity that is contingent, fluid, and emergent. This fluidity seems to apply as well to understandings of citizenship among the 1.5 and second generations. One young woman suggested that citizenship "is loyalty and respect, but not necessarily embracing its culture." Others indicated that you could be loyal to both places and have pride in both places without these really being divided loyalties. "Whenever I hear either the Indian or the U.S. national anthem, I always feel goose bumps. I have so much pride for both cultures, but in different ways." The concepts of pride and respect seem to be central to how the children of Indian immigrants understand patriotism, although for a few of them patriotism could be applied to India as much as to the United States. For example, one young man said he thought about his father when he thought of patriotism. His father came to the United States when he was twenty. He worked three jobs and every time he sat down for a meal he thought about his parents. "This is patriotism to me, this bond with a country. There are those Indians that come to America that block off all the poverty back in India, but a good citizen never forgets." Clearly this young man was operating with a broad conception of citizenship and he linked it to patriotism.

These youth also talked about the legal dimensions of citizenship. A student who was born in India but raised in the United States suggested that in India "nobody uses the term *citizens*. When you come to America," she continued, "you become much more aware of this concept as you apply for citizenship and think about citizenship and all that goes with it. The regulatory environment makes you come to terms with things in this way." As discussion of the meaning of citizenship continued, several of these college-age students also talked about the responsibilities of citizenship. One suggested that being or becoming a citizen is like being a member of a country club, "and with that come special privileges. Along with those privileges you also have civic responsibilities. Like, you can't just be an island; you sort of have to do stuff." Another put it this way: "Citizenship just means to be an active participant of your community. That's regardless of nationality. I think I'm a good citizen being an American. I still consider myself more Indian than American, but the people I go out and help are mostly American." Rather than talking about what it might mean to be a "good" or "bad" citizen, some of these young people preferred to distinguish between engaged and unengaged citizens. One group of students also discussed how much stronger the expression of citizenship is among those who have been naturalized and are proud to be citizens. "It's [such] a process to become an American citizen that I think if you have to go through it, you appreciate it more."

For several of these Indian students, adhering to the legal or rights and responsibilities definition of citizenship meant they could maintain their own culture and identity and still have a sense of belonging to American society and culture. They claimed that they experienced their Indian side most often when they were with their parents, during festivals and holidays, and when they went to temple. For many of them, speaking their parents' language—often a regional language such as Malayalam or Gujarati—is a key marker of being Indian. However, these young people also emphasize core values and family issues. A critical core value is respect for elders. Here is how one male college student put it:

> In an Indian setting, if someone older than you walks into the room, you are expected to stand up as a sign of respect. But in an American setting I just wave or something. In an Indian setting you wouldn't talk back; that is considered highly disrespectful. My parents taught me this as a child. When I was younger, I was kind of a rebellious child, and my parents would say, "This is not the way to behave."

Just as context was important to first-generation immigrants, so it is important to their children as they develop and negotiate their identities. One young man noted that when he returns to India he feels more American; in India he recognizes that he is different. He went on to describe the birthday party his mother had for him when he was still in high school. She invited his Indian friends from temple and his American friends from school. He said it "freaked me out," because he was keeping these two groups separate and all of a sudden they were in the same room and he had to acknowledge the two sides of himself.

Other students spoke less of a blended or hybrid identity than of two identities between which they could move. As one student put it, "It's an inside-outside thing. . . . There isn't really a lot of grey area." A young woman expressed it this way:

I think I didn't begin to embrace the Indian experience until college. I joined the Indian sorority and found out that I got completely immersed in it. I felt like there is a difference between your Indian heritage and your American heritage; it's like I'm bicultural but can turn on either side here at school. . . . It's like two separate lives that I fluctuate between. I've completely adapted and am comfortable functioning in both cultural worlds.

These young people also reflected on being accorded the right to be or feel American. One young woman who was born in India but largely raised in the United States poignantly noted that she is considered Indian in the United States because of the way she looks, but she is considered American in India because of the way she acts. She has become American in some of her behaviors, but she is denied a full sense of being American. Consequently, and unlike their parents, who are more "reluctant to be raced" (George 1997: 32), many of these young people embrace "brownness" as part of their identity (Kurien 2005).

If you're not black or white, in America you're brown. It's not really in the color of our skin; I don't know why we name it brown, but if you look at people, there are whites and blacks, and then this whole spectrum of Asians in-between. . . . It's like this slang term that we use. Not really even our parents. It's just easier than saying South Asian, or a region; we just say "brown." We all know what it means. We use it among each other all the time.

The struggle that these students are having with U.S. racial hierarchies and where they fit in was most poignantly expressed by a young man who firmly stated, "I am not a white person trapped in an Indian body, nor am I a black person trapped; when I look at myself I say, 'Hey, I'm Indian.'" This comment reflects an effort to find someplace in between to locate oneself, as well as, more generally, the ambiguous nonwhiteness of South Asians living in the United States (Kibria 1998; Morning 2001).[22] Racialization can be crucial "in keeping the South Asian Americans 'ethnic,' in spite of their integration in terms of residence, education, and related facets of their lives" (Purkayastha 2005: 55–56).

The brown identity that Indian youth embrace in order to capture their sense of in-betweenness is also fluid and situational. Further, it distinguishes them from their parents, who do not actively embrace brownness as a marker of who they are.[23] First-generation Indians have instead emphasized their class status, which is based on education, profession, and income, rather than any phenotypical markers. For them, "merit transcends color" (Bhatia 2007: 164). Further, they tend to emphasize their nationality—that is, being of Indian origin—instead of their race. A good deal of agency is involved here—that is, taking control of how one defines oneself in order not to be defined—but it is an agency that may be accorded precisely because of class and social position.[24] For those of the second generation, who have grown up with U.S. racial hierarchies and ethnic classifications, the issues are different and brownness is therefore invoked in certain contexts to emphasize being neither black nor white. Here is how one college student described the differences in attitudes about race and racism across the generations:

> [Our parents] see it but they are quieter about it because they don't feel that they can voice it. Our generation feels more like we can speak out. I get upset when my parents don't realize that they are being taken advantage of because of their race. I think that we can detect and understand it better having been brought up among the American culture. I got my car keyed after 9/11 in front of a sorority house. I got a lot of bad looks. I guess because I'm brown and somebody not from America did this.

Although the Indian youth who participated in our group interviews did not talk at length about Asian and Asian American identities, several admitted to being involved in Asian organizations on their college campuses. In other words, as was the case for Vietnamese American youth, they indicated more comfort with pan-Asian identities than did individuals from the first generation. One young woman said she was active in the university's Asian Council, an umbrella organization for seven Asian American organizations, in order to "connect with lots of different cultures. I like the fact that I get involved in lots of cultures and that I get to help bring people together." A young man who had served as treasurer for the Asian Council reinforced the idea that it was an organization aimed at bringing together students from diverse backgrounds to seek common ground. "We aim at freshmen because they leave the university because they don't feel comfortable here. It's been interesting to make a difference in their lives. I've learned more about what's going on against our society because I've learned a lot about hate crimes. [Asian Council] helps us to dialogue about these issues." More students were extensively involved in the Indian Student Association on campus but noted that it really included all South Asians. They indicated that the main purpose of this organization was to bridge diversity; to celebrate their culture, heritage, and traditions; and to educate others about their culture, which they do by hosting a few campuswide events each year, including a Diwali celebration, movie nights, and sports competitions.[25] Many students said they had chosen this organization over a sorority, to which they said they chose not to belong but from which they also acknowledged they were often excluded. One young woman said she was asked to rush and never "thought that anyone thought that I didn't belong. I really just didn't want to get into something that I couldn't get out of."

Shifting Boundaries of Identity and Participatory Citizenship

For research participants from both generations, being Indian or being Vietnamese is associated with cultural practices and traditions, with native languages, and with a core set of family values. Being in America and becoming a naturalized citizen accords some sense of belonging, but this is different from being or acting American. American identity is fluid, context specific, and more often associated with patterns of behavior than with a deeply felt identity, even among many youth who are American citizens by birth. Immigrants can certainly "act American," by adapting to the workplace, displaying the American flag, eating at McDonald's, cheering for football teams, and celebrating Thanksgiving and the Fourth of July. Individuals from both populations, especially those of the second generation, struggle with balancing their various identities.

The first-generation Indian and Vietnamese participants in our research expressed feeling discomfort with the pan-Asian and Asian American categories, although they recognized that these categories are assigned by others, particularly on official documents, including the census form.[26] They were also skeptical about any sort of collective political mobilization based on an Asian or Asian American identity. Individuals in both groups pointed to the multitude of linguistic and cultural differences across Asia. There is a political dimension to the discomfort that many Vietnamese feel with these categories, because being called Asian associates them with such groups as the Chinese, who dominated Vietnam for centuries and are currently communist. For first-generation Indians it is the *South Asian* category that is politically sensitive, because it puts Muslims and Hindus together and couples India with Pakistan, two countries that have looked upon one another with suspicion since India achieved its independence from Great Britain in 1947.[27]

Adults of the first generation recognized that their offspring may feel more comfortable than they do with the idea of being American or having a hyphenated identity, and youth of the second generation stressed the multifaceted identities that emerge in different combinations and in different situations.[28] Vietnamese youth identified a somewhat richer complexity of hyphenated categories (Viet-Viet, Vietnamese American, American Vietnamese) than did Indian youth, who placed more emphasis on behaviors appropriate to Indian contexts and those appropriate to American contexts, or on their brown, hybrid identity. We also found the Vietnamese youth more apt than the Indian youth to characterize themselves as Asian and to note that they are perceived as Asian by others. This is most likely related to the fact that this identity category is associated with East Asian phenotypes. Vietnamese youth therefore appear to enter more easily than their Indian counterparts into communities of practice associated with pan-ethnic Asian identity (such as the Asian Students Association).

The distinction between the so-called 1.5 generation—those born in the homeland—and the second generation is more cogent among Vietnamese youth because many Vietnamese families arrived as refugees with children already born whereas most Indian youth living in the United States were born here. It is more common for Indian immigrants to arrive younger and then have their families in the United States. Some Vietnamese families distinguish between the children born in the United States and the older children born in Vietnam. Although we can generalize somewhat about all of these youth as the children of immigrants, those who came to the United States as children are more conflicted about the relationship between their Vietnamese and American identities than are either the first-generation or those born in the United States. For the most part, however, those Vietnamese who are now entering public office are of the 1.5 generation and arrived in the United States as either young children or teenagers.

Whiteness figures prominently in understandings of what it means to be American. First-generation Indians are guided by their class status and hence tend to place less emphasis on their brownness than do their children. However, both generations of Vietnamese emphasize their "yellowness" as a barrier to full-fledged American identity. As one Vietnamese woman (quoted earlier in this chapter) said, "Look at this yellow skin and only yellow." The "banana" metaphor used by Vietnamese American youth reflects this inside-outside distinction. The Vietnamese of both generations, however, included African Americans among those who are "being American," even though they sometimes equated being American with being white. When *American* included all those who are not newcomers or immigrants, such as Asians and Latinos, then African Americans were included in this category. This view undoubtedly reflects the presence of African American soldiers, with an American identity and presenting the face of the United States, in Vietnam during the Vietnam War. Many Amerasian children were fathered by African American soldiers. Vietnamese immigrants, for whom *yellow* and *black* are distinct categories, situate themselves in relationship to both white and black Americans more than do Indians, who focus more on *white* as the defining American racial category. This approach may be connected to the desire of Indians (some of whom are quite dark in skin color) to minimize any hint of connection to "blackness." Further, in India itself, fair skin means higher caste or class status. Individuals of both sexes and across generations in both immigrant populations recognize that how they look raises questions in others' minds about who they are and where they belong.[29] How these issues of identity will play out as the children of immigrants move from their school and college environments into the working world and into broader social and political contexts is yet to be determined. Some scholars have already argued that a sense of nonwhiteness among the children and grandchildren of Asian immigrants can provide the foundation for a pan-minority Asian identity that shapes "quintessentially American" everyday practice (Zhou and Lee 2004: 14).

Our premise is that how people construct their identities as well as how they are identified by others influences the ways in which they participate in the public sphere and define meaningful citizenship practice. Despite a certain ambivalence about being American (in a cultural sense especially) and despite feeling that phenotypical differences can be a foundation for processes of exclusion, Vietnamese and Indian immigrants and their children find ways to become civically engaged, often from a position of difference and hence of cultural citizenship. Further, it is helpful to be mindful of Fredrik Barth's emphasis (1969) on situational identity and the fluidity of ethnic boundaries that are constructed in different ways depending on context. Immigrant newcomers can become engaged citizens through the prism of ethnic identity, through a pan-Asian identity, and as naturalized American citizens. In the following chapters of this book we explore how members of the Indian and Vietnamese populations develop their own sense of belonging through social practice. We turn to their participation in various communities of practice, including the religious institutions that are the subject of the next chapter, which not only are sites where they develop civic skills and practice forms of participatory citizenship, but also reflect the multiple situated identities that they claim for themselves.

3 Temples, Mosques, and Churches

Religious participation "prefigures" or prepares for citizenship?

THIS CHAPTER EXPLORES the relationship between civic engagement and religion. As we argue in this book, participatory citizenship does not always involve overt political acts, and that is certainly not the model adopted by the churches, mosques, and temples we studied. Vietnamese monks and Catholic priests uniformly reported that they resisted pressures from political leaders in the Vietnamese community to offer their institutions as venues for organizing or hosting political events (related to either homeland or U.S. domestic issues). Religious leaders serving the Indian immigrant community likewise stressed that their institutions were there primarily to provide spiritual guidance and training. Yet ethnographic observations at religious assemblies, as well as interviews with Indians and Vietnamese who were participating in them, showed that religion may play a role not only in civic engagement in general, but also in political mobilization more specifically. Religious assemblies are communities of practice for the acquisition and enhancement of civic skills by immigrants and their children. Moreover, the identities and moral values associated with particular forms of ethnoreligious expression shape both formal and informal citizenship practices.

The role of religion in the civic engagement of immigrants has been noted before but is only recently gaining renewed attention in relation to late twentieth- and early twenty-first-century immigration.[1] Urban historians have pointed to the importance of Catholic parishes in particular to the civic and political incorporation of earlier waves of immigrants. Building a church involved large-scale collective action (Sterne 2001). These churches claimed urban space, thereby visibly establishing the presence of immigrant populations. The diverse activities of the parishes offered laypeople opportunities to develop leadership and oratorical skills that they might not have been able to develop in the broader community (Hirschman 2004: 1223). Many immigrants therefore used their parishes "as springboards from which they became active in the larger community" (Sterne 2001: 54).

A major question posed in earlier studies of religion and immigration was whether ethnic religious assemblies were "mobility traps" (Greeley 1972) that prevented assimilation by promoting ethnic identity, or whether it was precisely their effort to "sustain ethnicity and religious convictions rooted in ethnic religions" that "helped ethnic groups adapt to American life" (Bankston and Zhou 1995: 524). These questions have guided previous studies of Vietnamese refugees. Rutledge (1985; 1992: 54), for example, argued that Vietnamese refugees in Oklahoma City adapt to American society through their religious participation, which provides a haven and reinforces ethnic identity, although this can also limit participation in the wider society. In contrast, Bankston and Zhou (1996: 19) found that while participation in Vietnamese religious institutions in New Orleans enhances "the network of ethnic social relations" and thereby increases feelings of being Vietnamese rather than American, religious participation can also help increase civic participation. Studies of Indian religious institutions in the United States suggest that they are "centers of cultural propagation and community" (Rangaswamy 2000) as well as "training grounds for participatory democracy," so that well before Indian immigrants will "stand for election to the school board, they will stand for election in the governing body of the Hindu temple" (Eck 2001: 336).[2] In New York City, Indian immigrants who are active in houses of worship "often become spokespersons for their religious communities in addressing the wider American public" (Khandelwal 2002: 88).

Vietnamese refugees and Indian immigrants who settled in Texas brought with them forms of religion that were new to this predominantly Christian, Bible Belt region. Although Roman Catholic and Protestant immigrants and refugees discovered established churches where they could find some common ground, Hindus, Buddhists, and Muslims initially arrived in a cultural landscape that contained few temples or mosques. By the time of this study, however, there were several well-established, ethnically based churches, temples, and mosques in the region.

In this chapter, we approach the relationship between religious institutions and civic engagement among the Vietnamese and Indian populations at both the institutional and individual levels. We focus on the history, structure, and organization of their respective religious institutions, as well as on what Warner (1998: 8) calls "congregations—local, face-to-face religious assemblies."[3] We are also interested, however, in how individual Vietnamese and Indian immigrants and their children may learn about and practice civic engagement by participating in religious communities of practice, and in how this participation is shaped by their moral beliefs. We therefore discuss their formal participation in the activities of their church, temple, or mosque; less formal social networking and activities in the wider civic sphere based on ties forged with other members of the religious community; and modes of leadership developed through contact with the congregation. Our emphasis is not on the micropolitics within these institutions, because our aim is to focus on the civic skills learned within them that translate to outside the religious realm. This chapter draws from participant observation at religious institutions, informal conversations and interviews with religious leaders as well as with laypeople who attend various types of religious assemblies, and our semi-structured interviews with first-generation Vietnamese and Indian parents. After discussing Vietnamese and Indian religious assemblies in turn, we draw comparisons between these two populations.

Vietnamese Religious Assemblies

I like to comfort people. I go to church every day. I go to pray with people in their homes also. I attend Vietnamese Martyrs Church and I am in the Rosary Division. Every day we take the rosary and we meet and go to help people. Two times a week we visit people who are ill in the hospital. Sometimes we go to the house, or if there is a problem in a marriage, or if the children do not obey their parents, we will help and explain that they need to respect and obey their parents. My friend lives at the corner of my street and we go together. Before, I helped with ESL classes. . . . My home is near the church. In Vietnam, houses are all near the church. [Eighty-year-old Roman Catholic woman, born in Vietnam, came to the United States in 1993 as a refugee with her husband]

We [a core group of older women at the temple] come here sometimes. We do something. If there is a celebration, we help with anything—food, cleaning, help the people. We help those who don't know things, who come here the first time; we help with translation and things like that. [DRD: why do you help?] It is good for my life. If I stay here [in the United States], I have to do something good for me. I feel good when I come to the temple. I can help other people here. I feel happy about that. [Sixty-five-year-old Buddhist woman, born in Vietnam, came to the United States in 1989 with her Amerasian son]

Although these two women participate in different religious traditions, their involvement is similar. Both get personal satisfaction from helping others through participation in their church or temple. Both also spoke of the centrality of religious institutions back home in Vietnam. For the Catholic woman, the church was the core of her former neighborhood—a sentiment voiced by many of this study's research participants. Vietnamese Buddhists also mentioned that the temple was the center of the village or neighborhood where they grew up. Most Vietnamese refugees in this region of Texas participate in ethnoreligious institutions headed by religious leaders who were born in Vietnam, rather than churches or temples attended by other ethnic groups. There are eight Vietnamese Catholic parishes that developed out of older congregations in the area, and six Vietnamese Buddhist temples and monasteries. There are also several small congregations of fundamentalist Christians, many of whom are associated with the Vietnamese Baptist Church. Some Vietnamese engage in spirit-possession rituals, and there are practitioners of both the Cao Dai and Hoa Hao religious sects in the region. Many people, even those involved in organized religions, practice ancestor worship. As one male interviewee put it, "Most people in Vietnam practice ancestor worship and are not part of a religion. In my village, everyone followed ancestor religion." Thirty percent of Vietnamese Americans are Catholic, a proportion far greater than the 8 percent of Catholics in Vietnam (Phan 2005: 98).[4] These trends are reflected in the local DFW Vietnamese population and were confirmed by the priest at one of the Vietnamese churches, who said in an interview that about one-third of the local Vietnamese population is Catholic.

Our in-depth interviews with thirty-three Vietnamese American parents provide information on the religious participation of this particular segment of the population—middle-aged adults of the first generation, most of whom are in the workforce and all of whom are also busy raising high school- or college-age children. When asked whether they were currently affiliated with a local church or temple, only two of the thirty-three responded no, showing a high level of religious affiliation. Among these parents, close to 40 percent (13) were Catholic, close to 60 percent (19) were Buddhist, and one person claimed only to practice "ancestor worship."[5] For both Buddhists and Catholics there are significant differences in religious participation across generations, having to do with stage of life as much as with immigrant status. Those in the workforce who are raising families are the least active, even though they may send their children to religious and cultural classes at the church or temple. Our interviews revealed that in order to understand religious participation, we must distinguish between religious affiliation, attendance at religious rituals, and volunteering or being involved in other social activities. Fifty-four percent of the Catholics in our parent interviews responded that they attend church on a regular basis, compared to only 21 percent of the Buddhists. However, Buddhism does not have a mandatory weekly ritual like the Catholic Mass, so attending the temple is not as important to being considered a practicing Buddhist as attending Mass is to being considered a Catholic. A more significant figure is that comparable numbers of the parents in each religion volunteer at their church or temple, and in each case it is less than half (42 percent of the Buddhists and 39 percent of the Catholics). When asked about her involvement at church, one Catholic mother responded, "We attend a Catholic church, but I am not very involved. I have no time. But my children have been more involved and taught religious classes at the church." For others, however, helping at the church on Sunday is an important weekly ritual. Another Catholic mother said, "My husband and I go every Sunday. We clean up on Monday at the church." And a father revealed, "I come to help. I help with the school at the church and with lunch. And I help with security at the church." The willingness to "help" is also expressed by the Buddhists. One single Buddhist mother, who co-owns and works in her family's restaurant with her son, explained, like one of the Catholic mothers just mentioned, "I don't participate. Maybe once in a while I go to the temple, but I don't have time. If they want me to sponsor something or donate to them, I help them." Some parents, however, are quite active. A father with four children of various ages told us, "I help teach Vietnamese to the fifth graders at the temple. I help volunteer for the holy days and at summer camp." His wife added that she cooks at the temple.

Just as historian Roberto Trevino (2006: 4) found it useful to describe "ethno-Catholicism" as a "Mexican American way of being Catholic," so too are there Vietnamese ways of being Catholic and Buddhist. Both Buddhist and Catholic respondents expressed a sense of responsibility to be involved in the church or temple even if they did not have time. One man said, "I go to temple because I am a child of Buddha. I have responsibilities to go to Temple, make offerings, and light incense." This sense of responsibility, often expressed with the phrase *trach nhiem*,[6] has connotations of familial and civic duty, and is a significant way of talking about participatory citizenship among first-generation Vietnamese Americans.

Vietnamese Catholic Churches

A Catholic man who was a teenager in 1975 when he fled to the United States with his refugee family said that when he arrived, "the only place where I felt at home was in church." Although he did not understand English, the rituals of the Mass were familiar to him. Now a college-educated engineer, he noted that in rural areas of Vietnam the priest would be the only person with outside contacts, and the church and priest would be the center of the village. In Vietnam, he noted, the priest had much more power than he does in the United States. This man had also observed that "Catholics adapt faster than Buddhists because of the universality of Catholicism. When the Buddhists arrived here, they found no temples."

Not only does the shared liturgy and ritual of the global Catholic Church link Vietnamese Catholics to both international and national organizations, but their shared sense of history as specifically Vietnamese Catholics also binds them together. Each Vietnamese parish is linked to other Vietnamese Catholics through such organizations as the Vietnamese Catholic Federation, founded in 1980. Vietnamese parishes are organized on the basis of the system used in Vietnam, with lay leaders (*truong khu*) responsible for providing services to parishioners in various districts (*khu*) within the parish. The leader of a district will be responsible to help families by bringing the Eucharist to sick people at home, registering births, notifying people of new directives from the church, and referring people to the priest to address family problems. Vietnamese ethno-Catholicism is also reinforced by local priests who come from two orders that are primarily Vietnamese—Domus Dei and the Congregation of the Mother Co-Redemptrix (CMC). Members of the CMC were encouraged to come to the United States as refugees, and many arrived at the refugee camp at Fort Chaffee, Arkansas, the camp nearest to the DFW region (National Conference of Catholic Bishops 1988). Vietnamese priests also arrived at Our Lady of the Ozarks camp in Carthage, Missouri, which is the home of the CMC. In 1978 this town became the site for an important annual pilgimage referred to as the Marian Days, reflecting "the Vietnamese special devotion to Mary and their Blessed Martyrs" (National Conference of Catholic Bishops 1988: 401). This important ritual event brings together Vietnamese Catholics from across North America. In one large DFW Vietnamese parish, during the days preceding this festival in the summer of 2007, about thirty adults gathered to prepare food and other provisions for the trip. Families often camp at the Missouri celebration, and teenagers look forward to it as an opportunity to meet other Vietnamese youth. This event has grown from about 1,000 people in 1978 to 22,000 in 1985 (National Conference of Catholic Bishops 1988), to between 40,000 and 60,000 in recent years (Red-den 2008). Another significant event for Vietnamese Catholics in the diaspora is the Feast of the Vietnamese Martyrs on November 24th. The largest parish in Arlington, Texas, is named in honor of at least 100,000 Catholics persecuted and killed in Vietnam in the early nineteenth century because of their religious practices. In 1988, 117 of these martyrs were canonized (Luong, n.d.). This story of religious persecution was evidently in the minds of those interviewed for this project. Many of them spoke of their family's migration from the north of Vietnam to the south after 1954, when the French left and Vietnam was divided in two. One participant spoke of an entire North Vietnamese village converting to Catholicism at one point, and later following their priest to the south.

The priests interviewed for this project referred to their parishes as "international parishes," although such ethnic parishes are also known as personal or multicultural parishes. About 75 percent of all Vietnamese Catholics in the United States attend one of these ethnic parishes (Luong n.d.). The first Vietnamese parishes in the DFW region were established during the 1990s, breaking off from other parishes as the number of Vietnamese grew. According to research participants who were involved in the founding of these churches, the Vietnamese raised the funds to build them (borrowing money from the diocese to help meet costs) and provided their own labor to construct them. Some of the parishes are very large and wealthy; for example, the Vietnamese Martyrs parish in Arlington built its own large church and outer buildings that take up more than a city block. According to the pastor of this church, there are 6,000 members and 1,300 families. Other churches are smaller. One in a nearby community has about 250 families and is located in a building originally built as a Protestant church. The large and small churches have similar elaborate organizational structures that involve both lay leaders and priests, but there are variations in how each parish operates.

The ways in which such churches foster civic skills and leadership is illustrated by the complex organization of the Vietnamese Martyrs parish in Arlington. All Masses at this church are in Vietnamese except for the so-called children's Mass, at 1 P.M. on Sunday, which includes a mixture of English and Vietnamese in order to accommodate those youth who are not fluent in Vietnamese. The parish is governed by a pastoral council of five male lay leaders in addition to the priests. The lay leaders run religious education classes on Sundays from 9 P.M. to 5 A.M., and the parish also sponsors a branch of the Vietnamese Eucharistic Youth Society (a group introduced to Vietnam by Jesuits in the mid-twentieth century), which meets each Sunday afternoon. There are several parish societies: the Association of the Sacred Heart, Catholic Mothers, the Rosary Society (known as the Blue Army of Our Lady of Fatima, due to Mary's association with the color blue), and the *Legio Mariae*, or Legion of Mary, an association brought to Vietnam by Irish missionaries and devoted to the Virgin Mary. According to one Legion of Mary member, this mostly male group cuts across the Vietnamese population and is also present in some Korean, Chinese, and American parishes, although Vietnamese branches are the most numerous. These parish societies brought to the United States from Vietnam express Vietnamese cultural identity, but they are also communities of practice in which adults and youth can develop leadership skills and practice forms of cooperative behavior.

When lay leaders of the Vietnamese Martyrs Church were interviewed, they distinguished between their service activities performed through the church and other forms of service outside of it. These were mostly older men of the first generation who had somewhat elite family backgrounds and had high-level military or government careers in Vietnam. One district leader and one leader of the Legion of Mary described their activities helping others in the parish, but they distinguished these activities from community service. Another man expressed the role of helping others at church in this way: "If I am Catholic, it is my responsibility to find a church and to serve God." The activities of the Legion of Mary include visiting the sick, helping with funeral and mourning services, providing transportation to Mass for those who cannot drive, organizing a retreat for Lent, and facilitating religious practices that occur outside of Mass. This group's activities can be contrasted with those of a military veterans association in which many members of the Legion also participate that, according to one research participant, does more community service. He said, "We try to help ourselves first." For example, the veterans group will raise $1,000 to help a family with funeral expenses. Here he was expressing an ethos of self-reliance—that the group would help its own members in order to help them avoid needing charity or other forms of assistance.

Most of the fundraising done at the Vietnamese Martyrs Church is for the purpose of sending money to Vietnam for charity work—for example, to help lepers or to support a local parish. This large parish did, however, get involved in Hurricane Katrina relief efforts, primarily because of the high number of Vietnamese families affected by the hurricane. The priest reported that about thirty families came to the church from New Orleans and slept there for about two weeks. He explained, however, that "we had no food, no facilities, not enough restrooms for them." In addition to offering housing and other forms of help to these hurricane victims, the parish raised about $30,000 that was distributed to various organizations involved in relief efforts, including the Federation of Vietnamese Catholics in the United States and the Red Cross.

At a smaller Vietnamese parish in a nearby city there are fewer resources for such charity work. Its parishioners are mostly working class families and therefore much of the fundraising is aimed at improvements to the parish facilities. The parish does not receive much financial assistance from the diocese. As the priest there put it, "The Vietnamese do not like to be in debt. They are afraid of debt. We have to support ourselves and be independent." Like the larger church, this smaller church has a parish council of lay leaders. The priest said he takes care of the sacraments and ministry, but "I told them they are in charge of the rest." This is different than in Vietnam, he said, where the priest would make all the decisions. He said that in one sense this parish is "Americanized," with lots of control over the parish by laypeople, who run many of the activities; but it is also somewhat traditional in that parishioners do not want females serving at the altar. The priest came to the United States as a refugee with his family in the 1990s and joined the priesthood after arriving. He emphasized the contrasts between the roles of the priest and church in Vietnam and their roles in America. Traditionally, in Vietnam the "priest was a small god" and highly respected. Although priests in the United States may feel they have less influence than priests have in Vietnam, one prominent leader of a secular Vietnamese voluntary association told me that "people will listen to their priest or monk before they will listen to me," and that these religious institutions wield a great deal of power and influence over their members.

The Eucharistic Youth Society at these churches is the community of practice that most explicitly serves as a "training ground" for participatory citizenship.[7] One Vietnamese Catholic college student described her own involvement and what it taught her. She had served as president of the Vietnamese Student Association on her campus and felt that her involvement in the Eucharistic Youth Society had enhanced her knowledge, leadership skills, and confidence. She was born in Vietnam, had spent seven years of her childhood in a refugee camp in Thailand, had subsequently served in the U.S. Army Reserve, and was studying to be a teacher. She noted that in the youth group "we discuss what is going on in the world." These parish youth groups do community service, and the members pass through several ranks (much like in scouting) as they age, including a group for young unmarried adults that helps to organize the lower ranks and whose members form part of the leadership corps for the association. There is a strong emphasis on youth working together and on developing peer leadership skills.

In addition to these activities and parish associations that provide pathways to wider civic participation through informal means, some events organized in the activities halls of these churches offer more direct forms of connection to formal politics. Although none of the Catholic churches we studied were explicitly involved in either domestic or homeland politics,[8] the lay leaders of the parish sometimes organized events to which local politicians were invited. One such event observed during our fieldwork was a commemoration of the Hung Kings, Vietnamese culture heroes who were the earliest leaders to unify Vietnam; and the Truong sisters, who led a successful rebellion against the Chinese in 40 A.D. but were eventually conquered and martyred themselves by committing suicide. This ceremony, held in a Catholic church hall, was neither explicitly religious nor political in the formal sense, and it evoked the shared cultural symbols of historic Vietnam, including the traditional altar to honor ancestors, and a tea ceremony. There was some mention of the relief efforts made by the local Vietnamese population for the victims of Hurricane Katrina, but otherwise the ceremony, mostly in Vietnamese, was dedicated to commemoration of these heroes. The politicians who attended, including the city council member from Arlington who represents Vietnamese interests, were invited as honored guests, to learn more about Vietnamese history, and to introduce themselves to those in the audience who might eventually vote for them. This event displays how the Vietnamese population draws politicians to cultural activities (and we will see this again in subsequent chapters) that simultaneously reinforce Vietnamese cultural traditions and provide links to the wider society.

Thus Catholic churches can be sites for activities that have implications for social and cultural citizenship. In these events, people work together for some common purpose and, even when that purpose is focused mainly on the Vietnamese population or on spiritual matters, they are encouraged to participate in spheres beyond their families. Parish societies in particular are communities of practice with implications for civic engagement. In addition, as the commemoration discussed in the last paragraph illustrates, the Vietnamese also use cultural traditions to engage in formal political arenas through events that take place on church grounds and to which elected officials are invited.

Vietnamese Buddhist Temples

Although many of the informal aspects of mutual aid and social support that take place in the Catholic churches are also found at Buddhist temples, the temples lack the highly organized structure of the churches. Also, attendance is sporadic for many who claim Buddhism (or Hinduism, as discussed later) to be their religion. There is no overarching Buddhist organization for these temples as there is for the Catholic churches, because there are different branches of Buddhism. Local temples are affiliated, however, with some large groups, such as the American Buddhist Congress, which encouraged the formation of the Texas Buddhist Council in 1993 (Texas Buddhist Council 1998) and whose mission is to foster Buddhist teaching across the various forms of Buddhism. The monk at the large Vietnamese Theravada Buddhist temple in the Mid-Cities area was one of the founders of this association. Also, the DFW Buddhist Association was formed locally by two Theravada temples, one in Irving and one in Fort Worth.[9] The Irving temple was established in the 1980s, before any ethnically Vietnamese Catholic churches were formed. A new Zen-based Vietnamese Buddhist monastery and temple were built south of Fort Worth in 2003 and are linked to a different organizational structure than the other two temples. The Zen temple is served mainly by Buddhist nuns and there is no resident monk, although they follow a spiritual leader in Vietnam who occasionally comes to visit. Some of the Vietnamese Buddhists have participated in a summer youth camp outside of Houston that is sponsored by a Buddhist charity foundation. In these ways the DFW Buddhists are linked to others across the Southwest, although on a much smaller scale than the Vietnamese Catholics who are linked nationwide through such gatherings as the Marian Days pilgrimage in Missouri that was described in the preceding pages. Buddhist religious participation is thus fragmented compared to the participation of Catholics.

In the DFW area there has been some Buddhist adaptation to the Christian model of Sunday church services, although to a lesser degree than elsewhere in the United States.[10] A Vietnamese Buddhist woman who often serves as a liaison with non-Vietnamese who visit her temple explained (in English) that there are similarities between what Buddhists do at the temple and what "Americans" do in church. In that way she was trying to find common ground. On Sundays, the Buddhist temples have chanting sessions, spiritual teaching (*dharma* talk) by the monk, and religious and cultural instruction for the children by the youth leaders. This type of activity is not done in Vietnam, according to research participants. Other than this accommodation to the American practice of religious observance taking place on Sundays, which is seen as a practical matter due to the structure of the American work week and school schedules, the Buddhist temples remain fairly traditional in architecture and practice.

Temples tend to be located on marginal side streets and therefore are not highly visible within the cityscape. They are noticeable only to those who live or work in the neighborhood and drive or walk by them. The largest temple in

Fort Worth is in an economically depressed area on the southern outskirts of the city. Another temple is in a more economically viable and suburban landscape, near a major highway and a working-class neighborhood but located on a side street that has little traffic. A third temple, built more recently, is located on a narrow winding road in the countryside outside Fort Worth, and another is located on a side street in an older suburban neighborhood.

When one approaches a Buddhist temple, including the four visited in the course of this research project, one is struck by its exotic architecture in contrast to the flat Texan prairie landscape. All have ornate gates close to the street, and the temples themselves are brightly colored. Large statues of Buddha are visible on the grounds. The Theravada temple in Fort Worth was constructed by members of the community who attend the temple and raised the money to build it. Since our fieldwork was completed, this temple community has built another temple on the grounds of the old one and now uses the former temple as a community hall and site for its "Sunday school." The ability of the lay leaders to organize, raise money, and build these structures on their own is impressive and demonstrates the ways in which leadership and cooperative skills are enhanced in this setting. The spiritual leaders of this temple are two monks and a nun, all born in Vietnam. The monks live in a modest one-story house on the grounds of the temple that was there before the temple was built, and the nun lives in a building at the back of the temple itself. A larger temple in the Mid-Cities area has more monks and an ornate meeting room for guests (where the head monk was interviewed) with imported wooden chairs and other furnishings. Several other buildings sit on the temple grounds.

Temples are open all week long for people to come into and pray or make offerings to Buddha, and people do stop by and do this when they have a special request or are facing a special problem. One does not find multiple religious associations, such as the societies found in the Catholic parishes. The leadership of the monk is paramount; however, lay leaders have some autonomy in the context of the Buddhist Youth Association. On any given Sunday, children are dropped off by their parents to attend classes in Buddhism and Vietnamese language and culture. They stay all day, from about 9 A.M. to 5 P.M. Older youth who belong to the Buddhist Youth Association help lead these classes under the direction of the youth director, a middle-aged Vietnamese man who works in law enforcement, speaks English, and is engaged in graduate studies in criminal justice. Some men and women also participate in activities during this time. The women—usually middle-aged or older—may be cooking for a special upcoming ceremony while a handful of men might be busy building or repairing various structures to improve the temple grounds. At around 1 P.M. a meditation, chanting, and prayer ceremony is held in the temple. The children as well as some parents and others attend this ceremony. The monk generally offers a *dharma* talk during this ceremony. When the ceremony ends, some children are picked up by their parents and others stay and play on the grounds.

Like the Catholic churches, Buddhist temples raise money for charities in Vietnam, such as hospitals and orphanages. One temple has photos of the hospital it sponsors on display. Also like the churches, the temples offered shelter and raised funds for victims of Hurricane Katrina. Because of their strong links to other Southeast Asian monks, the Theravada monks also raised funds for the 2004 tsunami and distributed them through the Red Cross. According to one monk, the basis for the Buddhist practice of helping others is the concept of karma. "This is consciousness, intention of mind. It is about the benefit of an action to yourself and others." He explained that "mindful awareness" has to do with controlling one's actions in order to control one's mind, eventually seeking "enlightenment" or truth. An enlightened person is one who can help you and whom you can trust. In his *dharma* talks, this monk stresses the concept of *loving-kindness*, which he says is connected to cause and effect: You must do good to have good come to you. Buddhists interviewed for this project often explained the purpose of their service to others as "for a good feeling or to give me a good feeling," which is a translation of the Vietnamese phrase *cho toi cam giac tot*. One woman explained that this means it gives a "person a good feeling to know that he or she has helped someone or done something good. If that person is Buddhist, he or she would say that by doing a good deed, he or she will receive good fortune or their sons or daughters will have good fortune later on." One Catholic man, stressing the commonalities between Buddhism and Catholicism, said, "Buddhists believe in reincarnation and Catholics don't, but [for both] you will have a reward if you do something good in your life."

The Vietnamese Buddhist temples in the DFW-area, like the one in Houston described by Thuan Huynh (2000), which is also part of the Texas Buddhist Council, do not provide social services to members in any organized way, in large part due to financial constraints, but also because "Buddhist temples have traditionally never provided social service programs; they have only been places of worship" (Huynh 2000: 53). The temple's role in civic engagement lies not so much in being an organization that provides social services to its members, although informally people do help each other, but in the central ritual role it plays in the wider Vietnamese community. For example, the Buddhist Youth Association organizes the lion dancers who perform at several community events throughout the year, including the Tet Festival and the Mid-Autumn Moon Festival.

Like the Catholic Eucharistic Youth Society, the Buddhist Youth Association encourages participatory forms of citizenship by training youth to become leaders and to work together on projects. One youth leader in training, who arrived in the United States as a teenager and works in the computer industry, said that "being involved in the Youth Association increased my self-confidence and helps me advance in my career, so now I want to help out as a youth leader." The lay youth leader mentioned earlier who works in law enforcement and is very concerned about gangs and other problems among Vietnamese American youth sees the youth group as a way to teach social and civic responsibility and leadership skills while also reinforcing Vietnamese cultural identity and Buddhist teachings. The youth group is a community of practice where youth learn social skills that they can take into the wider civic sphere.

Although Buddhist temples, like Catholic churches, do not regularly host events that involve direct engagement with politics, human rights and religious freedom for Buddhists in Vietnam has recently been a key issue among the leaders of the local Vietnamese population. An event hosted at a major university in the region during the spring of 2008 brought Buddhist activists from Europe to Arlington, Texas. This event involved the forced house arrest of the Venerable Thich Quang Do, a Buddhist monk living in Vietnam who was critical of the government. As participants at this event explained, the Unified Buddhist Church of Vietnam had been banned since 1981 and the communist government wanted to put in its place a Buddhist federation that it could control. The autonomy of Buddhists was the issue for the organizers of this event, which was highly political and focused on homeland politics while simultaneously aiming to unite all Vietnamese in the diaspora at a global level. The event was formally endorsed by the leaders of the Vietnamese American Communities of Dallas and Tarrant Counties, who spoke during the opening remarks. In addition, the event was attended by all of the major Vietnamese religious leaders in DFW—Catholic priests, Buddhist monks, and leaders of Cao Dai and Hoa Hao. Representatives from voluntary associations were also present, as were the Vietnamese American media. Approximately three hundred people (almost all Vietnamese American) filled the auditorium, and the event was timed to occur during celebrations of Buddha's birthday in Vietnam, at which religious freedom in Vietnam was being celebrated. The activists in the United States who organized and supported this event sought to protest what they felt were Vietnam's ongoing infringements on human rights and religious freedom. Although the monks and priests we interviewed stated that they did not view their institutions as politically engaged, this meeting demonstrates the type of mobilization that can occur around homeland politics and the issues of human rights and religious freedom in Vietnam. It also shows how diasporic Vietnamese come together across religious differences to rally for anticommunist causes.

Vietnamese Religious Syncretism and Civic Engagement

It is the shared culture and history of Vietnamese refugees in the United States—acknowledged and voiced by our research participants—rather than religious participation itself that provide the key to understanding how Vietnamese Americans engage with U.S. society. Vietnamese Americans in Tarrant County have multiple ties to others that cut across this ethnic group, through marriage and kinship, friendships formed both in the United States and (for older generations) in Vietnam, voluntary associations, employment, and religious participation. The dominant voluntary associations in this region are led by individuals from a range of religious affiliations—primarily Buddhist and Catholic, but also Protestant. Two prominent community leaders expressed the plurality of their own religious affiliations. Both of these men arrived in the first wave of refugees, soon after the fall of Saigon. One of the men, originally a Buddhist, married a Catholic Vietnamese woman in the United States, but he considers himself both Buddhist and Catholic and sees no contradiction in this. The other man, profiled in the next chapter, came from a Buddhist family in Vietnam, later converted to Catholicism, and after being sponsored by a Baptist congregation when he arrived in the United States, converted to that religion. His family attends major Christian holiday events at a Baptist church, but he considers himself influenced strongly by all three religions. These examples illustrate the ways in which immigrant leaders bridge religious differences across the population, with a common Vietnamese identity being the stronger link than religious affiliation for many people. The experience of colonization and foreign occupation of Vietnam was a recurrent theme during our interviews, and the fact that both Buddhism and Catholicism were brought to Vietnam from the outside was frequently noted by our research participants.

For both Buddhists and Catholics, the authority of the monk or priest is extremely important, a point noted by community leaders, who in some ways must compete with these religious leaders in order to get people to listen to their agendas and accept their secular authority. Although individual Vietnam-

ese immigrants have commonalities that transcend specific religions, the organization of Buddhist temples and Catholic churches leads to some differences.
As participants in a religion that originated in the West, Vietnamese Catholics
have religious ties to non-Asian Catholics and are part of a global Catholic hierarchy and structure. The complex organization of societies and associations
that characterizes many parishes encourages parish-based involvement but also
wider civic participation among adults and youth. Yet the lack of a strong organization or formal ritual practice among Buddhists leads to an openness to
other religions and ways of thinking that informs democratic practice.

The sense of responsibility (*trach nhiem*) to do good that Vietnamese of all
religious backgrounds expressed may arise from their shared roots in ancestor worship and from the importance of first taking responsibility within the
family and then taking it out into the wider world. *Trach nhiem* has connections to the Buddhist beliefs in karma and loving-kindness, discussed earlier.
The concept belies a contrast between an "individual moral project" and a
"collective moral project" (Kniss and Numrich 2007) because it expresses both
individual and collective forms of morality. When asked why they helped at a
church or temple, several people responded, "because it is my responsibility."
They considered this responsibility to be a moral issue whereby those who are
fortunate to have a better life should exercise *trach nhiem* and help those who
are less fortunate.[11] Both Catholics and Buddhists acknowledged individual
rewards after death for such behavior, but the notion is also rooted in a concern for the collective good. Issues of moral authority and moral responsibility inform Vietnamese civic practice. Helle Rydström (2003: 52) notes the use
of this concept in Vietnamese child training as one among several positive
sentiments (*thin cam*) related to a concept also observed in China that means
"good feeling."[12] The political connotations of this idea have historical roots in
Vietnam and are connected to values favoring community. In interviews with
South Vietnamese political actors during the Vietnam War, Allan Goodman
(1973: 81) reports, one of them said to him, "The basis of politics in Vietnam
is our sense of political responsibility, and we use the term *cong-dong trach
nhiem* to denote it." *Cong-dong* refers to community or collectivity (people
added together). Our Vietnamese research participants referred to *trach nhiem*
in terms of emotion, as doing things that provide a good feeling, as well as
in terms of social responsibility. This concept is very much related to Buddhist ideas about the necessity to be released from suffering (*dukkha*) at an
emotional-spiritual level as well as at a physical-material level; it is also a tenet
of the teachings of Catholicism.

Indian Religious Assemblies

My son is in the Chinmaya Mission programs and I take classes twice a week. I am thinking of becoming a teacher and my husband and I both volunteer. My husband does facilities and building maintenance part-time and I help provide food and decorations for events. Religion is very important. Back home, from day one your parents take you to the temple. It is in our blood. We try to teach our children the same. They sometimes rebel, but people say when they go away to college they come back to it. [Fifty-two-year-old housewife, born in North India, came to the United States as a bride in 1977]

I am a founder of a mosque in Plano and serve on the board of directors. I served as the secretary for four years. I also serve as president of the Islamic Association of Collin County. I go to weekly events at the mosque and daily prayers as time permits. I think community involvement is divine. I try to in-still in my children the virtue of service that my father gave me. Just yesterday I brought home some flyers that had to go out for the Islamic organization I am involved in. We are raising money for a children's school in an impoverished area of India. I called the family into the living room and we stuffed and licked envelopes together until it was done. [Forty-three-year-old Muslim male from Bangalore, India, came to the United States for education in 1989, currently president of an electronics company]

These two immigrants, who represent different religious traditions in India, forthrightly acknowledge the role that religious institutions play in com-munity building and in promoting volunteer activities by which individuals can "give back to the community." Whether the community is defined in rela-tion to India or as the wider American community, both are operative and important. Indians in DFW have founded numerous temples (including Jain, Sikh, Swaminarayan, and Hare Krishna temples). The woman quoted at the beginning of this section is a member of the very active Chinmaya Mission. Although the mosques serve Muslims across a range of national origins, a few are dominated by South Asian Muslims. In addition, Indians attend a number of Christian churches, four of them Mar Thoma churches founded by Indians from the state of Kerala in southwest India. Our research involved observing religious behavior across this broad range of religious traditions.

Reponses from the parents we interviewed give some indication of the ex-tent and diversity of religious participation among Indians, especially those in midlife. Of the thirty-four Indians who participated in the parent interviews, eighteen (53 percent) identified themselves as Hindu, one identified as Sikh and two as Jain, six were Christian (Mar Thoma, Syrian Orthodox, Protestant, or unspecified Christian), four were Muslim, and three said they were atheist, nonpracticing, or agnostic. When asked if they currently participated in a local church, temple, or mosque, 79 percent responded yes. Clearly the level and nature of their participation varied, with several of the Hindu respondents indicating that they attended their temple only on special occasions and for festivals.[13] Unlike in Christianity, in Hinduism the concept of congregational worship is foreign, and regular attendance is certainly not mandatory. Some individuals, especially those who own their own businesses and work every day, claim they do not have time to participate. Thus a high-school-educated Hindu in his early fifties who arrived in the United States in 1984 and is self-employed commented, "Our shop is open every day but Tuesdays, and the religious service and events are always on weekends, so we can never go. In India the religious events were a scheduled date and it fell on whatever day of the week it fell on. Here in America everything happens on the weekends. Those are our busiest days. We cannot afford to close down." Clearly the challenges of making a living can interfere with religious participation. The temples have adjusted to a U.S. timetable by concentrating their activities on Saturdays and Sundays.[14]

Those first-generation Indians we interviewed who do participate in religious institutions indicated that the primary reason for becoming involved in a temple, church, or mosque in this country is for spiritual guidance and to introduce one's children to one's religious and cultural traditions. One software engineer in his forties explained that he and his wife were interested in exposing their children to their culture so they would not miss any of it and then blame their parents later for not teaching them. He added that they liked to go to the temple from time to time because it made them feel like they were still in India. Clearly the bonding dimensions of these religious institutions remain as important for immigrants today as they were in the past. Many of these institutions are the venues for the celebration of major festivals, and many offer language classes in which parents are eager to enroll their children. Religious institutions in India were obviously not involved in language education, but like weekend scheduling, this is a common adaptation in the immigrant context.

A Christian research participant in his fifties who completed a bachelor's degree and worked as a corporate scientist said that his family attended church regularly. "My wife is in the choir and is involved in various activities and I am the secretary of the church board. We are very involved in our church . . . church is a big part of our life." Several other respondents talked about giving time to their religious organization, serving as chairman of a committee, teaching classes, or acting as a trustee. Some talked about being more active in the past and now turning it over to a new generation of leaders. A Hindu engineer in her early fifties summed up her involvement as follows: "First, the temple provides us with a place to worship. We, my family and I, feel it is very important to cultivate a spiritual life. Second, we enjoy the opportunity that these temples provide us to do community service." In articulating how first-generation Indians become civically engaged, one community leader suggested that individuals start out in religious organizations. From there, he continued, they move into other Indian community organizations, and eventually beyond the Indian community to serve within business chambers of congress, on school boards, and within the governance structures of mainstream organizations. "One is a stepping stone to the next. This is the path for the first generation." This individual was describing a significant trajectory of progressive entry into the civic sphere through various communities of practice, one that clearly represents the process by which new identities are embraced within organizational contexts as immigrants develop their sense of belonging and an increasing connection with American society and culture. It is to a discussion of participatory citizenship in the context of different Indian religious assemblies that we now turn.

Hinduism, Seva, and Civic Engagement

Hindus were least in number among the first wave of Indian immigrants to arrive in the United States, but they are now the largest and wealthiest of the South Asian populations here (Leonard 2007b: 464). In most cities where they have settled, these immigrants have constructed Hindu temples to serve as religious, cultural, and community centers.[15] The DFW Hindu Temple was one of the earliest Indian religious organizations founded in this area of Texas. It is located in Irving, an inner-ring suburb just to the west of Dallas.[16] The temple was built in several planned phases after the land was purchased in 1988. People first worshipped in an old house on the property whose living and dining rooms had been converted into prayer rooms. In 1991 the Ekta Mandir (*Ekta* means unity, *Mandir* means temple) was inaugurated, and in the mid-1990s, during phase two, a large cultural center was added. In the third phase, a school extension was built and carved decoration was added to the temple building to make it look more like a temple in India. This decorative work was completed in 2003–2004. Plans for the fourth and fifth phases include building living quarters for priests and a residence for old people along with a health clinic that will serve the entire population of Irving. The DFW Hindu Temple houses eleven deities in the main hall and four in an annex. In their deliberations about what deities to include, the temple leaders aimed to accommodate area Hindus who come from different regions of India, each with its own language and Hindu traditions. Their goal was to make the temple "an umbrella for everyone." This was an extremely important community-building decision that concentrated efforts and laid the foundation for successful collaboration in executing the project. This temple has become a gathering place as well as a symbolic center for the residentially dispersed and diverse Hindu population.

For Hindus, the idea of "giving back" that has become associated with and adapted to the practices of citizenship and civic engagement in the United States is rooted in the concept of *seva*, or selfless service to the poor and suffering without any expectation of return. Giving (*dana*) is a religious duty (*dharma*) and encompasses the principle that to serve humanity is to serve God. In the *Sanatana Dharma* (another term for Hinduism, sometimes translated "eternal religion"), *Vidya Daan*, or imparting spiritual knowledge, is the highest form of charity, followed by *Anna Daan* (donating food to the needy) and *Vastra Daan* (providing clothes to the poor). Modern usages of *seva* take two forms. One usage relates to the Hindu nationalist context: *seva* is seen as an expression of pride in the face of Christian missionary efforts and colonialism in the nineteenth century, as a principle that galvanized the freedom fighters in the first part of the twentieth century, and most recently as an idea adopted by right-wing politicians and Hindu militants. The second usage is more directly related to social service (Ruttonji 1968). This usage was popularized by the Ramakrishna Mission under a nineteenth-century Hindu leader named Vivekananda (1863–1902), who defined the main purpose of the Mission as to serve the poor through free hospitals and schools in rural areas.[17] Although the Ramakrishna Mission adopted the idea that liberation is possible through *seva*—which should be a collective enterprise rather than an individualistic undertaking—the idea that good deeds done through *seva* bring karmic benefits to individuals who engage in such activities has been more widely incorporated into mainstream Hindu consciousness. Thus the idea of not interfering with karma is counterbalanced by a powerful principle of social responsibility toward others that can enhance the karma of the good-doer and contribute to personal spiritual development (Satyanarayana 2008).[18]

In the United States it is this second usage of *seva*—as social responsibility—that is emphasized, but it takes on a more enhanced meaning than it perhaps carries in India, and one that fits well, at least as Hindus in the area perceive it, with the broader values of U.S. society. One male respondent suggested that everything that is done in the temple is *seva* because the temple serves the devotees. In India, he observed, people come to the temple for food, and at the DFW temple food is provided at all major events. More commonly, however, members of the DFW Hindu Temple take food out into the community—to shelters, to food banks, and to various places on holidays, particularly Thanksgiving. This activity, suggested one participant who was active in the temple, is how Hindu temples in the United States have incorporated "Western ways of giving charity." Although the youth group at the temple exists to help young people bridge the divide between the "mainstream" culture and Hindu culture and traditions, these youth also become involved in *seva* activities such as Meals On Wheels. The connection between *seva* and volunteerism is most apparent in the adoption of SEVA as the acronym for Students Engaged in Volunteer Activities by a group of second-generation Indian high school students in Plano, a northern suburb of Dallas. These students, as one of the participants in the group stated, are dedicated to "meaningful community service" and have adapted a set of principles from their own religious tradition to an American high school context. The SEVA students have volunteered at the Scottish Rite Hospital and at Lions Club eye clinics, and have held their own spelling bee for students who cannot otherwise compete.

Although there is no formal requirement for a temple to perform *seva* activities, at the DFW Hindu Temple a *seva* subcommittee has been in place for almost as long as the temple has existed. The goal of these *seva* activities, as one Hindu Temple member indicated, is to promote "good neighborship." *Neighborship* is both closely and broadly defined and thus these *seva* projects include bringing Christmas gifts to the children in a school located very close to the temple, as well as raising funds for the tsunami victims in late 2004 and early 2005. The temple has also partnered in some activities with the Dallas City Hall and with a homeless shelter where each month members of the temple go to cook a meal.[19] Like the members of Vietnamese religious organizations, members of the DFW Hindu Temple, as well as those who belong to other Hindu organizations in the area (such as the Chinmaya Mission and the Swaminarayan Temple),[20] became quite active in the aftermath of Hurricane Katrina and during Hurricane Rita. The temple hall was opened to Hurricane Rita evacuees (most of whom were Hispanics sent by the American Red Cross). By responding to these regional disasters in a fashion similar to that of other, nonimmigrant religious organizations, including collaborating with the Red Cross, the temple was claiming a rightful place in the American religio-civic sphere.

Beyond the *seva* activities and disaster responses that bring Indian immigrants out into the broader community, the DFW Hindu Temple offers other programs that are more social, such as a Diwali dinner. Local dignitaries—the mayor, the police chief, the fire chief—are invited to these events and thus outsiders are brought into the temple space and introduced to Hindu cultural and religious traditions. Christmas gifts are offered to the police chief and the fire marshal. Temple leaders suggest that these actions offer additional examples of good neighborship. The bottom line, one temple member suggested, "is that if I am a good citizen, this is precisely what I should be doing. The religion helps us do it." There is something else to consider, however, in the analysis of these particular actions and activities. Although members of the temple suggest that by their actions they are expressing their gratitude to the city of Irving, they are also clearly establishing their civic presence and the right to be both respected and heard as members of the broader local community.

Similar community involvement and engagement activities also occur at the much smaller Jain temple.[21] Organized at about the same time as the DFW Hindu Temple, the Jain temple is located in a house in Richardson, a suburb north of Dallas. The temple is locked, but the two hundred to three hundred members have access with a number code and can enter anytime to pray. However, like the Hindu Temple, the Jain Temple is most active on weekends, when most of the functions are scheduled. Newcomers to the city learn about these activities through the temple's Web site. They are also listed in various directories. Members make donations to support the temple; there are no dues. A governance structure is in place, with bylaws, a charter, a board of directors, officers, and a nomination process. Setting up and operating according to these mechanisms and structures is a good example of how civic skills are learned in a religious context. The languages used at the Jain Temple are Hindi, English, and Gujarati, and people come from as far away as Waco (approximately ninety miles south of Dallas) to participate. There is an active youth group that engages in activities such as food drives.

At the Jain temple, the *seva* group has helped retired people. First they target their services—such as medical camps—to the Indian community, whether Jain or not, and then to other senior citizens. These activities are modeled on the kinds of activities that occur in the main Jain temple in urban centers in India. Each temple has a *dharmashala*, a residence inn where travelers can stay and be fed (with first preference being given to Jains). Jain temples in India often support local charities or a school by providing scholarships for students. The Jain Temple in DFW continues these traditions. For example, members have delivered food (canned vegetables because they are vegetarians) to a homeless shelter. The temple also has projects to help the American Red Cross and the United Way, thereby collaborating, like the DFW Hindu Temple, with what they refer to as mainstream organizations.

When asked if he would link these activities with a concept of citizenship, one Jain leader, a retired software professional who moved to Dallas in 1978, used the term *social citizenship* and contrasted it with *political citizenship*, which he said "involves a power element." When pressed, he claimed that social citizenship is about helping others in need without the expectation of return. "And you don't just help people of the same religion; you help anybody. . . . You offer your help to another human being with no hidden agenda." He noted that this attitude emerges from religious teachings that emphasize being unselfish. When pushed for further explanation of his ideas about citizenship, this respondent first noted that a good citizen should be law-abiding, but after that he said a good citizen should be active in the community—by which he meant "your neighborhood, where you are living." This respondent was articulating the social responsibility dimension of citizenship, asserting his right to belong and his presence in the public sphere through the social practice of contributing to his community.

Perhaps the Indian Hindu organization with the most highly organized volunteer civic services is the Swaminarayan Temple in Irving. Adjacent to the temple building is a medical clinic that was built as part of the Bochasanwasi Shri Akshar Purushottam Swaminarayan Sanstha (BAPS) Pramukh Swami Hospital and Research Center. This organization has fourteen hospitals and clinics around the world, but only two in the United States—a large one in Atlanta and the Dallas-area clinic in Irving. According to one of the members of this temple, the Dallas area was chosen because it is a center for health care workers of Indian origin. Trained participants in this clinic not only donate time on Saturdays but also donated equipment to furnish it. They see anyone who does not have insurance, provide drug samples that they get from their private practices, and write out prescriptions and referrals. Most of their clientele are Indian because they come to know about the clinic largely through word of mouth and, as one informant suggested, "that does not go farther than the Indian community. We try to advertise by radio, flyers, at the grocery stores, so we do get some people who are not Indian, and we treat them just the same. But it has ended up to be mostly Indian." In addition to operating the clinic, the Swaminarayan temple also hosts a health fair each April. They contact agencies in the area that are engaged with health care issues and offer them free mammograms, X-rays, MRIs, blood pressure screening, physicals, eye exams, dental care, and blood work. For this project they partner with some of the local Indian Lions Clubs and with other churches and temples.

When asked to articulate why Swaminarayan adherents engage in such activities as the clinic and the health fair, one temple member said that service was fundamental to her religion. "We have a saying: Those who wish to sincerely serve society must be spiritually pure, and only those who are spiritually pure can serve society. We feel that other people are not your enemy; you are your own enemy. Your anger, fears, greed, bad thoughts and feelings are what make you bad. So we work on controlling the inner man. When you are free from those things, when you have yourself out of the way, you naturally want to think of the others around you." Good citizenship in this context, she thought, did not necessarily require a lot of money, although as physicians she and her husband are well-off. "It is a humbleness of heart; it's how you make life easier for other people, and that could be helping someone with a ride, or reading to children, or helping with labor." These comments reinforce that there is a general attitude among Hindus in the United States that the service component of their spiritual beliefs can be translated into aspects of good citizenship, and practiced by reaching out from the institutional space of their respective temples to the broader community of Indians as well as non-Indians.

The Mar Thoma Church: Christian Principles of Service

Christians represent slightly more than 2 percent of the total population of India, but they constitute a much higher proportion of Indians in the United States, largely the result of selective migration factors (Kurien 2004). Although Indian Christians who have settled in the United States are from diverse regional backgrounds, those from the state of Kerala are by far the largest group. Christian Keralan women have pursued nursing degrees in significant numbers and this has made them a hot commodity in the global labor market, facilitating the entry of Keralan families into the United States, among other places.[22] Christians from Kerala are among the most active in establishing churches in the United States (Alexander 2004: 74). The major denominations are Roman and Syrian Catholics, Mar Thoma Christians, and some Protestant denominations.

The history of the Mar Thoma Christians, or Marthomites, dates back to 52 A.D., when the Apostle Thomas, or Saint Thomas, is said to have arrived in India as a missionary.[23] For several centuries the Saint Thomas Christians maintained an affiliation with the Patriarch of Babylon and used a Syriac liturgy (Williams 1988: 104–105).[24] With the arrival of Portuguese explorer Vasco da Gama on the shores of India at the end of the fifteenth century, efforts were made to wean the Saint Thomas Christians from both Middle Eastern and traditional Indian practices. There was resistance to this effort to Latinize, and by

1665 the St. Thomas Christians had split into two churches: the Saint Thomas Christians of the Roman Catholic Church (Syro-Malabar Rite) and the Saint Thomas Christians affiliated with the Patriarch of Antioch. Anglican missionaries of the Church Missionary Society (founded in London in 1799) further complicated the picture by attracting some Syrian Christians to their practices and liturgy. As a result of its early founding and because of centuries of exposure to alternate Christian traditions, the history of the Saint Thomas Christians is both unique and complicated. In general, the Marthomite liturgy and modes of worship are today a blend of Orthodox characteristics and aspects of the Protestant Reformation. As a result of an agreement formulated in the early 1980s, the Mar Thoma Church in the United States has developed close ties with the Episcopal Church. The agreement "allows for the development of the Mar Thoma Church as a separate denomination, but it provides for a significant ecumenical relationship that broadens the contacts and influence of the Mar Thoma Church" (Williams 1988: 112).

In 1976, the first U.S. Mar Thoma congregation was established in New York (Williams 1988) and in 1978 the first DFW-area Mar Thoma church was established. At the time of our research there were four Mar Thoma churches in DFW—the largest located to the west of Dallas, in the inner-ring suburb of Farmers Branch. This particular church opened in 1996 and cost approximately two million dollars to build. The pastor serving this congregation outlined several of the regular activities of the church: a Sunday school, Sunday worship services conducted in English and in Malayalam (the language of Kerala) on alternating Sundays, a youth league (which meets on Tuesdays), a women's auxiliary, Bible study groups, a parish mission, an adult choir, and a youth choir. In order both to maintain Indian tradition (where men and women sit separately) and to adapt to life in the United States, the church has seating areas for men or women only as well as areas where families and couples can sit together. The congregation is governed by an executive committee elected annually by the full membership. This committee helps the pastor.

One leader, speaking about this congregation, said that the church "teaches you what it means to be a good Christian—to help your neighbors, that you can find the poor in your own backyard; you do not need to look to India, and you can take care of them here." He went on to observe that Eastern Christian churches are very community oriented. "We do not talk about 250 members, we talk about 250 families." The DFW congregation has ten prayer groups throughout the metropolitan area, each made up of 25 to 30 families. These tightly knit groups gather once during the week whereas the whole community gathers on Sundays. One member suggested that "the church is the most important way for people to get involved and interact with others." Another member said, "The mission of the church is to lead people to Christ, and some of the ways we execute that is by serving other people." At thanksgiving the members of this congregation give about a thousand turkeys to a social service organization in Farmers Branch, and they conduct some projects among the homeless. During Hurricane Rita they offered their homes to Houston-area Marthomites—who, according to one church member, are not strangers but like family.

The church collaborates with several mainstream organizations, such as the YMCA and the Salvation Army, as well as with other Christian churches from Kerala (but not Hindu or Muslim organizations). One church leader suggested that being involved in the broader community is the primary goal of the North American and European diocese of Mar Thoma churches. The Farmers Branch church also has missions abroad, including one in Mexico that has helped villagers to build homes, and another in India for tsunami relief. In some of these efforts this church participates with other Mar Thoma churches around the United States. One church leader emphasized how important these service activities are to the young people. They learn about real poverty, he suggested, and they are transformed. "They do not know what it means because they are in homes with five or six computers. They see people who have nothing," he said, "and it changes them."

Parents in the Mar Thoma Church are concerned about the very American outlook of their children. As a result, a good deal of emphasis is placed on the youth groups. The Farmers Branch church has four youth chaplains who were brought from India because they know the Indian way. One church member indicated that because people from Kerala tend to send their children to U.S. public schools, they rely on the church to help them sustain Indian values. The youth group accommodates individuals between ages twelve and thirty-five. In this congregation there are two youth fellowships, one that serves Indian Americans and operates primarily in English, and one for Indians who have emigrated as young adults. As one college-age participant suggested, this division accommodates the differences between those who grew up in the United States and those who grew up in India. Although the youth group is a social organization, its focus is primarily religious and centered on Bible study. However, it also offers young people the chance to assume leadership roles—which, according to one young man who was serving as joint secretary at the time he was interviewed, "gives you the opportunity to learn skills that can be transferred to other contexts." Another young man talked about how these skills were the foundation for the leadership roles he had assumed in student organizations at the university he attended.

The youth fellowship tries to complete several community service projects each quarter. After the 2004 tsunami, the entire church raised $30,000, including about $2,500 raised by the youth fellowship. The youth group also helped Hurricane Katrina evacuees by collecting twenty-five to thirty trash bags of used clothing, which they delivered to the Dallas Convention Center. They have engaged in Habitat for Humanity projects and visited nursing homes. When asked about the broader role of community service, a member of the youth fellowship suggested that it should be "integral to daily life, not something to fill hours, not something for recognition." He went on to observe that churches can encourage civic participation, "but you can fall into a trap if you think of it as something you have to do. It needs to be a daily concern. You have to get something out of it at a personal level." Another college-age Indian youth, when asked how the church in India is different from the church in the United States, drew on his experience during visits home to suggest that serving the community is not a pronounced idea in India "because there is no difference in cultures as there is here. Doing community service here is part of the process of assimilation into broader U.S. society. This is not necessary in India because there is no difference." In this single observation this young man articulated the necessity for immigrants in the United States to enter the civic sphere if they want to belong. Further, he suggested that this could be done from a platform within one's own culture and hence in a comfort zone where the skills for successful bridging activities can be developed. Although the Marthomites of the Farmers Branch church are, compared to the members of the DFW Hindu Temple, a much more tightly knit religious community of individuals who have constructed a culture of intimacy that revolves around their church and their faith, this does not obviate their participation in the broader U.S. community through acts of religious charity.

Indian Muslims: Zakat and Community Outreach in a Post-9/11 America

Only recently, and particularly after 9/11, have scholars begun to study Muslims in America, and some have observed that September 11 was a "watershed for Muslims, who from that point have become much more interested in involving themselves in American civic life" (Carnes and Yang 2004b: 30).[25] The largest and oldest mosque in DFW, located in the suburb of Richardson, held an open house soon after 9/11 to educate Americans about Islam. Copies of the Koran were handed out. The Plano mosque, where some negative graffiti was posted in the aftermath of 9/11, held an open house in December 2001 and since then has invited non-Muslims to participate in the activities surrounding Ramadan every year.[26]

There are various estimates of the number of Muslims (including African American Muslims) in the United States—anywhere from two to six million. They are diverse, with Friday prayers constituting "a weekly awakening to the scope and breadth of Islam" (Eck 2007: 215, 216–217). In the United States, Muslims operate under the umbrella of the Islamic Society of North America (ISNA), which was founded in the early 1990s and holds annual conferences in various U.S. cities (223). Anthropologist Karen Leonard (2003) describes South Asian Muslims who have gradually taken over leadership positions in some of the major Muslim organizations in the United States, such as ISNA and the American Muslim Alliance. Leonard also describes enhanced Muslim activities and politicization in the aftermath of 9/11, and changes in spokespersons as some individuals have risen to prominence through media influence. In Chicago in particular, Muslims from Hyderabad, India, have assumed leadership roles in downtown institutions, thereby challenging Arab leadership (Leonard 2007a: 159).

A significant number of Muslim South Asians have settled in the Dallas suburb of Plano. Planning for the construction of a mosque for about 1,200 registered members began in the late 1980s, and in 1991 a space was rented in an office complex where they could come together to worship (which they had previously done in individual homes). At the time there was no formal organization—just a collection box and volunteers. However, in 1997, the members established the Islamic Association of Collin County, a tax-exempt 501c3 non-profit corporation with a constitution and governing bylaws. A board president and six other board members were elected and began to focus on building a mosque. Establishing the formal structure and working on the goals they set for themselves, including raising the necessary funds, launched a group of leaders along a path of civic learning and engaged a broader community, some of whom were very generous donors.

The mosque was officially opened in 2001. In addition to its board of governors there are several committees appointed by the board, including a security committee, a construction committee, and a sisters committee, composed of female participants. An outreach committee has been tackling the negative image of Islam among the general American public. This committee has sponsored several open-house events to bridge the communication divide by helping people to understand what Muslims believe and to find commonalities.

A member of this committee observed, however, that Muslims also need to understand other religions. The first open house, in December 2001, had fifteen hundred visitors. To promote it, fliers were distributed across the city, including in churches. There were radio spots, and mosque members invited coworkers and neighbors. Every principal from the Plano Independent School District, as well as city mayors and managers and many non-Muslim community leaders, were also invited. "We were really prepared," said one board member. "We involved our young people, who gave gift packages to guests. And the ladies did a program to change the perception that people have of women in Islam." Another board member, who is also a member of the multicultural board of the Plano Independent School District, said they take a proactive stance, such as writing articles for the local newspaper whenever there is something negative about Muslims in the news. He characterized what is going on in the post-9/11 world not as a clash of civilizations but as a "clash of the uncivil. These people are a fringe element, doing things that get the rest of us in trouble." He went on to note that Muslims have to "assimilate into society; this is the purpose of the outreach activities. We came here to be part of the community and to contribute to society." After their first open house, members of the mosque paid a visit to a synagogue.

These outreach activities have been a major effort of those involved with the Plano mosque. However, they have also been active in other forms of civic engagement that are fundamental to the Muslim religion and closely allied to *zakat*, the third of the Five Pillars of Islam. *Zakat* requires spending a fixed portion of one's wealth for the poor and needy. Members of the Plano mosque have used their *zakat* fund to help other Muslims—for example, refugees from Kosovo, Bosnia, and Afghanistan who have come to the region. They have partnered with refugee organizations in this effort. During Hurricane Katrina the mosque was opened to those displaced by the storm, and mosque funds were used to cover rent for several families for two to three months. The mosque also sent volunteers to the American Airlines Center in downtown Dallas, a holding ground for Katrina evacuees. One mosque leader described these activities as mandatory for the faith. When asked if these activities were part of being a good citizen, another Mosque leader insisted that Islam does not separate who you are from your belief in God, nor does it separate your civic duty from your duty to God. "Anything you do should be for the pleasure of the Creator, even obeying the law. It is part of the whole package, part of being human. Doing good in the world is a form of indirect worship." In the planning stage at the Plano mosque is an effort to open a free clinic for routine health care. Like the Hindu community, the South Asian Muslim community includes a number of health professionals. Members of the board acknowledged that this would be a good way to "pay back the community," by which they meant the larger DFW area.

Unlike the various Hindu temples already discussed, and the Indian Mar Thoma congregation, the Plano mosque has been overtly political, no doubt a result of the post-9/11 context within which they have had to cope. In the 2004 election, the mosque was a polling place. The goal was to share the facility and be part of the political process "so that people could see that we are not secluded." Although there was some protest (people arrived with placards on election day), in general it was a successful move. The mosque took a leadership role in organizing efforts to ensure civil rights, gain political voice, and establish Muslims as part of the larger DFW community.

Indian Religious Diversity and Civic Engagement

First-generation Indian immigrants, whether Hindu, Christian, or Muslim, draw on the principles of service, charity, and the obligation to take care of others that are embedded in their respective religions and they adapt these to the ideas of giving back to the community and volunteerism, which they view as organized American manifestations of these service principles.

Invoking the phrase that Hilary Clinton popularized, "It takes a village to raise a child," one study participant drew subtle distinctions between behavior in his home context and behavior in the United States. He recalled throwing a water balloon at a car when he was a child. By the time he arrived home his parents were already aware of what he had done and he was punished. "In America," he continued, "everyone lives so individually, so they create these organizations to provide opportunities for people to get involved in other peoples' lives. In India we do not have this idea of organized giving back to the community. You live in a community and you are part of it and everyone gives back to each other all the time. So when I say 'giving back to the community,' it makes me feel American." This individual, and others quoted earlier, also appear to be suggesting that through these kinds of activities they can establish their right to belong and construct their American identity. As the young man in the Mar Thoma youth fellowship suggested, community service is part of the process of assimilation, a way to minimize the difference between insider and outsider—a difference, as he so astutely noted, that does not exist in India.

In India there is no concept of membership in a Hindu temple, but the idea has evolved in the United States in order to secure tax-exempt status and ensure the smooth operation of the institution and its activities. This approach contrasts with the Indian Christian tradition, in which individuals do belong to particular churches, but as families more than as individuals. Further, Mar Thoma Christians are part of a diocesan structure (the Diocese of North America and Europe) with its own bishop, as well as part of a global organization linked to Kerala. The mother church in Kerala sends out pastors for three-year assignments in the United States. In the spring of 2008, Dr. Joseph Mar Thoma Metropolitan and Dr. Philipose Mar Chrysostom Mar Thoma Valiya Metropolitan traveled to the United States to visit several Mar Thoma churches, including those in DFW, as well as to visit the Mexican mission in Matamoros. Members of all four local Mar Thoma churches gathered at the Dallas Convention Center for a collective Holy Communion service. The partnerships forged by Marthomites are largely within the local, national, and global Mar Thoma spheres.

Hindus have perhaps most strongly equated community with good neighborship, reaching out into the public sphere to serve or partner with local as well as national and international charities on projects to help those in need. Hindus in the United States have a level of wealth and education that allows them to support clinics like the one opened by the Swaminarayan temple. The Mar Thoma Christians focus their energies to a much greater extent on collective mission projects abroad, in India or in Mexico, but they do support local projects as well. Neither the Hindus nor the Mar Thoma Christians view their activities as political, but they do emphasize the civic dimension. "It is a civic duty," said one male interviewee. "Since you get a lot in one way or another, and you live here and take advantage of the library and the schools, you need to give back. If you have time, that is the best way to give back. If you don't have time you can give money, but giving time is better."

In contrast with Hindus and Mar Thoma Christians, the Muslims focus first on helping their own—that is, other Muslims within the local, national, and Muslim spheres—and second, and since 9/11, on serving the community by demonstrating overtly to non-Muslims the peaceful and generous dimensions of their religion. The mosque has increasingly been used as an arena for organizing in the face of the discrimination and distrust that has emerged in the post-9/11 world. Unlike some of the local Hindu missions (such as Swaminarayan and Chinmaya), which are connected to national and international organizations, and the Mar Thoma Church, which has similar diasporic links, DFW-area mosques are relatively autonomous, although they of course have a sense of linkage to global Islam, as manifested in the symbolic importance of Mecca and the effort to fulfill the Five Pillars of Islam.

Children of the first generation of immigrants learn about service activities and hence about civic engagement within their respective religious institutions. For example, one young man said that he was president of the youth organization at his temple and that around age seventeen he became involved in various charitable tasks, including starting a library at the temple. The most active youth organizations, however, are those in the Indian Christian churches, perhaps because there is greater emphasis on families actually belonging to and participating in a particular church. Across all three religious traditions, adults learn leadership and organization skills, and become aware of the governance structures that are so fundamental to getting things done in American organizational life. Such lay leadership is certainly not nearly as strong within the Indian Hinduism and South Asian Muslim traditions. The skills and knowledge that it takes just to set up these religious institutions cannot be underestimated and perhaps point most directly to how these various religious assemblies function as communities of practice for civic engagement and responsible citizenship.

Religious Assemblies as Communities of Practice

Some scholars of the most recent wave of immigration to the United States have suggested that religious organizations play "a much weaker role in immigrant civic and political adaptation than they have in the past" (DeSipio 2001: 90) and that immigrants in general reflect the broader U.S. population in their low level of civic engagement (Skocpol and Fiorina 1999). Our ethnographic research has revealed, however, that although the religious institutions built by Vietnamese and Indians certainly are primarily places where Vietnamese meet and interact with other Vietnamese or where Indians meet and interact with other Indians,[27] they have also become important spaces for civic learning and, by extension, for a host of activities that allow new immigrants and their born-in-America children to practice forms of participatory citizenship and claim civic presence in the broader public sphere.[28]

For both groups, the religious practices they brought with them have changed to accommodate a different lifestyle in the United States. Immigrant religious communities adapt and adjust, absorbing some American practices into their individual and collective civic involvement projects. Vietnamese Buddhist and Indian Hindu temples have concentrated their activities on Sundays, and the Hindu temples have adopted a more congregational or membership (in a loose sense of the word) approach than is characteristic in India. This change shows an attempt to coordinate temple activities with those of the wider society and is a practical response to the school and work schedules of families in the United States. Perhaps more important, across the diversity of religions represented, including the Christian traditions, the lay population takes a much more active role in the governance of their respective sacred assemblies than is true in their respective home countries. This activity is critical to the process by which civic engagement is learned and practiced, as well as to the principles of democratic behavior.[29] Youth involvement in churches and temples is another common theme in our research, and we see that leadership skills are taught and youth are encouraged to engage in the wider social sphere through community service and other cooperative activities.

Alongside the many features common to both Indian and Vietnamese religious assemblies, we have also found some interesting differences. One example is the approach to providing social services. Although the Hindu Temple and the Mar Thoma Church both have strongly organized social service activities that reach beyond the members of their congregations, this approach is not significant for Vietnamese temples or churches.[30] Among Vietnamese refugees, social services are already well coordinated through refugee agencies and through forms of mutual aid developed soon after the refugees started to arrive, which was long before the religious institutions described in this chapter were established as independent organizations. Early forms of mutual aid were not based in religious institutions, and they eventually led to the establishment of voluntary associations that cut across religions. It is these associations that today organize health fairs and other forms of charitable social service. In addition, in contrast to the Indian approach, any charitable work or other social assistance offered by the Vietnamese temples and churches is generally aimed at homeland causes (orphanages and hospitals) or at members of the religious group itself. An exception occurred during Hurricane Katrina, when these institutions, like their counterparts in the Indian community, mobilized resources to assist victims of this natural disaster. The Vietnamese expressed a strong desire to help themselves by accepting assistance from family members, and they were sensitive about having had to take charity when they arrived in the United States. This attitude fits well with the dominant values of the United States, and may also reflect the influence of the Republican Party among the Vietnamese in this part of Texas.

For both Indians and Vietnamese, charitable work is connected to notions of social responsibility—*seva* and *trach nhiem*. Among Hindus and Muslims in particular, conscious efforts are made to build bridges to and to collaborate with other local mainstream organizations. Such efforts are seen less in the Vietnamese religious institutions, although the Catholic Church is far reaching and some lay leaders in the church come into contact with those of other ethnic groups through their parish societies. Some of the Indians who participated in this research were able to articulate quite clearly the concepts of social citizenship and civic duty that are manifested in the activities in which they are involved in their respective religious organizations. They could also articulate how these "good works" facilitated a process of "assimilation"—a term used to suggest acceptance rather than abandonment of cultural practices and religious distinctions. Instead, core religious principles become the foundation for entering the larger American public sphere and exercising civic responsibility. Whereas the Indians we interviewed spoke about "giving back to the community," using an idiom familiar in U.S. society, many of the Vietnamese American parents we interviewed did not use or recognize this idiom. One explanation for this discrepancy is that many first-generation Vietnamese refugees lack the English skills and command of American vernacular speech that would make them familiar with such an idiom. As we show in subsequent chapters, Vietnamese youth and young adults are more apt to use this concept than those of the first generation who were participants in the parent interviews. When this concept was explained, however, to those without good English skills, they recognized the importance of both service to others and helping those who have helped you. People mentioned Vietnamese expressions for "paying back" that could be used in such situations, but they were also sensitive to overly explicit expressions of reciprocity. One woman quoted the English expression "It is better to give than to receive," but she also translated what she saw as a related Vietnamese expression, "Who sows the wind will reap the whirlwind," which means that being selfish can have bad consequences. In most cases, when the concept of giving back was explained, the Vietnamese parents we interviewed said they gave back through charity donations.

In any case, the notion of giving back uses the metaphors of gift and exchange to talk about social responsibility. Although this concept may seem to resonate with the idea of *seva*, the notion of *trach nhiem*, which guides Vietnamese forms of social responsibility, is more about release from suffering and getting the "good feeling" that comes from helping others rather than about reciprocity. It may be that the first generation of Indian immigrants—especially Hindus, who are influenced by the morality of *seva* and also have a better command of English—adjust more quickly than Vietnamese Americans of the first generation to the rhetoric of giving back that is so prevalent in American ways of talking about civic engagement. Among the Vietnamese, this idea has taken hold more among the younger generations. We see, therefore, that similar impulses to assume social responsibility are articulated differently among our two populations, and with slightly different implications for the role of religious institutions in fostering charitable activities.

Another contrast between Indian and Vietnamese forms of civic engagement through religious participation is that such engagement is more direct among Indians (for example, in the ways that churches and temples provide social services, such as the health clinic operated by the Swaminarayan temple) than among the Vietnamese. For Vietnamese Americans, churches and temples provide space for the development of the organizational networks and leadership skills that are on occasion mobilized for civic action and then lead individuals to greater forms of participation outside their churches and temples.[31] Moreover, Vietnamese cooperate in civic activities with other Vietnamese outside their specific religious groups. Many Vietnamese people have a syncretic view of religion and thus move back and forth between Buddhism, Catholicism, and ancestor worship.[32] This movement permits Vietnamese American leaders to mobilize the population across religious lines for political purposes. This religious fluidity is not found among Indians, who do not talk, for example, about moving between Catholicism and Hinduism.[33]

Vietnamese churches and temples provide resources for political mobilization that depend on their shared history and cultural traditions that transcend religion. The commemoration of Vietnamese culture heroes at a Catholic church, to which elected officials were invited, and the forum to protest the persecution of a Buddhist monk in Vietnam that attracted religious leaders from all the major Vietnamese American institutions illustrate how formal politics is intertwined with religious expression in ways that may, however, be more indirect than direct. Political mobilization in which people from different religious organizations work together is less common among the Indians, although since 9/11 such mobilization has become a facet of mosque activity. In terms of homeland politics, what is politicized for the Vietnamese is framed by the communist/anticommunist divisions in Vietnam, a conflict that draws Catholic and Buddhist refugees to work together. In contrast, among the Indians it is the homeland divisions related to centuries-old religious conflicts that are most polarizing.[34] Indian immigrants therefore choose either not to bring the intensity of these religious divisions with them or to keep them as tightly controlled as possible.[35] In DFW, Indians work together through secular organizations for collaborative pan-Indian and transreligious purposes. However, even within the more secular pan-Indian associations, efforts are made not to engage in any activities or make any position statements that might indicate

support for either Hindu or Muslim causes in India—that is, choosing between being Indian and being Hindu or Muslim or Christian. Thus the India
Association of North Texas (IANT) acted to raise funds after the earthquake
in Gujarat in the early 2000s but made no statement about nor took any action in relation to the Hindu-Muslim confrontations in Gujarat province in
February 2002, when Hindu mobs attacked Muslims and burned a mosque
and other Islamic facilities in retaliation for the Muslim firebombing of a train
that was transporting Hindu activists from Ayodhya, a disputed holy site. Two
thousand people died.[36]

Among both Vietnamese and Indians, ethnic associations (such as those
profiled in the next chapter) and the commercial malls and restaurants that
contribute to the cultural landscapes described in Chapter 1 are more visible
and have a greater civic presence in the wider society than do the religious institutions we have profiled here. The Vietnamese American Community, a nonprofit association, is the "face" of this ethnic group,[37] and with the exception
of the large Vietnamese Martyrs Church in Arlington, the Vietnamese shopping malls and restaurants are better known among the general public than the
temples and churches. The Indians are most visibly present through organizations such as the IANT and commercial enterprises like FunAsia (mentioned
in Chapter 1).[38] Yet even though they are less visible to the wider society, immigrant religious institutions are, as Alex Stepick (2005: 27) has written, sites that
help us understand how immigrants "negotiate their identities, social stature,
legitimacy, and power in complex social arenas." Our research suggests that individual Indians and Vietnamese can enhance their civic skills within religious
institutions and then take these skills into other communities of practice with
greater civic and perhaps even political presence.

4 Ethnic Associations

IN THIS CHAPTER we explore the role of ethnic associations in facilitating participatory citizenship and civic leadership. Although we found that fewer Indian and Vietnamese immigrants participate in ethnically based voluntary associations than in the religious assemblies we discussed in the previous chapter, these associations are significant. Through them, immigrants become aware of the problems and possibilities of American civic life. Some associations involve and are visible only to members of the immigrant group, both domestically and internationally; others operate as interlocutors between the immigrant population and the broader American society, and serve as the immigrant community's public face in the DFW region and sometimes beyond.

We add a new dimension to the existing scholarship through our analysis of the socialization processes that occur "on the ground" in these social spaces. Although the significance of voluntary associations and mutual aid societies in the life of immigrants in the United States has long been recognized,[1] recent work has drawn particular attention to the role of immigrant associations in the processes of civic and political integration.[2] Some of this work takes a top-down approach, emphasizing the political opportunity structures that facilitate the development of immigrant associations at the local level, as well as the resources extended to them, whereas other work takes a bottom-up approach, examining whether those immigrants who are more active in associations are better integrated politically.[3] By viewing immigrant voluntary associations as communities of practice, we emphasize the transition that newcomers make toward being "insiders" and hence social citizens. As with our analysis of religious assemblies, the main focus here is on the acquisition of civic skills rather than on the internal struggles of associations as a form of micropolitics. In fact, we have found that learning to minimize such internal struggles and provide a more unified front to others is an important civic skill practiced by both Vietnamese and Indian associations.

The Organizational Spaces of Indian and Vietnamese Immigrants

No matter where they have settled in the United States, Indian and Vietnamese immigrants appear to have developed a rich array of organizations. In the DFW area, there is no precise list of all the Indian associations, but estimates from various sources run between eighty and one hundred.[4] Many are religious, but others are regional—that is, focused on the culture of the Indian region or state from which a critical mass of Indians have emigrated (such as Gujarat, Kerala, or Bengal). There are also professional and business associations, as well as Indian organizations within big corporate entities such as American Airlines and Texas Instruments. In addition, charity associations such as Pratham USA and ASHA for Education (http://www.ashanet.org) raise funds for the education of underprivileged children in India. There are also cultural associations, alumni associations, and associations that are chapters of national organizations such as the American Federation of Muslims of Indian Origin and the Indian American Friendship Council. Many of these associations are loosely gathered under the broad umbrella of the India Association of North Texas (IANT), the oldest organization established by Indian immigrants in DFW and one that is widely known within the Indian community. At least once a year the IANT, which was recognized in the fall of 2006 by the Greater Dallas Asian American Chamber of Commerce for its contributions, holds a meeting for all the Indian associations in the city, with the goal of facilitating joint activities and promoting common goals.

Many Indians belong to multiple associations and are active in several of them, while others are active primarily in a religious institution and little else, or not active in any association. One indication of this is that among those Indian parents we interviewed, 71 percent said they were involved in an ethnic association, 73 percent in a religious institution, 53 percent in a service organization, 82 percent in a school organization (the Parent-Teacher Association, or PTA, for example), 23 percent in a political organization, 18 percent in a pan-Asian organization, and 44 percent in a broader U.S. organization. Further, 23.5 percent indicated that they were involved in some other organization. This is of course only a partial portrait of the dimensions of organizational participation among Indian immigrants, which can vary by gender, stage of life, and individual interest.[5]

When asked how important these associations are to the Indian community, 71 percent described them as very important and 18 percent described them as moderately important. Close to 60 percent said they had held a leadership position in an organization. This proportion is high by contrast with the general U.S. population, indicating that Indian immigrants have both an interest in involvement and a desire to develop social relationships in the absence of an extended family. Although many research participants pointed to the sense of community, even kinship, provided by these organizations, others emphasized that they facilitate charity work and help to establish unity—the latter a desirable image to present to the outside. Still others emphasized that associations are spaces for learning civic skills and becoming American. For example, a Muslim businesswoman in her fifties commented that associations have a positive effect because "they have made me learn how the U.S. works. Americans lead busy lives with work and family, but they still have time to get involved." Another research participant made an even more significant comment. These associations, she said, are "our way of coming out in American society." Like religious assemblies, ethnic organizations help Indian newcomers to claim civic presence and the right to belong.

The Vietnamese also have a large number of associations. According to research participants, there are at least a hundred—some of which are chapters of national or transnational associations—in the DFW region. These organizations are in addition to the parish societies and youth organizations discussed in the previous chapter. This proliferation of associations is somewhat typical of Vietnamese diaspora communities and continues a tradition from Vietnam of multiple voluntary associations in both rural and urban settings (Dorais 1992: 79).[6]

The Vietnamese do not have a comparable "umbrella" association that plays the same role as the IANT plays for Indians. However, there are three major associations that animate events and activities across a broad spectrum of the Vietnamese population in the DFW region: the Vietnamese American Community of Dallas, the Vietnamese American Community of Tarrant County, and the Vietnamese Culture and Science Association (VCSA), an organization based in Houston with branches not only in DFW but also throughout the United States and in Toronto. In addition, there are smaller associations that sometimes overlap in membership. Few of these organizations are known outside of the ethnic community, and their activities and events are announced primarily through informal channels or in Vietnamese print media or on Vietnamese radio stations. The range of associations includes those for military veterans, homeland associations, alumni associations connected to schools attended in Vietnam, organizations within large corporations that group Vietnamese with other Asians primarily for social activities, medical associations, and politically explicit groups, such as the Vietnamese American Public Affairs Committee. There are also groups specific to youth, such as Vietnamese American student associations at colleges and universities, and groups focused on Vovinam, a Vietnamese form of martial art.

Despite the plethora of Vietnamese associations, and in contrast to responses from Indians, few (27 percent) of the Vietnamese parents we interviewed reported that they were active members of an ethnic association. Also, most of these Vietnamese parents reported that they were not involved in associations beyond their ethnic group, and none disclosed that they participated in a political organization (although many reported that they attended political events, especially events related to homeland politics). Half of the Vietnamese men we interviewed claimed to have assumed a leadership role in an association (including religious associations), whereas only 16 percent of women did so. Although direct participation was low, almost all of the parents we interviewed considered ethnic associations important, and 78 percent ranked them as very important. They viewed associations as sites for working to help others and to promote positive social change. Only a third of respondents looked to associations for social support, because many families had been helped in their initial settlement by refugee agencies or family members instead of ethnic organizations. One person explained, "At first families came to help us when we arrived. A friend at Catholic Charities, he saw my husband's name on the list of refugees coming and helped sponsor us. He came to the airport to meet us. There are about fifteen people who came. They were so loving and friendly, like family. They took us to their homes, gave us clothing, food." The parents we interviewed were keenly aware of the importance of associative life for their children, and they described their children's participation in youth groups at churches and temples, in scouting, and in school clubs. One mother explained that through this participation "they get leadership skills. They learn to work well with others, not just to be an individual but to be part of the whole. . . . " As with the Indian population, participation in associations varies with gender, generation, and stage of life.

The differences in participation between Vietnamese and Indian parents may be partially explained by the profound significance of regional identity for many Indian immigrants that manifests itself in many organizations that, among other things, foster the perpetuation of various Indian languages. Many Indian parents want their children to learn these languages. Although there are many hometown and regional associations for Vietnamese Americans, these are not connected to distinct languages, and the Vietnamese diaspora as a whole is associated with South Vietnam (even though many people trace their origins to North Vietnam before 1954). Another difference is that more of the Vietnamese mothers than Indian mothers we interviewed were working, more families were struggling financially and working long hours, and many did not feel they had time for such participation. This information reflects the specifics of the age cohort of the parents we interviewed, who represent only a subset of the entire population. On the basis of our participant-observation research, which gave us a wider view than the interviews, we can say it is evident that there is more participation among the older Vietnamese generation, who came soon after the fall of Saigon, and among younger Vietnamese of both genders who are not actively engaged in raising families. Yet another factor is the ambivalence that some Vietnamese expressed toward the leadership struggles that occur within ethnic organizations. One parent voiced this sentiment with the following observation: "Being a leader among the Vietnamese is 'too political.' . . . The men I work with, Americans, they volunteer at places like Habitat for Humanity, at other places. They just do it. They don't have to be a leader. I am like that. They do not do it as individuals, but as a team, as a whole." In both this remark and the earlier ones regarding their children, we see first-generation Vietnamese adults adopting the rhetoric of being part of a "team," a rhetoric that is prevalent in American associative and corporate life, thus demonstrating that they are engaged in a process of learning about the civic skills (including teamwork) that are valued in the United States.

To elucidate the ways in which particular individuals have entered into collaborative activities in the public sphere through the door of ethnic associations, in the following pages we weave into our discussion of four ethnic associations as communities of practice the personal narratives of men and women who have adopted leadership roles in such associations. Each of the associations profiled displays both formal political engagement and less formal modes of civic engagement, or participatory citizenship, but their emphases vary. We begin with one Indian and one Vietnamese organization that emphasize formal political engagement, and then relate the narratives of two men who shared with us their experiences as leaders within ethnic associations. We then turn to two associations that direct their energies more toward participatory citizenship in a broader sense. We end with the narratives of one Vietnamese and one Indian woman, each of whom who has been active in associative life.

Political Engagement Through Ethnic Associations

The Indian American Friendship Council

The mission of the Indian American Friendship Council (IAFC), founded in 1990 by Dr. Krishna Reddy, a physician of Indian origin living in California, is ambitious: "to create political awareness among Indian Americans, and maintain an ongoing dialogue with local, national, and international policy makers as well as to educate, encourage, and involve Asian Indian Americans with voter registration, volunteerism, community service, and youth leadership training, better the ties between USA and India, protect the interests of the Indian-American community, promote global democracy, and support the developing countries" (IAFC, Texas chapter, banquet program, March 11, 2006).[7] IAFC was launched nationwide in 1996 and the Texas chapter was established in Dallas in 2003 by a past president of the IANT—a good example of overlapping membership and the multiple communities of practice with which individuals can be engaged.

The logo of IAFC shows an arm draped in an American flag shaking the hand of an arm draped in an Indian flag. This logo clearly symbolizes the key goal of shaping and influencing the relationship between India and the United States, and building the visibility of the Indian American community. The latter goal is largely achieved at the annual national convention, where members from across the nation gather with the power brokers in Washington, D.C. According to a member of the Texas chapter, one of the major issues that IAFC has been working on is securing India a seat on the United Nations Security Council. Other issues that have preoccupied the organization are the backlash against outsourcing and the nuclear arms agreement between the United States and India. This agreement in fact galvanized many Indians in the United States, was debated for several weeks on the pages of the national newspaper *India Abroad*, and provided the theme for the third annual banquet of the Texas chapter of IAFC—Strategy, Stability, and Security.

During the period of this research, the activities of the Dallas-based Texas chapter were focused largely on these annual banquets, which raise funds to support congressmen and senators who are supportive of IAFC's causes. Members of this organization have clearly learned, through their observations of the U.S. political process, as well as through the activities of mainstream organizations, that money leads to influence in the American political process. Just as they are at most major events sponsored by the Indian community, both the American and Indian flags are displayed at IAFC banquets, and each banquet is opened with the singing of both national anthems. These actions and symbols, in this and other Indian-sponsored contexts, reflect the balancing of identities discussed in Chapter 2. They are perhaps less about patriotism than they are expressions of being placed in America and showing respect for a country that has been welcoming and that has become home for first-generation Indian immigrants and their offspring.

Each year important dignitaries, including local mayors, state legislators, and U.S. congressional representatives, were invited to the IAFC banquet, and the local chapter announces contributions to important American charity organizations, such as the Boy Scouts or the American Cancer Society. Through these charitable contributions and invitations, Indians in the U.S. convert their financial capital into symbolic, social, and political capital. These banquets are also an arena in which the political accomplishments of Indian Americans nationwide can be highlighted, thus offering role models from whom Indians can learn successful strategies for running for political office. Among the guests who have been honored are New Jersey State Assemblyman Upendra Chivukulu, Iowa State Representative Swati Dandekar, South Carolina State Representative Nikki Randhawa Haley, Minnesota Democratic State Senator Satveer Chaudhary, Kansas State Representative Raj Goyle, and Ohio Representative Jay Goyal.[8] Some of these individuals are first or 1.5 generation, others are members of the second generation.

In 2006, President Bush's trip to India and the nuclear arms accord were of central interest to Indians in the United States. The editor of *India Abroad*, Aziz Haniffa, received an award at the DFW-area's IAFC banquet and was one of the featured speakers. His speech emphasized the growing pro-India stance of the U.S. government, but it also called on Indians in the United States to help bring about social change in India by adopting local communities in India. The president of the Texas chapter of IAFC used the platform that year to represent IAFC as an organization that builds bridges with U.S. policymakers and brings the concerns of the Indian community in the United States to politicians and helps them to form pro-India relations. He raised the themes of community service, reciprocity, and political engagement with elected officials. Pride in the growing stature of India on the global stage as well as pride in the strengthening national political presence of Asian Indians in America were palpable in the room and reinforced when Republican Congressman Bobby Jindal of Louisiana, a second-generation Indian American who in October 2007 was elected governor of Louisiana, was introduced. He thanked the Indian American community in Texas and the state as a whole for the support they gave to Hurricane Katrina and Rita victims. Jindal described a new kind of U.S.-India relationship that is no longer dominated by the Cold

War, and he noted specific policies that affect Indian Americans (for example, laws shaping the lives of motel owners or those engaged in international business). He called on the assembled audience to become more involved in order to define the debate about these and other policies. Jindal thus outlined issues around which Indians in the United States could organize, illustrating that there is something in politics for everyone, no matter what their background. Of equal importance was the message that one could be a good American citizen and a diasporic citizen at the same time—that is, be both American and Indian with equal pride.

In 2007, the theme of the banquet was Innovation, Inspiration, and Involvement. The American charitable organization recognized with a monetary award was Help Hospitalized Veterans—an appropriate gesture to call attention to the impact of the Iraq war, and evidence that this organization makes every effort to be current and to link its members with issues of broad concern in the United States. Toward that end, a U.S. Army sergeant of Indian ancestry who had just completed service in Iraq was recognized, and when he came onto the stage he announced that he had a brother working for Halliburton in Afghanistan. In his speech that year, Ohio State Representative Jay Goyal talked about being galvanized by the 2004 election in Ohio—a battleground state that year—and then deciding to run himself—-at the age of twenty-six. As if echoing the comments about race and identity articulated by Indian youth that we discussed in Chapter 2, Goyal noted that his campaign was tough "because I was brown, in the middle of Ohio, and people would say you are not an American." He won with 63 percent of the vote—as a Democrat in a conservative region of Ohio. He received extensive support from the Indian community—locally, statewide, and even nationally. The powerful message here was that by working together, Indians across the United States could enhance their voice and, by extension, their power in the political process.

As a community of practice, IAFC links Indians together locally as well as nationally. It involves them in the shared enterprise of strengthening their profile in the national political arena, including shaping how the United States and India interact. Both local gatherings and national conventions provide venues for the activities of the organization and for the exchange of critical information about political participation as well as about national and international issues of importance. First- and second-generation Indians from across the country who hold political office are invited to share their personal stories of success; such narratives are clearly a powerful educational tool, used here to great effect. The presence of these individuals also illustrates how Indians in local communities

can build connections on a national scale and collaborate to enhance their polit-
ical visibility and voice. At the local level, the most revealing evidence of the civic
presence of IAFC is that they were able to lobby the city of Dallas to recognize
Diwali—complete with a ceremony at Dallas City Hall.[9] In the spring of 2010,
IAFC announced their success in convincing the city of Dallas to erect a statue of
Mahatma Gandhi near the Dallas Convention Center. The nine-foot-tall bronze
status was made in India at a cost of $10,000, paid for by IAFC. Members of the
IACF board of directors had assembled an advisory committee of individuals
from various backgrounds, including prominent "Anglos" from the city, who
agreed to attend the inauguration ceremonies when the project was completed.
Not only does this initiative represent a powerful action of claiming civic space,
but it also demonstrates the effort made to build connections outside the Indian
community to accomplish public goals.

A final event indicates how effective IAFC has been as a venue for the political
incorporation of Indian immigrants, and how quickly they have learned how to
muster political influence in the United States. Texas Senator John Cornyn was
brought to Dallas in the fall of 2006 to meet with a group of twenty to twenty-
five invited IAFC members. The cost to attend the community dinner reception
was upwards of $1,000. Cornyn was billed in the invitation as chairman of the
Senate's Immigration, Border Security, and Citizenship subcommittee and as
a dedicated defender of free markets, traditional values, and individual liberty.

The Vietnamese American Community of Tarrant County

Since the 1990s, nonprofit associations with official names translated into the
Vietnamese American Community (VAC) of (fill in the blank) have formed
in many cities across the United States. There are two such nonprofits in the
DFW region. The VAC of Tarrant County (also known in some Vietnamese-
language materials as the Vietnamese Nationals Community of Greater Fort
Worth) was founded in 1985 and became incorporated as a nonprofit in 1997.
Another group, which works closely with the first, is the VAC of Greater Dallas,
founded in 1983. Other associations in Texas include the VAC of Austin and the
Vietnamese Community of Houston and Vicinity.

The VAC of Tarrant County is a highly visible symbol of Vietnamese presence and the main interlocutor between this population and the wider population. Its leaders consider themselves to be spokespersons for the Vietnamese
and they interact with local politicians in that capacity. The role of the VAC is
similar to that played by IANT, although the VAC is not recognized, as is IANT,
as an umbrella association. In fact, the role that its leaders adopt, as representa-

tives of all the Vietnamese in the region, is sometimes contested by leaders of other associations. That there are two VACs (Tarrant County and Dallas) in this metropolitan region, even though they frequently work together on events and issues, also demonstrates the segmented nature of Vietnamese associative life. As one research participant said, with a touch of irony, "Among the Vietnamese, everyone wants to be a leader, and so they form their own association."

The VAC of Tarrant County primarily draws people living in Fort Worth, Arlington, and Grand Prairie—all to the immediate west of Dallas. It took an active role in raising money for Hurricanes Katrina and Rita relief efforts. Although it was not the only organization active in this way, its leaders have become the spokespeople in local media outlets that reach a broad audience. The VAC of Tarrant County collaborates with the VAC of Dallas to organize the Tet Festival each winter (described in more detail in Chapter 5) and has been a major participant in the Egg Roll Festival and Health Fair each spring (organized by the Tarrant County Asian American Chamber of Commerce). It has also cosponsored, again with the VAC of Dallas, the annual commemoration each April of the fall of Saigon (known as Black April among Vietnamese Americans). Although the VCSA has traditionally been the group to organize the Mid-Autumn Moon Festival for this region each year, members of the VAC of Tarrant County attend and participate. In 2006, the VAC of Tarrant County started offering English as a second language (ESL) classes on a regular basis and organized computer skills classes for the elderly. It rents out office space to a few other associations (such as an association of elders, a hometown association, and a veterans group). The VAC of Tarrant County also participates in Arlington's Fourth of July parade by entering a float, and in 2006 it won the mayor's award, given to one float each year and a high honor that permitted the float to come right after the mayor in the parade.[10]

The logo for the VAC of Tarrant County, designed in the mid-2000s by a young college student and former refugee who came to the United States as a child, includes a map of Vietnam with figures of two adults and four children moving out from south Vietnam and extending toward the west (in the direction of the United States). The logo is circular, with the map in the center and a ring around this image in the colors of the U.S. flag. On the association's Web site, the American flag provides a background to this logo and is flanked by the freedom and heritage flag of the former Republic of South Vietnam. This logo represents the desire of the VAC of Tarrant County to serve as a bridging organization between former refugees and their new homeland, where they will raise their children.

The VAC of Tarrant County is known among the Vietnamese population as a *political* organization, one that lobbies on behalf of Vietnamese issues both in the United States and back home in Vietnam. Many of its members are concerned about homeland politics and distribute frequent e-mails to each other about events in Vietnam. This group mobilizes protests of various sorts and sends delegations to protest visits to Washington by Vietnamese officials. It is also, however, active in local politics and helps to organize "get out the vote" drives. Local politicians take note of the VAC's role in mobilizing voters to support various candidates and many regularly appear at events sponsored by the VAC, such as the grand opening of the new Vietnamese American Community Center in 2006. Local politicians and Texas legislative candidates also attend (and campaign at) the Tet Festival. The Vietnamese population in this region has a high rate of naturalization and a high rate of voter turnout, mainly as a consequence of the efforts of leaders of the VAC of Tarrant County and other Vietnamese associations to mobilize voters.

Members of the VAC of Tarrant County took part in a large voter registration drive, Viet Vote, conducted during the 2004 presidential election and spearheaded by the DFW chapter of the VCSA. This effort helped to galvanize Vietnamese American political participation in this region on a large scale, and it was tied to a pending referendum to approve the construction of a new stadium in Arlington for the Dallas Cowboys football team, moving it from its previous location in Irving. Dat Nguyen, a Vietnamese American who was then a member of the Cowboys, helped to rally support among Vietnamese through a series of events, including a large concert.

Members of the VAC of Tarrant County try to influence politicians on issues such as improving access to citizenship and other rights for Amerasians, human trafficking in Vietnam, and pressuring the Vietnamese government to increase religious freedom and freedom of speech. They also work to get financial support at the local level for the community center and its activities. An example of the ways in which this organization has learned to work with and through the political system was a town hall meeting held in summer 2007 that was organized by a group called the Amerasian Citizenship Initiative, whose leaders are also influential in the VAC of Tarrant County. Representatives from the office of Congresswoman Kay Granger attended the meeting on her behalf and promised to report back to her. The forum was facilitated by the owner of a Vietnamese restaurant in Fort Worth who provided a venue and a free family-style meal for the participants. The documentary film *Mother Tongue, Fatherland: Stories of the Vietnamese Amerasians* (2005) was shown, followed by an informational presentation on the paperwork necessary to apply for citizenship, distribution of forms, and an open question-and-answer session.

In spring 2006, in a more public demonstration of its growing political presence, the VAC of Tarrant County mobilized its networks to protest the display of the flag of the Socialist Republic of Vietnam (the current government) at a large public university.[11] The flag was displayed in the context of an international student festival to celebrate Vietnamese international students studying at the university. The flag provoked protest by a vocal group of Vietnamese American students who were initially prohibited from displaying what they felt was the flag that represented them as former refugees and as Vietnamese Americans—the freedom and heritage flag mentioned earlier. The Vietnamese American students were supported in their protest by the VAC of Tarrant County (as well as other VACs in Texas and in other states). The anticommunist activists in these organizations argued that the only Vietnamese flag displayed should be the one that represents the Vietnamese American population: the yellow flag with three red horizontal stripes. This population, they argued, cannot and should not be represented by the red flag with a gold star in the center that represents the regime in Vietnam from which they had fled. A protest at the university gathered thousands of supporters, including people from as far away as California and Washington, D.C. Letters were written to politicians, including the governor of Texas, and several city council members spoke in support of the VAC's efforts. State Representative Hubert Vo, the only Vietnamese elected official in Texas at that time, voiced his support. By engaging in this protest, the VAC was following in the footsteps of Vietnamese groups in other American cities who had also protested the display of the official flag of the Socialist Republic of Vietnam.[12] The VAC protesters and their supporters put pressure on the president of the university to alter its course, and they were rumored to be connected to threats by allied politicians to withhold funding for the university if it did not back down. Eventually all displays of flags were suspended while a committee on diversity met to carve out new ways to honor international students without alienating Vietnamese American students and their families. This committee included a Vietnamese lawyer and alumnus of the university who had a more moderate view than the VAC activists.

As a community of practice, the VAC of Tarrant County includes both insiders and those more peripheral to its activities. The VAC both has old-timers (those who helped establish the organization) and tries to recruit newcomers from among the younger generation. Active members range from retired generals who arrived in 1975 and started the group for Vietnamese "Nationals" to business-owners who arrived as children and now interact regularly with clients of various ethnic backgrounds. Some Vietnamese American college students were initially drawn into this group through the flag controversy and are now actively engaged in *situated learning*, that is, they are observing how their elders pressure American politicians—what has been successful and what has not been successful. The VAC of Tarrant County provides a context for social learning, for learning ways to engage in civic activities and practice citizenship. It is the Vietnamese association in this region of Texas with the most political presence and weight. It gets the attention of the media, of local elected officials, and of the public. For many non-Vietnamese in the region it represents the public face of the Vietnamese. As further evidence of the political clout of the VAC and the role it plays as a training ground for broader civic and political skills, its former president, Andy Nguyen, was elected Tarrant County commissioner for Precinct 2 (a district that includes much of the city of Arlington) in the November 2010 election.

Enhancing Political Awareness and Mobilization: Cao H. and Vishal P.

Cao H. and Vishal P. are two immigrants who transitioned from newcomer to insider and assumed active leadership roles in ethnic organizations. By juxtaposing their life stories, we show that even though they are of different generations and came to the United States under different circumstances, each man developed leadership skills through participation in associations as communities of practice.

Cao H. was born into an elite, educated family in Saigon that had ties to the French colonial regime. He also had relatives in political positions in South Vietnam. Cao's grandfather had been a physician and Cao followed in his footsteps to become a medical doctor, serving as a military doctor during the Vietnam War. He sent his wife and children to a rural area to be safe during the war, but he eventually sent his children to live with his parents in Paris. "I did not trust the United States at that time," he said. At the fall of Saigon he was part of a group escorted by the United States to Guam, where he spent time in a refugee camp before being transferred to Camp Pendleton in California. Cao mentioned that when his group arrived in Guam, they had to put away their South Vietnamese flag, but he "vowed to return [to Vietnam] one day with the flag." He and his family were soon reunited in California, where they were sponsored by a Baptist church that helped them settle. Cao attended medical school in California and although he struggled with English he was able to pass the medical boards. By 1980 they had moved to Dallas, where he found work as a general practitioner. He currently has a medical practice in Tarrant County, and many connections to other physicians who are not Vietnamese. He claims that his wife and children are quite "Americanized."

Cao assumed leadership positions in a military veterans group and in the VAC of Tarrant County, for which he served as president during the 1990s. He has been involved with both the Dallas and Tarrant County VACs. His civic involvement in the United States is based very much on his experiences as a young man in Vietnam. Much of what fuels his participatory citizenship is his passion for homeland politics and anticommunism. Cao feels strongly that Vietnam "needs a strong overseas community" to help change the political culture there. He believes that this will be achieved first through economic prosperity, which will develop because "many of the younger generation in Vietnam support capitalism." The next step will be to guarantee "freedom and democracy" in Vietnam. Cao is involved in groups that pressure the United States to in turn place pressure on Vietnam, and he supports elected officials (at both the state and federal levels) whom he feels will work on behalf of this cause. Cao is very mindful of the psychological trauma affecting the older generation. As he puts it, "those who escaped and came here feel sinful as deserters, because for most Asian soldiers, if you surrender you should kill yourself for honor. Those who came thought at first that it was only temporary, but now that they have stayed, they feel that they have betrayed their country and their ancestors." Cao's engagement in the civic sphere is primarily on behalf of those of his generation. He asked rhetorically, "Why do we need a community? We need to stick together, to get out from under the domination of China. And for our ancestors' memory." He has taken on leadership roles reluctantly, he said, but was pressured to do so by those who felt he could help.

Cao's religious stance—he says he now identifies mainly as Baptist, since his conversion in California—illustrates his adaption to his host society, and is also an example of what we described in the previous chapter as religious syncretism among the Vietnamese. His initial religion was Buddhist, but Cao "secretly converted" to Catholicism against the wishes of his family while a student in Vietnam. He said, "I stay in the middle of Buddhists and Catholics, but I am more of a Baptist." He admires what he considers the "altruism" of Baptists, and feels that "they are the future of the religions." Cao's political and religious life experiences demonstrate a fluidity that helps him adapt to new circumstances. He is representative of the earliest wave of Vietnamese refugees, those who first established ethnic associations in the United States and, by virtue of their previous experiences, English language skills, and high social status in Vietnam, were able to adapt fairly rapidly to life in their host country.

Vishal P., an Indian immigrant who became active in IAFC, arrived in the United States as a child in the company of his parents, who had been sponsored by his mother's brother, a U.S. resident since 1970 and a citizen since 1986. Vishal's father, trained as a nuclear engineer in India, found a job in drafting after arriving in New Jersey, but after improving his language skills in ESL classes, he eventually found work as an engineer. The family lived in several parts of the country before moving in 1996 to Texas, where Vishal received his high school diploma and then completed an engineering degree at a DFW-area university.

In high school Vishal belonged to the more academically oriented groups, such as the math team. "For Indian parents," he said, "education is big. I was not encouraged by my parents to be involved in political or service organizations." After his graduation from college, Vishal found a job in Houston, working in information technology for a waste management company. In 2003 he returned to India to marry, and in 2004 he was laid off; he described this as a "rough period." He moved to Dallas and within two months found another job, but he commented that the experience of being unemployed is what sparked his interest in becoming more involved in politics. "The issue that drove me to greater action was outsourcing, because it affected me most directly." His parents were never active in this way and hence he found his role models in other people who were successful as community leaders or at organizing events that he attended. "They were inspiration enough."

During the 2004 elections, Vishal worked for the Democratic Party and closely with the League of Women Voters. His interest at that time was to register people to vote. He set up tables at Taj Mahal Imports, at several local temples, and at the Anand Bazaar (the annual event sponsored by IANT to celebrate India's Independence Day, mentioned in Chapter 1). Vishal said that at first the IANT was a bit skeptical about his activities at the Bazaar, "because they are not a political organization; they have a different agenda; they are a community organization focused on cultural events." But ultimately, he said, they decided it was a positive thing.

Through his involvement with the Anand Bazaar, Vishal met the president of the IAFC, who asked him to become involved in IAFC, telling him, "We need people like you, someone young, with enthusiasm, willing to get involved." Vishal had not heard of the organization until that time, but he decided to join the board of directors because he had job stability and freedom to be active. Vishal helps with the annual banquet for the local chapter and with fundraising events that IAFC has sponsored for local congressmen who are "sympathetic to our issues." Like others who are involved with IAFC, Vishal acknowledges that right now its focus is on improving U.S.-India relations. "In the 1980s and 1990s," he noted, "there was very little dialogue between the U.S. and India. That is changing." But Vishal also said that he would like to change the emphasis of the local chapter of IAFC to focus more on what he referred to as grass-roots issues. "The IAFC should be a clearing house for information on local amendments." He further suggested that the Indians who have been successful at getting elected to political office have learned to stress issues of concern to the general population. "Everyone wants better education systems; that is an issue that affects everyone." He observed that many Indians do not know how to get involved and hence one of his major goals is to raise awareness and to show people connections between their daily concerns—whether outsourcing, student loans, or better funding for public universities—and political action.

While Vishal has been working to increase political participation among Indians in the United States, Cao has been focusing on homeland politics. Cao's level of activity in Vietnamese associations was facilitated by the fact that he was raised in Vietnam in a wealthy family and arrived in the United States with English skills and, perhaps, the confidence that comes with the privilege he experienced during his childhood. His experience in the military probably also served him well, not least of all because it helped him to become familiar with Americans. He brought significant civic skills with him, but he also adapted these to his new environment. Vishal had some exposure to organizational activity during his years in high school and college in the United States and hence represents the attitudes and experiences of the 1.5- and second-generation youth. Although he uses an ethnic organization as a base, he has developed an awareness of important American organizations, such as the League of Women Voters, with whom he has collaborated. His role, as he defines it, is to educate people about issues in which they can find common ground despite their differences—whether within the Indian community or between the Indian community and Americans outside it. Vishal treads less lightly than his elders because he was brought up in America and feels as American as he feels Indian. He has a different sense of ownership with regard to American culture and American politics.

Vishal and Cao have participated and taken on leadership roles in associations that primarily are devoted to increasing political participation but also sponsor a variety of events and activities. In the next section, we turn to two ethnic associations that place more emphasis on charity and cultural events, even though formal political engagement is not absent from their respective agendas. Unlike the VAC and IAFC, both of these associations are linked to global organizational structures.

Participatory Citizenship Through Ethnic Associations

The Irving DFW Indian Lions Club

There are several Indian Lions Club chapters in the DFW area. One of the more active of these is the Irving DFW Indian Lions Club. All Lions Clubs are part of the district convention, and representatives are expected to attend both local and national conventions. Most Clubs take on one annual eye clinic service project because this is the primary charitable cause of Lions Clubs globally. Beyond this obligation, however, they can define their own activities and projects.

Many Indians who come to the United States are already familiar with Lions Clubs International, but they view the Lions as operating differently in the United States. In an interview, one of the past presidents of the Irving DFW Indian Lions Club indicated that initially he had no interest in becoming a member of the Club. He explained:

> We have lots of Lions Clubs back in India, but they are usually associated with status. Only the rich or upper class are members. When someone says they are a member of the Lions Club, you know they have money. I didn't have a lot of money and have never been much concerned with status, so I was not interested. My friend who was trying to recruit me said, "No, no, it's not like that here; it's all about serving." So I went to check out a meeting, and eventually went through the process of application and was finally accepted.

Although this individual was using status in the ascribed sense (as the fixed criteria associated loosely with caste and inherited wealth and position in the Indian context) to describe how Lions Clubs work in India, clearly he himself could achieve social status and recognition through his involvement in the Lions Club in the United States. He could give his time rather than his money, in an arena that is more open to individual opportunity than the hierarchized (by class or caste) society of India.

The motto of the Irving DFW Indian Lions Club, which has between thirty and forty members of all faiths but primarily from the Indian state of Kerala, is "We serve." One of the past presidents described this as a high calling, "higher than those who are called to serve only themselves and not their community." When asked what he meant by *community*, he noted that there are two communities: the geographical community of those in DFW, and the greater Indian community, including people in India. Another member noted that by establishing an Indian Lions Club it was possible to support charitable causes in India as well as in the United States. The former, he observed, would not be of much interest to a mainstream Lions Club. This observation reflects the complex identities that immigrants juggle as they enter the civic sphere. They maintain transnational interests alongside efforts to claim recognition locally. Thus, whereas about 40 percent of the funds raised by this Club, largely through the annual banquet, support service projects in India, including an India Habitat for Humanity project and tsunami relief, 60 percent is spent in the United States on projects such as Habitat for Humanity, eyeglass recycling, and a sports extravaganza for the physically challenged.

The median age of members of the Irving DFW Indian Lions Club is sixty (whereas in India the average age, one member suggested, would be the mid-thirties). Leadership in this organization rotates each year to fulfill the explicit goal of leadership development. One past president said he had previously served in his church and had a good deal of experience organizing events, facilitating meetings, and communicating in front of audiences. He brought these skills from one community of practice to the next.

When asked about the role that serving plays in being a "good citizen," a past president of the Club responded that they go hand in hand, "especially here in America.[13] I feel it is a citizen's duty to give back, or contribute to the well-being of the community in which he lives." He underscored the learning process that goes on within an organization like the Lions Club when he observed that in India citizenly duty is not connected with service, but in the United States Indians make the connection.

> I think it's the environment that influences us. It's not a change of values
> because I would like to think that I still hold the same values toward mankind;
> however, those values are worn more on America's shirtsleeves. They are acted
> out in a bolder way, and that environment sucks you in. Eventually you learn
> to express your values in the same way.

This respondent was calling attention to a subtle process of "Americanization" by which he had learned both the behaviors and the rhetoric of participatory citizenship. Further, he suggested that a certain amount of economic success in the United States facilitates "bold" acts of citizenship.

One of these bold acts of citizenship, and a major accomplishment of the Irving DFW Indian Lions Club, is its support of a clinic for the uninsured in the general population. Located in the Dallas suburb of Lewisville, it serves an average of four thousand people a year. It is open every Saturday morning and is staffed by volunteers from the Lions Club and volunteer physicians and nurses of different backgrounds. The fee for all visits is $30 and there is a nominal charge of $8–10 for lab work. If a patient needs specialty services, the clinic has prearranged referral agreements with other physicians in the Indian community, again with a nominal fee for service. According to one Club member, patients are 40 percent Anglo, 40 percent Hispanic, 10 percent "Oriental," 5 percent African American, and 15 percent Indian (and these are mostly Indians who are visiting from overseas and do not have insurance). It is important to emphasize that several other local Indian associations sponsor health clinics—for example, the India Association of North Texas, the Indian Physicians Network, and as noted in the previous chapter, the Swaminarayan Temple—but in these cases the patients are largely Indian. It is certainly possible that the reputation and name recognition of the Lions Club makes the Irving DFW Indian Lions Club clinic more visible and hence heightens its civic presence relative to other associations within the Indian community.

The commitment to and support of this clinic reflects the concern that the Club has about the rising cost of health care and declining coverage—a concern that is shared by everyone in the Lions Club. By acting on this mutual interest, the members of this club have become civically engaged. For them, participatory citizenship follows a rule of reciprocity. They have become naturalized citizens of the United States, with all the rights that this accords, and it is their duty to serve. Equally, however, by serving they can be recognized as good citizens who take the responsibilities of citizenship seriously. As a community they can "give back" (through their practice of mutual engagement) by drawing on a critical mass of expertise in the medical arena—the high proportion of Indian or Indian-ancestry individuals who are doctors or nurses. A similar outlook was expressed by an Indian woman who spearheaded the formation in the fall of 2005 of the Dallas Women's Lions Club, composed largely of women of Indian origin or ancestry.[14] She began by observing that political participation is not the only behavior that defines good citizenship.

> Politics exists no matter where you are. Politics involves the decisions of the few and you cannot really see what your impact is. Being a good citizen means doing the right things for the people of a country. It is not about placing people in leadership roles. It is rather about who is making the community the way it is. . . . You are living in your community and you can work to make it better.

Although participants in these ethnic-based Lions Clubs are largely focused on civic engagement, and hence on the broader meaning of citizenship that is central to our discussion of the learning that takes place in communities of practice, they also use their Club to build a local civic and political presence. They do so by inviting local political officials to their annual banquet, at which they also recognize non-Indian individuals for their service, and by making monetary donations to American charities. Two candidates for governor of Texas participated in the 2006 annual banquet of the Irving DFW Indian Lions Club—one virtually, through video, and one in person. This participation demonstrates that individuals running for political office have become aware of the monetary resources of Indians in the United States, and of their ability and likelihood to vote.

The Vietnamese Professionals Society

Although it is currently inactive,[15] during the time of the fieldwork conducted for this book the Dallas chapter of the Vietnamese Professionals Society (VPS) was an active member of the international network of twenty-five chapters of the VPS in North America, Europe, Australia, and Asia, and one of nine chapters in the United States. The English version of the VPS Web site (http://www.vps.org) states that its mission was to "increase the knowledge and understanding of the social and economic conditions in Vietnam, to promote the welfare of the Vietnamese people and, through international cooperative effort, to apply science, technology, and humanity to the renovation of Vietnam." The goals of the Dallas VPS were both civic and political. Membership was based on having a university-level degree and being of Vietnamese descent, although the latter could be waived in certain cases, and members tended to be in their late twenties to early forties. Although most of the activities they organized were not explicitly political, some members of the Dallas VPS were active in more politically explicit associations. One former board member, for example, is still active in Texas party politics and works on political campaigns.

The Dallas chapter, founded in 1991, served as a social network for its members as much as it functioned as a community of practice for civic and political engagement. Whereas many VAC members are first-generation Vietnamese who arrived in the United States as adults, most VPS members either arrived in the United States as the children of refugees or were born here. The last active president of the Dallas VPS arrived in the early 1990s as a young adult, but his predecessor arrived with her family when she was a child. Also in contrast to the VAC, in the VPS more women had visible positions of leadership, including one who served as its president.

The VPS organized social activities such as parties and other get-togethers for its members, and it functioned as a networking organization for young Vietnamese professionals. It was equally active, however, in community and volunteer events. The VPS raised money for Hurricane Katrina victims, and in 2006 it arranged a work party in response to a call from Vietnamese living in the New Orleans area to help address continuing problems related to the hurricane. This type of charity work was one of the main missions of the VPS, and Hurricane Katrina was a particularly salient cause for this association at the time of our research. Some VPS members also traveled to Vietnam to undertake charity work there. The Dallas chapter of VPS organized health fairs and other events throughout the year, including an academic challenge event and a Vietnamese film festival, discussed below.

One leader identified the association's major function as "professional networking." He added, however, that it also served as an "advocate for the Vietnamese community," citing as an example the lobbying done by the VPS to the U.S. State Department against human trafficking of Vietnamese girls who were sold as brides. He also mentioned the lack of religious freedom in Vietnam as an important political issue. Members of the VPS referred to their volunteer and charity work, both in the United States and in Vietnam, as "giving back" to the community—a phrase heard more often among Indian immigrants (most of whom are professionals) than among the older Vietnamese Americans who were interviewed for this project, whose responses have been discussed in previous chapters. This terminology indicates that the younger generation of professional Vietnamese, whose linguistic skills are equal to those of Indian professionals, are adopting more of this discourse. They have learned a vocabulary for talking about civic engagement that resonates in the United States and thus have learned a civic skill.

Two major events organized by the VPS were a Vietnamese film festival and an academic challenge event. The goal of the film festival (held for three years in a row from 2005 to 2007), as expressed by an organizer, was both to help form a broader audience for Vietnamese American films and to educate local Vietnamese youth about possible careers in the arts. A dinner held for VPS members after the event included those involved in the films as directors, producers, and actors, as well as audience members who wished to attend. In 2005 there was a gala fundraiser for Hurricane Katrina after the festival.

The academic challenge was aimed at children under age sixteen. It was held at a local community college. One of the organizers reported that this event was patterned on Japanese competitions they had seen on television. It featured teams from churches, temples, and other groups that instruct Vietnamese children in the language and culture of Vietnam. The children were quizzed on their knowledge of Vietnamese language and culture. Whereas the film festival was primarily an English-language environment, with occasional translation between Vietnamese and English, the academic challenge was conducted exclusively in Vietnamese. Special gifts were given to the winning teams, but all children received gift packages for participating. As stated in the VPS March 2006 newsletter (published in both an English and a Vietnamese version), the organizers of the academic challenge hoped that participating students would "find in themselves the pride of their roots, and would realize that they too have a harmonious and sacred relationship with Vietnam the culture and Vietnam the origin." Both the academic challenge and the film festival were aimed at youth of the second generation; both were also aimed at instilling an appreciation for Vietnamese culture and history; but the film festival was also intended to extend this beyond a Vietnamese audience.

The VPS operated as a community of practice that provided a context for situated learning about American civic and political engagement, both for its members and, by extension, for those other, younger Vietnamese who attended its events. Because it was part of an international organization, it also brought members from the Dallas chapter into contact with a global professional network. The International VPS holds an annual conference each year, most recently in European cities. Members of the Dallas VPS were civically engaged in ways similar to those of the Indian Lions Club, whose members organized to help victims of natural disasters and engaged in charity work in their home country. In its civic participation, the VPS adopted a dual focus—first, to reinforce the preservation of Vietnamese cultural traditions and promote new forms of cultural production (such as film), and second, to do charity work—such as the health fair and the work party for victims of Hurricane Katrina. Its activities were also aimed at both the Vietnamese population, including charity work in Vietnam itself, and at the wider society in the United States. In contrast to the VAC, whose activities are mainly oriented toward the interests of the first generation, often looking back toward the Vietnamese War, the VPS focused on the second generation and its future in the United States and beyond.

Immigrant Women and Ethnic Leadership: Ngo L. and Sundari B.

Men—like Cao and Vishal, profiled earlier in this chapter—tend to be more visible in ethnic organizations, particularly in positions of authority and leadership, but women have also assumed leadership roles. One first-generation

Vietnamese woman, for example, has served in several leadership capacities, including as president of the Dallas VAC. In Fort Worth, another first-generation Vietnamese American female has an important position in the school district and is active in the political sphere, although she has not run for office. Within the Indian population, women have stepped into leadership roles by serving on religious and other voluntary association committees, in one case as president of the IANT, in another case as a board member of DFW International Community Alliance (an umbrella organization for all the foreign born in the area), and in a third case as a member of the board of a Dallas-area adult literacy organization. There are also organizations directed toward women's issues (domestic violence, for example) that Indian women have been instrumental in forming. Among the women leaders we interviewed were Ngo L. and Sundari B.

Ngo L. arrived in the United States when she was twenty-one years old, having escaped from Saigon with siblings by boat in the early 1980s. Her parents remained behind in Vietnam and have never relocated to the United States. After spending some time in a refugee camp overseas, Ngo and her siblings were settled by a church group in the western part of the United States, where she remained for a few years and attended college. Eventually, however, she and her husband (also a refugee and "boat person" whom she met in America) moved to Dallas, where their two children were born. They moved to Dallas to join Ngo's sister, who had arrived in the United States after Ngo and settled in Dallas. Ngo and her husband liked the warm weather ("It was just like in Vietnam") and the economic prosperity of a growing economy. Ngo was born into a wealthy family that was persecuted after the communist takeover of Saigon. She was not able to continue her education there because, as she reported, the communists in control of the examination process did not let her pass the entrance exams for college. Ngo and her husband both attended college in the United States and now have a successful business; Ngo also works full-time in a semiprofessional job in industry.

Unlike many of the first-generation Vietnamese women we interviewed—especially the parents who said they were not that involved or interested in politics—Ngo freely expressed an interest in both homeland and domestic politics, and a desire to participate in American society. She and her husband are both naturalized citizens. She articulated her own desire to be a citizen thus: "I think I belong to the U.S. It is my homeland now. I want to be part of the society." She also believes that voting is a very meaningful activity because, as she put it, "I believe my voice can make a difference. The voice of the citizen influences the government." Like many of the Vietnamese research participants whose views were expressed in Chapter 2, she does not, however, feel 100 percent American. As she explained, "I am adapted to American culture; I work with Americans and American culture. I combine both cultures, but I am not 50/50; I am more like 30/70 [Vietnamese/American]." Ngo has worked on political campaigns and handed out literature on behalf of candidates at the local, state, and national levels, but she was reluctant to express a strong political party affiliation. She says she votes for the best candidate.

Ngo's entire family is involved in activities related to the civic sphere. Both she and her husband are active in a Vietnamese ethnic association, and her two children, young adults, have been active in school associations, sports, and their Buddhist temple youth group. One of her children started a multicultural youth group at her high school that does a lot of volunteer work. Ngo feels it is important for her children to get involved; she bases this in part on her Buddhist beliefs: "They learn to make their own decisions, learn not to be selfish and to live for others. This comes from Buddhism—enlightenment." The best way to teach children to participate in this way, she feels, is to "be a role model, be involved, respond to others." Since arriving in the United States as a young woman, Ngo has acquired excellent English language skills, and she works for a company where she interacts exclusively in English. Therefore she does not experience the language barrier that prohibits many first-generation refugees from getting involved beyond ethnic associations. When her children were in elementary school, she was active in the PTA, as a room mother, and as a volunteer; she also spoke to classes about her job a couple of times. She did this because, as she said, "I want to stay close to my children."

In 2002, Ngo got involved in an ethnic association. She had previously attended the annual DFW Tet Festival and had learned from more senior members of the Vietnamese population about what she perceived to be some disturbing developments in Vietnam regarding China's claim to some lands along the Sino-Vietnam border. She took the position that the current Vietnamese government did not stand up to the Chinese and this had eroded the strength of the country.[16] Ngo attended another meeting on this topic and thereafter got involved in this ethnic association, becoming an officer and helping in a variety of ways. She noted that she acquired some leadership skills through workshops offered by another Vietnamese ethnic association, and through involvement in a professional network at work.

Although it was homeland politics that first sparked her involvement in ethnic associations, Ngo feels it is important to "make our community stronger" in the United States. She is involved in such associations in order to help educate Vietnamese immigrants so they can adapt to American culture, and to "get our voice heard." As she explained, many former refugees are separated from one another, and they focus on their own family, and their own church or temple. They feel sad because of their difficult circumstances and "don't want to get involved; they look out for their own interest." She wants to help stop this and to get Vietnamese Americans more involved in the wider society through education and through participation in the U.S. government by voting. According to Ngo, to be a good citizen in Vietnam meant to stay involved with your own family and children but not get too involved in politics. She feels, however, that in the United States to be a good citizen is "to vote, to help others when they need it, and to participate in American activities like Katrina, 9/11, and the PTA." Here Ngo expresses a notion of citizenship that is legal and formal as well as participatory and informal. Ngo also feels it is important, however, not to be ashamed of being Vietnamese, and to retain some of that identity. She was one of the few Vietnamese we interviewed who openly expressed ambivalence about the stereotype of the "ugly American," and one of the few to have a critical eye toward some American ways of operating. She wondered aloud if the government of the United States always reflected the will of the people. This attitude may be an indication of her adaptation to American life, which includes the right to debate and disagree.

Like the other first-generation leaders who were interviewed, Ngo cited the Truong sisters (who, as described in the last chapter, were the subject of a commemoration in a Catholic church hall) and other historic culture heroes and heroines as her role models and mentors rather than people she had met in her life.[17] Ngo is oriented toward both her Vietnamese past and the American future of her children, who "were born here; they don't carry our culture, so we must be flexible." She sees ethnic associations as important spheres in which to "balance the old and new ways." She feels strongly that her involvement with this association helps "make our community better; my influence will make our community better." She continued, saying that "somebody has to go beyond the culture. I believe in America, and that we can improve and adjust. My people should have the benefits that the rest of the U.S. has." Although she was not familiar with the phrase "give back to the community" (which was often used by our Indian informants and by younger members of the VPS), she certainly operates within the spirit of this phrase. Ngo also, however, cited her Buddhist beliefs as informing her desire to help others (as a path to enlightenment and in keeping with the values of *trach nhiem* mentioned in Chapter 3).

Like Ngo, Sundari B. is active in an organization that focuses on her homeland, but the mission of this organization and the focus of her involvement in it are educational rather than overtly political.[18] Sundari was born and raised in Bombay, but her experience prior to arriving in the United States was international. After graduating from a university, she worked in a bank in India and was then sent to Australia and later to Germany. She had also visited Boston and eventually took a sabbatical year to study there in 1992. She was then sent for a one-year training program in New York City. It was there that she met her husband, who is of Indian background but at that time was a legal permanent resident of the United States. They married and eventually both became U.S. citizens. Reflecting the dual identities mentioned by other research participants that were outlined in Chapter 2, Sundari stated, "I feel totally American and totally Indian." She continued: "Countries are man-made. There is little difference. The important thing is what you value, what your moral fiber is."

Sundari's daughter was born in New York and in 1999 the family moved to Houston. In their early years in Houston Sundari was a stay-at-home mom. Her daughter was enrolled in a Montessori school where there were many other Indian children. One day the head of an organization called Pratham USA came to speak at the Sunday school of their temple. Pratham's mission is to spread literacy in India. The presentation, she said, was powerful. The founder was an Indian man whose mother died when he was three-years-old. His village came together to educate him. When he was admitted to the University of Oklahoma to pursue a doctorate, the villagers collected money to pay for his trip to the United States. Education, he said, had saved his life and he wanted to give back so that education would change the lives of other children in India. With the aid of a small grant from UNICEF, this individual founded Pratham in 1994. He had been teaching chemistry at the University of Houston and had returned to India to do charitable work. There he saw the need to focus on preschool education.[19] "When I heard his story," Sundari said, "I was ready to write a check."

With great passion Sundari observed that there are four hundred million illiterate people in India, one hundred million children with no access to primary education, and children in schools with no access to computers. Pratham, she said, "tries to address these issues, tending also to the basic deficiencies, including the absence of preschool preparation." Over the course of a few years Sundari became active in this transnational organization, moving quickly from being a donor to developing fundraising projects. Initially she approached the Houston area Pratham chapter about sponsoring a literacy week in the Montessori school. Her goal was to involve the children in Pratham through a read-a-thon. She did find a community sponsor and the event was quite successful, raising $3,000. "This is the way to introduce Pratham to a general audience,"

Sundari observed. "If the children are exposed, they go home and convince the parents that it is a worthy cause. The children also learn gratitude for what they have and what other children do not have, and that they can help." Before leaving the Houston area, Sundari developed a Thanksgiving read-a-thon in the Houston Independent School District for Pratham. Seventy children were involved. Sundari said she was able to introduce the program because in the school where her daughter was enrolled there were programs to teach children how to be good global citizens. The hurdle, she said, was that sponsoring a program that raised money was not allowed, so they did it under the auspices of another literacy program in the city.

Sundari's daughter has been very active in the read-a-thon, continuing it after they moved to DFW in 2004. "She has sponsors in India and among relatives and friends across the United States. She e-mails them to tell them how many books she plans to read over the holidays, and people send in donations. With e-mail you can create global sponsorship." Sundari was approached to join the board of the local chapter of Pratham USA. She became active in the annual gala, which one year raised $350,000. Sundari said she does not enjoy the board meetings. Rather, she prefers to be involved with the children, inventing strategies for raising money with and through them.

One of Sundari's role models for civic engagement, she said, is an uncle she never knew who she was told was very involved in raising funds for schools. She also talked about a grandfather who was a justice of the peace who helped people and settled disputes. Sundari also described the concentric circle of caring within Indian tradition. "You take care of yourself, and then you take care of your immediate family, then of your extended family, then of your neighbors, then of your community, and then the rest." As you go through life, she suggested, the circle of caring expands. She contrasted this circle-of-caring model with the monetary model found in the West, where the amount you give increases as your income increases. "For Indians," she suggested, "giving begins once you feel secure psychologically. Many Indians need to establish themselves, be in a place where they feel less anxious about money, and then they can give easily." She also observed that once you have started giving, you cannot stop. It becomes a habit from which you receive "peace and satisfaction—for having done something good." She emphasized how important it was to teach her daughter, to give her "the right perspective on life." Through this work, she said, her daughter has met the best kind of people—those with a similar mind-set. Sundari has, in other words, brought her daughter into this particular community of practice and taught her at a very young age the value of civic responsibility. Of significance in all these comments is that learning about civic engagement can also occur within families. Sundari had her own role models and is attempting to be a role model to her own daughter. Ngo's eldest daughter had been influenced in a similar fashion by her parent's involvement to become an active youth leader.

Sundari described her fundraising strategies. She said that when she raises money she uses a kind of "emotional blackmail." She asks people how many times they say "My child is in good health, thanks to God"—and then suggests, "Do thank God by giving for the good things that we have." She observed, "Many people can give $100 a month and not miss it at all." She asks her friends, If you had $100 that was stolen or lost, would you miss it? and most admit they would not. Sundari thinks that younger Indians are becoming more involved and are more generous and more confident than their parents. She expressed confidence in the way Indian parents are raising their children in the United States—"they will synthesize the best of both worlds." She suggested that they were creating a generation of good citizens, which she defined as "being honest and true to your core values, especially when no one is looking."

Sundari B. and Ngo L. are good examples of the ways in which first-generation female immigrants become involved in American civic life. They expressed deep concern for cultural and charitable enterprises as well as for teaching the next generation about service and responsibility, thereby serving a bridging function between the first and second generations. They described being gradually drawn into participation in those communities of practice in which they eventually assumed leadership positions. Their motivations for participation were a blend of circumstances, structures already in place, and a strong desire to contribute. Ngo, for example, who was already interested in homeland politics and desired to help other Vietnamese immigrants, happened upon a controversy being discussed at the Tet Festival and was thereby drawn into fuller participation in an ethnic association. This seemingly chance encounter occurred, however, when she was ready to get involved, having already been involved in the PTA. Sundari originally heard about Pratham by chance at her daughter's Montessori school, decided she wanted to become involved, and did so by organizing read-a-thons for children.

Interest in the civic engagement of post-1965 immigrant women in particular is just beginning to develop and has largely been examined within religious contexts.[20] Writing specifically in relation to religious assemblies, anthropologist Alex Stepick (2005: 19) poses a question that is equally germane to ethnic associations: Under what conditions do women assume more public responsibilities? It is certainly commonly assumed, and some literature reflects this, that in religious and ethnic associations women are active in the background rather than the foreground—a reflection, Stepick suggests, of patriarchal values that accord men the more formal and public roles. However, Ngo's and Sundari's narratives suggest that time (both in the country and in terms of availability in relation to other work and family responsibilities) allows at least some immigrant women to become more civically engaged, to serve on committees and boards, to make sure their voices are heard, and to help lead organizations. In some cases, as alluded to in the case of the Indian women who formed their own Lions Club, immigrant women launch their own organizations, often ones that address family issues, including domestic violence and the development and needs of children.

Spaces for Civic Learning, Participatory Citizenship, and Political Incorporation

Both the Indian and Vietnamese populations have created a host of associations at the local level that offer opportunities for participating in community service and other shared activities, for learning about the political process, and for acting politically. Their activities in these arenas illustrate the complex and multiple dimensions of civic engagement among immigrant newcomers and their children. Both populations have organizations that facilitate civic engagement through forms of social or cultural citizenship, and others that explicitly emphasize strategic political action, whether in the United States or directed toward the homeland. We suggest that these organizations are communities of practice where learning involves both the acquisition of knowledge and social participation (Smith 2003: 4). Both are important to participatory citizenship and hence to political incorporation. Indeed, even those involved in organizations that are not overtly political in their mission statements recognize the political dimensions of those organizations. One Indian parent, an engineer in his early fifties, commented that many of these associations "offer cultural contexts and also social and political awareness; even though they are nonpolitical on the surface, it is always in the background."

We found that certain associations may eclipse other voices within an immigrant population when it comes to representing their interests within the wider society, but this silencing is not always evident to outsiders. Debates in some Vietnamese associations about the importance of being anticommunist, for example, create didfficulties for those who are critical of the current regime in Vietnam but also want to focus on other issues and look more toward the future. The common experience of having arrived in the United States as refugees helped many of the first-generation Vietnamese to create bonds they would not necessarily have had at home in Vietnam. A shared history of military service brought many first-generation men together. At the same time, the war experience has also created tensions because those who served in the war and are strongly anticommunist claim a higher moral authority than those who seek a more moderate approach to contemporary Vietnam. Homeland politics is thus a highly charged issue for many people. Leadership in Vietnamese ethnic associations was also a topic of much discussion among research participants. Some suggested that there are so many associations because, as one man put it, "everyone wants to be a leader." A female respondent expressed her view that "the Vietnamese will only get involved in the community, in helping, if they can get something out of it. They all have ulterior motives, trying to help themselves get something. There is not enough of a sense of community."[21] These views, expressed privately among Vietnamese Americans and shared with the interviewer, seem to contradict the perception from outside that the members of associations work very well together.

We see, however, that Vietnamese Americans have come to realize that learning to put aside these differences and petty criticisms in order to provide a more unified image to the wider society is an effective strategy for gaining the respect of local politicians and elected officials. One local (non-Asian) politician observed that "the Vietnamese community is the most organized of all the other ethnic groups." When asked why he said that, he replied, "They have their own culture, they have an established community, they come together. This is partly because they are relatively new to the community and have only been here twenty-five to thirty years. They have stayed as an individual community." He compared the Vietnamese to Latinos, who, he noted, "come from different countries and don't have much in common." His comments reflect the success of the Vietnamese in learning to minimize publicly any factions and tensions within associations and to project an image of working together effectively.

Like the Vietnamese, Indians have been able to provide a coherent portrait of themselves and to minimize internal factional differences when interacting with those outside their ethnic group. In some Indian organizations there are debates between those who want to take a more vocal and public position regarding religious violence in India and those who want to maintain political neutrality. Within the Indian community a core group of people has been propelled into leadership roles, moving up the hierarchy within different associations. They are well-recognized and to some extent they gain prestige through this recognition. They are equally aware, however, of not overstepping their bounds, because the potential to be criticized for becoming too full of themselves is always beneath the surface. Further, efforts are made to try to contain conflict and differences, particularly within the "umbrella" associations, so that the public face of the Indian community (that is, the face presented to the broader American society) can be one of harmony and working together. The vast array of religious and regional associations offers venues for fostering difference and displaying diversity. This variety makes it possible for associations such as the Irving DFW Indian Lions Club and the Texas chapter of IAFC to rise above differences. The emphasis placed on presenting a harmonious public face may be enhanced by the character of the DFW region. Dallas, in particular, has cultivated a can-do business culture, to which the highly educated and extensively professional Indian community may be responding.[22] In the context of associations like those discussed in this chapter, Indians are managing to present themselves within the broader American society. Sociologist Pawan Dhingra (2003) found similar behavior among second-generation Korean and Indian professionals in DFW. He describes an effort among these populations to promote a model minority image in order to gain acceptance and counter their image as foreigners and outsiders.

The growing financial clout of the Indian immigrant population, in DFW and nationwide, facilitates these forays into the American public sphere in general and into the political arena in particular, whether as individuals or as members of organizations such as the Indian American Friendship Council. Increasingly Indians can afford to pay to attend an event where a mainstream political figure is present. As will become more evident in the following chapters, the Vietnamese are also able to enter the U.S. political arena. Although they may not have the same level of wealth as the Indians, the Vietnamese are very effective in mobilizing voters to support political candidates; this has been noted by local politicians, who appear at their events and court their support. Some Vietnamese Americans have also run successful political campaigns and been elected to political office.

Our ethnographic research on ethnic associations provides important information on the social practices of their members and on the institutional structures that organize such practices. The narratives of Ngo, Sundari, Cao, and Vishal offer insights into the processes by which immigrants and their offspring move from the peripheral position of outsiders to the position of engaged and involved citizens in the context of a diverse range of ethnic voluntary associations. The idea that voluntary associations can serve as arenas for socialization is not new. Anthropologist Clifford Geertz (1962: 160) noted that in mid-twentieth-century Asia and Africa, "the rotating credit fund is . . . a socializing mechanism, in that broad sense in which 'socialization' refers not simply to the process by which the child learns to be an adult, but the learning of any new patterns of behavior which are of functional importance in society, even by adults." Through their participation in these associations, he wrote, peasants "learn to be traders, not merely in the narrow occupational sense, but in the broad cultural sense" (261). We have argued here that Vietnamese and Indian immigrants undergo a similar experience in the context of ethnic associations that operate as "communities of practice" in which newcomers learn effective ways to become participatory citizens.

In the contexts of the associations we have described, Indian and Vietnamese immigrants construct dual or multiple identities and engage multiple communities. First-generation Indians speak about "the [Indian] community" and "the community at large." One person articulated the relationship as follows: "We live in one community, Indian, and engage the other, American." A similar comment was made by a former Vietnamese refugee: "There are two communities: first, the American community, and second, the Vietnamese community. To 'give back to the community' means that when you have reached your place in life, when you are productive as a citizen, you get involved. You must think of yourself as a citizen."

In summary, associations such as those we have described are communities of practice that can be both inward and outward focused at the same time. Formal political participation often develops in the context of informal participation in multiple communities of practice. Both types of participation are expressions of civic engagement.

5 Festivals and Banquets

IN THIS CHAPTER we focus on ethnic festivals and banquets—events that tell us something about how immigrants perceive and manage their civic and political presence. These are cultural spectacles—that is, they are organized events "in which a group represents itself both to its own members and to non-members," events that may "enrich civic participation by creating social spaces in which people from a variety of backgrounds can come together to learn about each other ... " (Bramadat 2001: 79, 89).[1] As spaces of cultural citizenship, festivals and banquets are ritualized activities that illustrate "civic engagement in an expressive context" (Stepick, Stepick, and Labissiere 2008) with significant political meanings.[2]

Anthropologist David Kertzer (1988: 14) has emphasized the role of ritual in building political organizations, in creating political legitimacy and solidarity, and in shaping people's understandings of the world.[3] We see some of these dimensions at work, perhaps more covertly than overtly, in the two ethnic festivals (one Vietnamese and one Indian) and the pan-Asian banquet we discuss in this chapter. Each festival and banquet has its own style and format, repeated every time it takes place. There are particular beginnings, middles, and endings. There are communal aspects (with an audience listening to a speaker or watching a performance) and individual aspects (speeches and interpersonal networking). These ritual occasions are, in Clifford Geertz's terms (1973), "models of" and "models for." That is, on the one hand, they are *models of* the relationships that Vietnamese immigrants currently have with other Vietnamese immigrants or that Indian immigrants currently have with other Indian immigrants. In some cases, they are also models of relationships with Asians more generally, and of the current positioning of these immigrants vis-à-vis the wider society. On the other hand, they are *models for* the possibilities for communal action and for future roles within the broader civic and political spheres in the United States. In this chapter we discuss two festivals that focus on cultural traditions but have political meanings, and one pan-Asian banquet with an explicit political agenda that brings together Asians of different national origins.

Ethnic Festivals: Tet Festival and India Nite

Historians and other scholars have described ethnic celebrations and com-memorations among earlier European immigrants to the United States,[4] but these have often been dismissed as forms of a nostalgic "symbolic ethnicity" (Gans 1979) that lacks political import.[5] There are numerous examples to the contrary, however. The celebration of Nisei Week by Japanese Americans in Los Angeles has become an occasion for working out complex racial politics and constructing political identities (Kurashige 2002). An annual Latino festival in Washington, D.C., allows diverse Latino immigrants to "self-Americanize" as they define spaces and stake claims as an ethnic group in the American civil sphere (Cadaval 1998: 3, 5). Italians in a Brooklyn neighborhood "retake the streets" and transmit "a public message of territorial proprietorship and local power" through their religious processions (Sciorra 1999: 330). In other neigh-borhoods of New York City, West Indians, Puerto Ricans, and Haitians, negoti-ate the cultural politics of race, express ethnic pride, and engage in civic politics through their carnivals and parades (Kasinitz and Freidenberg 1987; McAlister 1998). Ethnic festivals are an "entrée into a community's symbolic, economic, social and political life, especially because they are organized and presented to members of the community by members of the community" (Farber 1983: 33).[6]

The Tet Festival and India Nite, organized and sponsored by the Vietnamese American Communities of Tarrant County and Dallas and by the India Asso-ciation of North Texas (IANT), respectively, are examples of the ways in which ethnic associations reach out to both co-ethnics and the wider public. Because immigrant festive culture has deep roots in the United States, it has been posited that ethnic groups have been "inspired by the festivals of American democracy" to create their own celebrations (Fabre and Heideking 2001: 12). The Tet Festival and India Nite are not, however, solely derivative of American ceremonial life. Tet has long been celebrated in Vietnam,[7] even if aspects of its celebration have changed in new settings; India Nite is an "invented tradition" (Hobsbawn and Ranger 1983) that brings Indians together in the new civic space of the United

States. Our particular interest lies in what these festivals reveal about the ways in which Vietnamese and Indians choose to emplace themselves in the wider civic sphere and make claims of cultural citizenship and belonging. Of equal interest is how these festivals operate as "learning activities" (Lave 1996) for developing civic skills and hence as communities of practice for Vietnamese and Indian immigrants.[8]

Tet: A Vietnamese Cultural Spectacle

The Tet Festival, a celebration of the Lunar New Year held in late January or early February, is the largest of three major yearly public events organized specifically by and for the Vietnamese American population and which a broad spectrum of people attend. The other two events are the commemoration of Black April, or the fall of Saigon, in the spring; and the Mid-Autumn Moon Festival, aimed primarily at children and held in the fall. Although religious institutions also hold separate Tet festivals for their congregants, and families celebrate this holiday at home with gifts (particularly special foods and money for good luck), this public festival transcends family and religious affiliations and is open to the entire population. In all regions of the United States where there is a strong Vietnamese American presence, a community Tet festival is held.[9] Although significant historical and cultural meanings connect the Tet celebration to religious and civic practices in Vietnam, when former refugees in the United States hold public festivals to mark this holiday, new meanings related to civic engagement emerge.

During the three years of this research project, the location of the DFW Tet Festival changed each year. In 2006 it was held under a large white tent on the grounds of a Vietnamese shopping mall. One of the organizers later remarked that "this tent symbolized our struggles as refugees and the refugee camps that were set up under tents." In 2007, Tet was celebrated in an empty warehouse connected to what was then the headquarters of the VAC of Tarrant County. In 2008, the festival was moved to Traders Village—a large, privately owned flea market located in Grand Prairie, a town next to Arlington, that rents out space for events.[10] Traders Village consists of a series of small buildings, most with open stalls, in which vendors sell goods and food. It boasts on its Web site that "for almost 40 years [since 1973], Traders Village has offered millions of guests a little piece of Americana; a glimpse back to a time when small businesses were the norm and haggling with the shop owner brought great bargains."[11] This commentary links Traders Village to a spirit of free enterprise that is highly salient in the business ethos of this region of the country. Traders Village is well-known for having long been the site of an annual Native American Pow Wow (http://tradersvillage.com/grand-prairie/events/49th-annual-national-championship-indian-pow-wow). It has increasingly, however, become a hub for other ethnic festivals; in the summer of 2010 the Web site indicated that Filipino, Caribbean, and Mexican festivals would be held there. By moving the Tet Festival from its previous venues (places associated with Asian ethnicity), the festival's organizers made it more accessible to a wider audience, including the primarily working-class Anglo and Hispanic families who go to Traders Village to shop and meet friends, especially on Sundays.

The VAC of Tarrant County, profiled in Chapter 4, and the VAC of Dallas work together and join with representatives of other organizations (such as the Vietnamese Culture and Science Association and Vietnamese student organizations at area universities) to plan the event, solicit funding from major donors, and send out publicity. Planning for the 2008 event, from which most of the following ethnographic description is drawn, began in fall 2007. At a meeting held on a Sunday early in December, representatives from various organizations met at the Vietnamese American community center in Arlington to plan the festival. Approximately twenty-five people attended, including a reporter from a local Vietnamese-language newspaper, and were seated in chairs arranged in a circle to maximize discussion. The main business was to confirm the division of labor among the volunteer organizers, including coordination of the booths, performances, and fundraising. The meeting went very smoothly and displayed a remarkable spirit of working together to accomplish the event. Tasks were assigned and representatives of the various organizations promised to mobilize volunteers.

The organizers later prepared a fourteen-page "Tet in DFW" sponsorship package to solicit support from corporations, small businesses, municipalities, and other nonprofits. This brochure underscored what it referred to as the need for "cultural and heritage values" among the Vietnamese at the same time that it reminded potential sponsors of the market for goods and services that this growing population represents. Also stressed in the brochure was the "collaborative effort" embodied in the festival—evident in the organizational meeting described in the previous paragraph. The brochure included a description of Tet and a range of sponsorship levels, as well as several photos of the activities of the VAC of Tarrant County. The photos highlighted the civic engagement of the VAC with shots of the commemoration of the fall of Saigon as well as of Vietnamese Americans participating in "multicultural day" at a local library, the Fourth of July parade in Arlington, registering voters, and addressing the Arlington City Council. The brochure attempts to demon-strate that the Vietnamese population has already entered the civic sphere and learned many skills for marketing its "cultural" products.[12]

The 2008 Tet Festival was held at Traders Village in a large structure that had a roof but was open along its sides so there were many points of entry.[13] The spatial layout of the festival included a main stage on which opening ceremonies and the blessing of the event by elders took place in front of a backdrop patterned after an altar that combined traditional elements of Viet-namese culture compatible with both Catholic and Buddhist traditions. Chairs and benches were arranged in front of the stage so that many people could sit to watch the speakers, singers, and dancers perform. Around the periphery of the tentlike structure were many smaller booths, as well as clusters of people talking, eating, and investigating the offerings at the booths. Many things are going on at any one time during the Tet Festival. People come and go; little children leave their seats to get up and dance or mimic the martial arts per-formers; groups of older women chat quietly with each other, sharing family news and commenting on the performances. As they strolled around Traders Village that weekend, non-Vietnamese patrons were drawn inside the structure to see the performances and visit the booths. While non-Vietnamese families were purchasing *banh mie* sandwiches and watching Vietnamese dance, song, and martial arts performances, the Vietnamese attendees were outside buying Mexican roasted corn on the cob (*elote*) and other specialties sold by vendors in Traders Village.

The festival opens on Saturday morning and goes into Sunday. The most highly ritualized part of the festival takes place near and on the stage. The open-ing ceremony (followed at each of the festivals observed during our research) begins with a performance by the lion dancers (part of a youth group from a nearby Buddhist temple) outside of the structure that includes a fireworks display. This is followed by a procession into the structure by a color guard of Vietnamese military veterans who served in the Vietnam War; as in other Vietnamese American public ceremonies, they carry both the United States flag and the freedom and heritage flag of the former Republic of South Vietnam. Next, the altar is blessed by a group of elders, and honored invited guests are introduced. The ceremony ends with a patriotic sequence and the color guard standing at attendance in front of the stage. This procession from outside to inside helps create a Vietnamese social space within the structure, claiming it for the two days of the festival.

The two flags displayed and used by the color guard express the dual nature of Vietnamese American identity and sense of belonging. The so-called freedom and heritage flag, a potent symbol of the Vietnamese diaspora that has already been mentioned at several points in this book, is officially recognized by the local government of Arlington, Texas, and by the state of Texas as the flag of the Vietnamese American community. At the Tet Festival, the two flags flank what is at first an altar and then becomes a performance stage. The national anthems of the United States and South Vietnam are both sung, as they are at other Vietnamese American public events. Although we observed (as detailed later in our discussion of India Nite) that Indians also display two flags and sing two anthems at their public ceremonies (and we presume that other immigrant groups also do this), for the Vietnamese there is an added layer of meaning, because when they display the South Vietnamese flag and sing the national anthem of South Vietnam, they are making a political statement as a diaspora community vis-à-vis the current government of Vietnam. One research participant, a Vietnamese college student, observed that the display of both the U.S. and South Vietnamese flags at the Tet Festival was similar to the use of both the Texas and American flags in public school classrooms. For her, the layering of identities was similar: you can be both Texan and American, and you can be both Vietnamese and American. But being Vietnamese in this way is a particular form of Vietnameseness, related to anticommunism.

The Tet Festival draws in young and old, Vietnamese and non-Vietnamese, to the performances, food, and other events that take place within the space of the festival. At the same time, the festival is a social space connected to the internal "cultural intimacy" of the Vietnamese population, which according to Herzfeld (2005: 3) is "aspects of a cultural identity that are considered a source of external embarrassment but that nevertheless provide insiders with their assurance of common sociality." The various Tet activities take place with some accompanying internal fissures and tensions, which are not evident to the casual attendee looking for entertainment but are examples of cultural intimacy. There are booths with political displays related to homeland politics, where Vietnamese American participants are heard discussing those issues. For example, a booth was organized by a Vietnamese military veterans group about the dispute over the Paracel and Spratly Islands off the coast of Vietnam. An organizer of the display explained that before the Olympics that would be held in Beijing they hoped to turn the attention of Americans to their protest of China's control of the islands and of the Vietnamese government's acquiescence to China in this matter.[14] At another booth, DVDs of the flag protest at a local university were distributed,[15] and people could purchase T-shirts printed with the South Vietnamese flag and other anticommunist symbols. Another source of interpersonal tension related to homeland politics at the festival that was not evident to non-Vietnamese was the display of a map of Vietnam at a booth intended to promote awareness of Vietnamese culture. The map labeled the site of Saigon with both Saigon and Ho Chi Minh City, the newer name, and a handful of activists associated with the VAC put another map that labeled this city only Saigon over the offending one. Because such tensions are not overtly displayed to casual attendees, and because language barriers keep non-Vietnamese speakers from understanding the discussions of homeland politics, the use of the Tet Festival as a forum for internal political struggles is not evident to outsiders.

Not only does the festival have meanings within the Vietnamese American population—meanings related to cultural expression and internal politics—but it also reaches an "external" audience in its display of the growing political and economic clout of Vietnamese Americans, and it is a vehicle for increasing this influence. Local elected officials (and political candidates in election years) are invited to attend the Tet Festival. They are treated as honored guests, introduced to the crowd during the opening ceremony, and permitted to address the audience. These politicians are not privy to the factions within the Vietnamese American population; they depend on the leaders of the VAC to serve as spokespeople for this group. Elected officials from Arlington and other nearby cities, several of whom depend on the Vietnamese vote in their districts, attended the Tet Festival in 2008. One Anglo mayor expressed his admiration for the Vietnamese population and its leadership by remarking, "The Vietnamese understand retail politics. They understand that you need to have grassroots connections." A new development in the political realm was observed during the festival in 2008: for the first time a Vietnamese political candidate—Sandra VuLe—attended the Tet Festival. VuLe was at that time a candidate for state representative from Dallas District 112 in the Democratic primary. She addressed the crowd in Vietnamese, even though she is fluent in English, and asked for Vietnamese American support in her bid for office. Although she did not win the general election, despite her success in the primary, her presence underscored that Vietnamese Americans are starting to produce elected officials. By the time of the Tet Festival in 2010, a former president of the VAC of Tarrant County was running for county office (as mentioned in the last chapter) and his campaign was a major sponsor of the festival. (We return to his election in our concluding chapter.)

Associated with this political role of the festival is its display of the growing economic strength of the Vietnamese consumer market. Various businesses (such as insurance companies, telecommunication providers, and medical offices) interact with and promote their services to Vietnamese and non-Vietnamese attendees alike. Many of these businesses are Vietnamese run, but larger corporations also take part. In 2008, the Tet Festival was underwritten by two corporations—OnPac Energy and the Horseshoe Casino in Bossier City, Louisiana. OnPac Energy is an electric company formed after the 2002 deregulation of such utilities in Texas. It has a Vietnamese director of marketing. The Horseshoe Casino attracts many Vietnamese clients, and hosts large shows with Vietnamese performers.[16] By sponsoring the Tet Festival, these two groups sought to enlarge their Vietnamese client base as well as to show their goodwill toward existing clients. Another major sponsor was McDonald's.

In the Tet Festival of 2008 we see collaboration among a large group of Vietnamese Americans, well-established after previous years of organizing the festival, having learned a few things about where to hold their festival in order to get the greatest turnout, and demonstrating their civic presence and political clout in the region. By engaging in a form of placemaking and spacemaking, if only for a long weekend each winter in this quintessentially American flea market, Vietnamese Americans strengthen internal networks as they engage more fully with the wider civic sphere and work to influence local politicians. While the Tet Festival is a site for Vietnamese Americans to learn new civic skills, it is also a place where those non-Vietnamese who attend and those who interact with the Vietnamese in planning the festival (including corporate donors) learn about this group and its growing presence and influence in this region of Texas. The Tet Festival is a critical social space and community of practice in which to explore the ways in which Vietnamese Americans are engaging with the wider public sphere. It is a "model of" Vietnamese American cultural resilience and growing political and economic clout, and a "model for" increasing Vietnamese American presence in the American civic sphere.

India Nite: An Indian Cultural Spectacle

Each year, the IANT sponsors two community-wide events, one on August 15 to commemorate India's Independence Day (when the British officially left India in 1947) and the other on January 26 to commemorate Indian Republic Day (when the Indian Constitution came into effect in 1950). Although these events are largely for the Indian community, to bring together a dispersed and heterogeneous population, they are, like Vietnamese American festivals and commemorations, also communities of practice where individuals acquire organizational skills, exercise leadership, and practice civic engagement. In addition, these occasions offer opportunities for attendees to learn about the broader public and political spheres, as well as to remember their own history and celebrate their culture.

Although hosted in various venues, since January 2002 India Nite has been held in a large auditorium (with just under 2,400 seats) on the campus of a private university in Dallas. At a November 2001 meeting between university officials and the leadership of IANT that launched the move to a new venue, the guidelines for hosting the event on the campus were discussed. The meeting itself represented a process of civic education and cross-cultural negotiation. IANT leaders recognized that they had a problem reconciling what university officials perceived as chaos and contrary to the rules and regulations of a U.S. college campus with what they acknowledged as almost unalterable characteristics of Indian society, including having "too many chiefs" and the tendency for Indians to get up and down during events rather than sit in one place for three or four hours. As the president of IANT put it, "At non-Indian events they behave, but at Indian events they think it is their own—as if they are on their own territory. They see so many other Indians and they get excited." One of the sticking points for university officials was the food service; people would not be allowed to bring their own burners and cook food in the lower foyer. The food would have to be prepared in advance. Further, IANT would have "to move people to their seats in order to avoid too much crowding in the foyer." Another moment of cultural difference came in the discussion of the timing of the program; in an American context, events generally start on time, but Indians operate on "Indian standard time"—that is, behind schedule. Over the years, IANT has attempted to move the program along to conform better to an American standard. IANT acquiesced on the food service, but university officials accepted that little could be done about the mobility of the audience during the afternoon and evening.

Another problem that had to be ironed out was the prohibition on individuals handing out fliers for their own businesses. From the university (American) side this activity created chaos; from the Indian side it was understandable because the campus was a place where entrepreneurial people could reach a captive audience. The IANT leaders at this meeting came to an agreement with the university staff, but they admitted that they had little authority over their fellow Indians, and that if they tried to exercise too much control, people would think they were being self-important. There was also a long conversation about

tickets and finally a workable will-call strategy was developed that accommo-
dated both parties. Normally tickets for events like this are sold in advance
through IANT and are often available at prominent Indian stores in the region.
All of these negotiations illustrate a difference between India Nite and the Tet
Festival: that in the more restricted environment of a university auditorium
both parties must accommodate one another and their differences, whereas in
the more open commercial space of Traders Village a freer flow of people and
activities is possible.

Planning for India Nite—an evening of dance performances interrupted by
ceremonial activities and speeches—begins in the spring with sporadic meetings of a small group of IANT board members. Meanwhile, various groups,
including local dance academies, begin to prepare for auditions. A set of guidelines is available and all performers are encouraged to produce "fast-paced,, folk,
regional, patriotic, semi-classical and movie-song entries." As the date draws
closer, groups of IANT leaders and members and other volunteers meet regularly to organize the evening, including signing the contract with the university,
organizing the responsibilities of those working the front and back stages, securing business sponsorships, and deciding which restaurants will serve food.
Notices for the event are posted in centers of Indian activity throughout the city
and announcements are read on Indian radio stations. On the day of the event,
IANT sends automatic voice messages or e-mails to all its members to remind
them about India Nite.

The program begins at about 4 P.M. and lasts about three and a half hours.[17]
Like the Tet Festival, India Nite is routinely opened with a patriotic display, including the singing of the Star-Spangled Banner (generally by second-generation
youth) and the Indian national anthem (by an older performer). In the auditorium, advertising slides for the business sponsors (a form of civic involvement
for them) are continuously projected on two screens. The sponsors are also listed
on the back of the ticket and in the printed program. One year a prominent
travel agency served as the grand sponsor and its name appeared on a banner
at the back of the stage; later in the evening the owner was recognized from
the stage. That year, Zee TV, a cable network, was also recognized, as were New
York Life Insurance Company, and two local restaurants that provided the Indian snacks available on the lower level of the building. Among the slides are
also social service messages, such as one warning people about the dangers of
drugs and another about how to become a foster parent. The slides also include
pictures of various IANT events and programs, and information on major charitable contributions made by the organization, such as a large donation to disas-

ter relief following a cyclone in the Indian state of Orissa. One general-message slide read, "Support your community; become a member of the India Association of North Texas." The slides offer an occasion to promote the IANT, and local Indian-owned enterprises, as well as non-Indian enterprises that want to reach out to this generally well-to-do immigrant population. As they are with the Tet Festival, commercial functions are an important dimension of this cultural spectacle.

The dance performances are introduced by a group of Indian American youth who rotate serving as emcees and often issue a general thank-you to the audience "for letting them serve the community" or "for the opportunity to give back to the community." One year an emcee made a somewhat more patriotic statement: "Service to our country is service to our Lord of lords. Our prayers and homage go out to all our soldiers serving in Iraq." The afternoon always begins with the youngest performers (children aged four to eight) and progresses through the afternoon and early evening to the older children. Some of the dances are rooted in traditional folk dances from various regions of India; others are dances that draw on the various classical traditions that characterize Indian dance. Still others offer a blend of traditional elements and contemporary dance movements and are often performed to Bollywood film songs that are very familiar to the people in the audience. Some dances tell stories, occasionally with political or patriotic messages. One year, for example, a dance involved several children waving both Indian and American flags. The theme of the dance was "let us bow to the motherland," and the use of both flags indicated that both countries are now the motherland.

Throughout the evening there are also various ceremonial activities. Each year the outgoing officers and board of directors of IANT are introduced to the assembled audience along with the incoming officers. "These are your community leaders" is the message transmitted. The outgoing president (whose spouse is also always introduced) gives a short speech about the accomplishments of IANT over the course of the year. One year an Asian charity ball for which IANT had served as host was mentioned. At India Nite in 2002, the incoming president gave a very passionate speech about how freedom and capitalism had been attacked on 9/11, and also discussed some of the recent troubles between India and Pakistan. He concluded by talking about the "80,000-strong Indian community in the DFW area" and claiming that they were "living in the best country but could also be nostalgic for India"—a clear message about transnational identity. Another year, the incoming president, a woman who was prominent in the community, read a message from the consul general in Houston and then talked about the Indian diaspora as well as about the values that Indians and Americans share—democracy and pluralism. "We are birds of the same nest; though we are different, we share the same home," she said, and then noted that "man can only survive collectively." Each president emphasizes that membership dollars help the association to "serve the community" and acknowledges the more than four hundred youth who perform each year to help celebrate both Republic Day and Indian culture.

Each year community leaders are recognized with plaques, and one year a college need-based scholarship, underwritten by United Central Bank, was presented to a student of Indian descent. Another year the winner of the talented-youth award was a young Indian doctor who had graduated from a medical school in north Texas and was now living in California. Her parents came to the stage to accept the award on her behalf. The volunteer-of-the-year award that year went to an Indian who owns a photography studio who regularly records various community events; and the outstanding service award went to the owner of Taj Mahal Imports. In 2003, a check for $12,000 was presented to Mrs. Alka Patel, whose husband was shot shortly after 9/11 while he was working at his gas station in Mesquite. The funds had been collected to set up an education fund for her two children.

Finally, each year guests of honor are recognized and asked to address the crowd. One year it was the district director of the FBI, a Latino. He noted that he had met a Muslim, a Christian, and several Hindu people that evening and spoke with admiration of the coexistence of these faiths. He also referred to the importance of protecting freedom and the American way of life. Another year the IANT recognized the president of the university that hosts India Nite. In 2006, the Indian consul general from Houston was the honored guest. He emphasized that India has become a place where things are happening, and that community events like India Nite "provide us with opportunities to take stock of our achievements and shortcomings. We've had trials, tribulations, and tragedies," he went on, but "today we see tremendous optimism and high confidence levels. India is emerging as a major player on the world stage." He noted that the economic growth in India in the previous year was 7 percent and concluded by suggesting that it is a wonderful time to be Indian and that Indian Americans play an important role in the emergence of their country.

Sometimes the honored guests have been people whose presence has suggested the developing political capital of Indians both nationally and locally. One year Frank Pallone, founder of the Congressional Caucus on India and Indian Americans (colloquially known as the India Caucus) in the U.S. Congress,[18] was recognized. Pallone encouraged the audience to spread their heritage and maintain their level of community involvement. "Indians can make themselves heard," he said, "by contacting their congressmen." He also stressed the important relationship between the United States and India, suggesting that Indians in the United States could help promote trade and corporate investment in India. Referring to the high level of education of the Indian community, which "made them somewhat unique," Pallone concluded by urging the audience to "take the next step, get involved, [and] act politically."

Congressman Pete Sessions was another prominent guest of honor one year. He began his address by announcing that, at the urging of IANT, he was going to join the India caucus. (There was applause.). Noting the similarities between India and the United States—"both countries are democracies, both countries are pluralistic, both countries believe in the rule of law"—Sessions called on those present to help America build the bridge to India so that the two countries could cooperate in the war on terrorism. He went on to comment on how wonderful it was to have children grow up with their own heritage. You can be a good American, he suggested, but also hold on to cultural traditions. He praised the Indian community of DFW for its contributions to Texas, for its sense of family, and for its emphasis on young people. He concluded by complimenting the IANT for its work and telling those assembled, "You are part of our country; you make us better. We share a common bond and vision of the future."

India Nite is permeated with allusions to community service, political participation, and the role that Indian immigrants can play not only in the American public sphere but also in the global sphere. It is as much a civic and political performance as it is a celebration of culture. The leaders of IANT stand before the audience as models of community service, as do the youthful emcees and the local Indian entrepreneurs who offer substantive sponsorship for the event. Throughout the evening various individuals are recognized for their contributions to the local community or to humankind, and the guests who are invited to speak not only stress the rising importance of Indians in the economic and political arena, but also by their very presence indicate the growing political and social capital of this immigrant population.

At India Nite (and within the IANT) there is an effort to emphasize unity across differences of region, language, and faith, both behind the scenes and prior to the event, as well as in the front stage performances.[19] The backstage negotiations are primarily with the American "other" in the form of university officials and hence require such unity and collaboration. This emphasis is in contrast to the situation at the Tet Festival, where backstage tensions over homeland politics have erupted among the Vietnamese organizers. In a posts-9/11 world this display of unity has become particularly important because a portion of the Indian American population is Muslim. Finally, in the context of the celebration of the day when India became a republic with its own constitution, and by extension a celebration of Indian culture, there are always many references to being an Indian in America or an American of Indian descent, which reflect the fluid identities with which Indians in the United States wrestle and the balancing act of political and cultural belonging.

The Tet Festival and India Nite demonstrate the ways in which Vietnamese and Indian immigrants are establishing themselves, through a process of emplacement, as persons morally situated within a broader American context. They seek common ground with the wider society, albeit in a slightly different register. Whereas the Vietnamese are proclaiming, "We are like you because we are also anticommunist and share a love of democracy and freedom," the Indians are proclaiming, "We come from the world's largest democracy and share your democratic traditions." It is curious and paradoxical, however, that whereas Indian individuals, as evidenced in previous chapters, are more extensively involved than Vietnamese are in mainstream associations, it is the Vietnamese American organizers of the Tet Festival who reach out to and operate in a public sphere that invites outsiders in. India Nite, by contrast, operates more within the Indian population, albeit bridging regional, religious, and linguistic differences. Although non-Indians are not excluded, they are there because they have been invited, and often because they will be honored. In other words, each population interfaces with the broader American society in different ways and through different communities of practice.

Feasting, Displaying, and Networking:
The Fifth Annual Banquet of the DFW Asian-American Citizens Council

During our ethnographic research, in addition to attending the festivals already described, we each attended several banquets sponsored by various groups and organizations. As indicated in Chapter 4, such banquets are particularly important for several Indian ethnic associations, and a fundamental part of the activities of various Vietnamese associations. We conducted participant observation research not only at banquets specific to Indians and Vietnamese Americans, but also at banquets hosted by pan-Asian organizations. One of these, to which we now turn, was the 2005 banquet of the DFW Asian-American Citizens Council (DFW AACC), held at the Westin Hotel in the Galleria, a major commercial center in the region.[20]

Although previous scholarship has paid some attention to ethnic festivals, the role of banquets among immigrant populations has been neglected. However, anthropologists and other scholars have been interested for some time in the political and social dimensions of banquets and feasting.[21] Writing of the practice in ancient Rome, historian Katherine Dunbabin (2003: 2) has observed that "communal banqueting played an essential role in the relationship of members of the elite to their dependents, with their potential supporters, or even with their entire community." Yang (1994) demonstrates how banquets in contemporary China enhance social connections (*guanxi*), an observation quite apt for the banquet we describe here. We found in our research that banquets often have a more focused agenda than festivals and draw on a more select segment of the population. But like festivals, banquets follow ritual patterns through which civic and political presence are performed and communicated. Like the Tet Festival and India Nite, this Asian American banquet can be read as a community of practice for civic engagement.

The DFW AACC was founded in 2001 with the mission to assist the local Asian American community to participate in the wider civic sphere through voter education and registration and other activities. In its invitation letter for the fifth annual banquet, the DFW AACC was described as "an affiliation of approximately fifty Asian chambers of commerce and community organizations."[22] This organization stresses that it is nonpartisan, and members of both the Republican and Democratic parties are members. The chairwoman of DFW AACC in 2005 was Angie Chen Button, originally from Taiwan, and a Republican who subsequently won election as a Texas state representative from Dallas in 2008. DFW AACC sponsors a youth symposium for high school students, a competitive internship program for high school and college students, and a leadership training program for young adults.

The theme of the 2005 DFW AACC banquet was Key People in Key Roles (an explicit reference to leadership). It was well attended, with many tables sponsored by companies or organizations. The forty-two "community tables" were sponsored by twenty-nine associations (eight pan-Asian, seven Chinese, seven Korean, three Taiwanese, two Indian, and two Vietnamese), four individuals, six businesses, two educational institutions (Garland Independent School District and Southern Methodist University Dedman School of Law), and one government agency (Taipei Economic and Cultural Office in Houston). The majority of people attending were Chinese, Taiwanese, and Korean. There were, however, some Indians and Southeast Asians, including Vietnamese, in attendance. Not only was the chairwoman of the DFW AACC that year female, but the banquet chair was a Vietnamese American woman who had been active in the Dallas VAC (and in 2008 she became president of DFW AACC). A board member of the IANT was there as a liaison to that organization. Several Anglo elected officials also attended the banquet, as did a few Hispanic officials, such as State Representative Rafael Anchia. Joining us at our table, which had a marked display of ethnic diversity, were a district judge and his wife, three Anglo women from the Democratic Party of Collin County, a Chinese woman who came to the United States in the mid-1990s and was employed at Texas Instruments, and an African American woman serving in the Texas Legislature.

Like the two festivals described earlier, the evening started with a patriotic display. After the honor guard entered (flanking the stage with U.S. and Texas flags), the American national anthem was sung by a Chinese music professor from a local public university who was also director of the Dallas Asian American Youth Orchestra. Many people put their hands over their hearts. Unlike the Tet Festival and India Nite, where homeland flags were displayed, this event focused on shared belonging to the United States and Texas and minimizing the distinctions of national origin among Asian groups. An Indonesian woman came to the stage to lead everyone in the U.S. Pledge of Allegiance, and then a Japanese woman who worked for the local public radio station began her duties as emcee for the evening. The banquet committee members, as well as the DFW AACC board members, were introduced. Opening remarks were made by the banquet chairperson, who mentioned several of the important activities of the organization, including a fundraiser for Asian tsunami victims, the candidates forum held in advance of the 2004 elections, and the celebration of Asian Heritage Month. She indicated to those present that her great passion was community service. She went on to introduce her husband and someone at our table jokingly observed that "behind every active service woman is a patient man."

The evening then proceeded with opening speeches by local politicians, cultural performances by a traditional Korean dance troupe and a musician playing a Chinese opera instrument, a keynote speech, and an awards ceremony. U.S. Congresswoman Eddie Bernice Johnson, an African American Democrat, noted that DFW AACC demonstrates and fosters Asians working together. When Kenny Marchant, an Anglo and Republican Congressman from the 24th District of Texas, spoke, he mentioned that the "Asian American community is an important part of the Texas fabric." Republican Congressman Pete Sessions, also a guest at India Nite one year, noted approvingly that Asians were beginning to run for and get elected to office. Observing that many companies in the DFW region were strong trading partners across Asia, Sessions suggested that the local Asian community could reinforce this trade by maintaining their ties with family and friends in their home countries. He also suggested that the people sitting in the room were those who might best disseminate the ideas of freedom and opportunity that characterize America. His speech suggested that Asians in America could be the "face" of our country, a "voice of reason" telling others that "America is their friend." Sessions was embracing those present as Americans, but also recognizing their transnational reach and hence calling on them to be ambassadors for the United States. The one Asian politician who spoke during the opening remarks was Joe Chow, an immigrant from Taiwan who at the time was the newly elected Mayor of Addison, Texas. He talked about how tough his political race had been but indicated that with perseverance he had succeeded. He was a key leader in a key role.[23]

By the time keynote speaker Texas State Representative Hubert Vo was introduced, people had finished their meals. Mentioned in previous chapters because of his prominence as a Vietnamese elected official, Vo is a successful businessman in the Houston area who attended college at the University of Houston. He is a Democrat and was first elected in 2004 from Texas District 149 in West Houston. He won reelection in 2006, 2008, and 2010. Vo began his remarks by referring to the important role of DFW AACC in building alliances, fostering prosperity, and opening doors to opportunity. Noting that Asians constituted a "young community" in America, he nevertheless proposed three goals for them: economic prosperity, the preservation of culture, and political participation. Vo then launched into an autobiographical narrative of his immigration experience, telling the crowd about his arrival as a Vietnamese refugee in 1975 with no knowledge of English, and describing the cultural dislocation and discrimination he faced. He came to America, he said, "with little more than the shirt on my back" and he observed that it was through the "grace and generosity of neighbors who opened their arms" that he was able to find the opportunity to work hard and achieve the American Dream. "The American Dream should belong to all," Vo continued. "America gave us the opportunity to work hard, and we did. We built businesses, we introduced our culture in the places where we lived." Vo called on his audience to be proactive as individuals and as a group—to get involved, to participate in such organizations as chambers of commerce. He also urged them to be vigilant in preserving their cultures, in teaching their children and reminding them where they come from.

Vo expressed pride in a newcomer group that had accomplished so much, including entering a range of professions and raising children who are valedictorians and studying at major universities. Although the goal of economic prosperity has been attained by many Asians, Vo told the audience, it is in the political realm that more efforts are needed. He said that he and Mayor Chow had opened the doors for Asians in Texas and that they are a population poised to take off politically. However, given their population numbers, Asians are underrepresented in politics and the level of participation is, he argued, minimal. They must "repay the kindness and generosity" they have received here, he said, and they have "the right and obligation to take their seat at the table of politics." He said that Asians must get to know their elected officials, adding that "we will support elected officials who best represent our values." Hubert Vo ended his inspiring speech by returning to autobiography and talking about his own core values; he is pro-faith (he emphasized the religious value of "living in harmony with others" taught by Moses, Allah, Buddha, and Jesus), pro-education, pro-civil rights, and pro-business. He reminded the audience that success depends on "values, education, and hard work."

Vo's autobiographical approach in his speech reflects his having adopted discursive strategies that are common in American political life. Politicians and political candidates use personal histories and "narratives of belonging" (Duranti 2006) to connect with audiences and to explain their motivations for entering public service.[24] He linked his own story of being a Vietnamese refugee with the values and goals of the other Asian Americans at the banquet and of Americans in general. The newcomers to a community of practice are learning from the life stories of banquet speakers like Vo what Etienne Wenger (1998: 156) calls the "paradigmatic trajectories" of "old-timers" who have moved closer to the center of American public life. We have seen these techniques before in the context of other banquets—for example, those sponsored by the IAFC, discussed in Chapter 4.

After Vo's speech, various awards were presented. The Pioneer Award was given to a well-known leader in the Taiwanese Chinese community. Another award went to the Korean American Coalition to recognize their work in voter registration. The banquet chairperson commented how important it is to explain the electoral process to immigrants. At the end, all of the new board members were called up and sworn in by Judge Karen Johnson of Dallas County, who was born in Tokyo to a Japanese American mother and a father of Polish ancestry and is the first (and only) Asian American judge in Dallas County.

This banquet brought together many constituencies across a range of Asian ethnicities. As a ritual, it reinforced the solidarity of the Asian population, despite its many divisions. At the same time, it also reinforced the dominance of Chinese and Korean social actors in the political sphere, even as Vietnamese participants in particular were gaining prominence in the organization. Indians remain somewhat marginal to the DFW AACC in comparison with East and Southeast Asian groups, undoubtedly because they really do not have a well-developed sense of Asian identity and because they have so many of their own organizations through which to make their civic and political presence visible and heard. As we noted in Chapter 2, an Asian identity is not easily adopted by many first-generation Vietnamese and Indian newcomers who are not directly engaged in political activities. The DFW AACC banquet, which was held in Dallas, also reinforced the dominance of that city as a center of pan-Asian power that was eclipsing the activities of other groups in Fort Worth and Tarrant County (where Chinese and Koreans are less visible and the Vietnamese and Filipino populations dominate). The banquet can be viewed, therefore, both as a "model of" the current regime of Asian pan-ethnicity in this region, one dominated by East Asians, and as a "model for" greater unity and joint political activism.

Although the DFW AACC has many programs that specifically train youth and adults in leadership and political participation, the annual banquet is a more symbolic and expressive spectacle that highlights the political and civic weight of the Asian population and offers them an occasion to interact with elected officials. As Hubert Vo emphasized, the educational and economic strength of the Asian population is evident and growing, and hence the time for greater political clout is close at hand. The 2008 election for state representative in the Dallas area that pitted Republican Angie Chen Button (the 2005 DFW AAC banquet chair) against Democrat Sandra VuLe reinforced Vo's assessment and offers a strong indication of the emerging political participation of Asians in the region.

From Festivals and Banquets to Civic Participation

It is quite evident that as the Vietnamese, Indian, and other Asian immigrant populations become established in the United States, they use festivals and banquets as vehicles for communicating their growing economic and political importance to what they regard as the mainstream. The fact that these events, and others that we have described in previous chapters, occur at hubs of prominent commercial activity, as well as on major university campuses in the area, is itself a statement of civic presence. The decision by the two VACs to hold the Tet Festival at Traders Village, a venue frequented by a broad range of people, rather than at an Asian shopping mall, was clearly made with the goal of enhancing both the civic and economic visibility of Vietnamese among the general population. The location of the DFW AACC banquet at the Galleria, well-known as a high-end shopping mall in Dallas, also signals the use of public spaces as sites for emplacement and claims of belonging. Holding India Nite at the largest private university in Dallas also demonstrates a strategy of linking up with centers of power and influence in the region.

We have argued in this chapter that festivals and banquets have much in common with other forms of political ritual. In the cases we have described here, we found patterns of behavior and formats that were repeated from one year to the next. In the case of banquets, this includes adopting a theme and celebrating the achievements of particular individuals as role models of leadership. Included in all the events were displays of flags and other patriotic symbols. Through these events, the prominence of particular organizations within the broader public sphere is enhanced, civic and political legitimacy are established, and networks of solidarity are forged. We have also argued that these events offer excellent examples of "civic engagement in an expressive context" and, by extension, cultural citizenship. Both Vietnamese and Indian immigrants hope to retain subsequent generations' interest in their cultural roots, while at the same time claiming space in the wider public sphere. The Tet Festival and India Nite both work toward these goals. Guest speakers praise these dual identities and emphasize the contributions that Asian American populations can make in helping to build global bridges.

The Tet Festival and India Nite, as community celebrations that establish the civic presence of their respective sponsoring populations, have much in common, but we have also pointed out some subtle differences. India Nite is a new tradition invented in the immigrant context; the Tet Festival is a traditional Vietnamese celebration that has been transported and adapted to the immigrant context. As they do in the other Vietnamese communities of practice described in this book, the tensions of homeland politics can also emerge in the context of the Tet Festival, even though such tensions are minimized in contacts with audiences outside the ethnic group in order to display a more unified image. The Tet Festival exhibits the religious syncretism mentioned in Chapter 3, with its altar that includes symbols of ancestor worship that speak to both Catholics and Buddhists and thereby bring people together as Vietnamese across religions. Many symbols related to the refugee experience (including the freedom and heritage flag) also draw people together in spite of their disagreements about how best to respond to homeland issues. By contrast, no religious symbols are present at India Nite and no references are made to homeland politics. As in other Indian communities of practice described in this book, the religio-political divisions that characterize the Indian homeland are controlled and submerged in India Nite to present a unified community both to themselves and to the outsiders who are invited to be present and whose very presence reinforces the civic and political weight of the Indian immigrant community both locally and nationally. Both festivals, in other words, are characterized by important political activities, but they take different forms.

The DFW AACC banquet is primarily an event for a particular subset of Asians—those who are most educated and have professional jobs. They come together with the dual purpose of furthering the interests of Asian Americans in the United States and contributing to U.S. society through participatory citizenship that includes both informal civic engagement and more formal political engagement. Vietnamese and Indian individuals who have been drawn into the community of practice of this pan-Asian organization attend the banquet and there participate on a different plane of the civic sphere than they do when attending either the Tet Festival or India Nite. As we have noted, they are less visible in the DFW AACC than other Asians, but those who do attend certainly learn about the merits and strategic purposes of pan-Asian collective action.

6 Pathways to Wider Participation

MUCH OF THE DISCUSSION in this book so far has centered on the first generation of immigrants and the communities of practice they have established in order to develop civic skills and enhance participatory citizenship. In this chapter we turn to sites that may have more direct implications for subsequent generations, even though members of the first generation are involved in the cases and stories we discuss. Communities of practice, according to Lave and Wenger (1991), are sites for both teaching and learning. It is therefore useful to differentiate between a *teaching curriculum* and a *learning curriculum* in communities of practice—with the former "structuring resources for learning" through an instructor's participation, and the latter evolving "out of participation in a specific community of practice" (47). Although most of the communities of practice that we have already discussed focus on a learning curriculum, there are other contexts in which a teaching curriculum is more obvious and where the development of social networks and leadership skills is an explicit goal of the activity.

We begin this chapter with a discussion of deliberate forms of leadership training fostered by pan-Asian chambers of commerce and an Asian leadership forum aimed at young professionals that has a strong teaching curriculum. These are, we suggest, communities of practice in a business context, with outcomes for the development of both workplace and broader civic skills. We then turn to spheres in which Indian and Vietnamese American youth are participating in what are often viewed as mainstream cultural spectacles (beauty pageants and spelling bees) that also illustrate communities of practice with a teaching curriculum. Finally, we end this chapter with the civic engagement narratives of four people who have come to participate in activities and organizations that extend beyond immigrant-group-based associational life. These individuals are in a sense developing their own forms of both teaching and learning curricula.

Learning Civic Skills in Pan-Asian Contexts

As discussed in Chapter 2, members of the younger generation of college-age youth who participated in the group interviews were more comfortable with pan-ethnic categories than the Vietnamese and Indian parents we interviewed, who expressed ambivalence about Asian and Asian American identities. However, in our interviews with adult community leaders from both groups, and in our observations at events such as the banquet described in the last chapter, we found many individuals who embrace pan-Asian ethnicity. These leaders, many of whom are also active in ethnic associations, viewed pan-Asian associations as strategic arenas within which to extend their social networks, as organizations that provide them access to economic and political resources, and as an alternative platform on which to engage with the dominant American society and be recognized.

The meaning of *pan-ethnicity* for political mobilization is a question frequently raised in the context of Asian American studies. Sociologist Yen Le Espiritu (1992: 6) has argued that pan-ethnicity is "an imposed category [that] ignores subgroup boundaries, lumping together diverse peoples in a single expanded 'ethnic' framework." She acknowledges, however, that pan-ethnicity can also be a political resource for insiders through which they can mobilize into groups that are "products of political and social processes, rather than of cultural bonds" (1992: 13). We find it particularly important to discuss how Indians and Vietnamese, as Asian newcomers, learn to use pan-Asian networks to engage the broader business and civic environment of the DFW region that we profiled in Chapter 1. One way they do this is through participation in Asian-American business chambers of commerce.

Learning to Network: Pan-Asian Chambers of Commerce

In the DFW region there are three pan-Asian chambers of commerce that foster business cooperation: the Greater Dallas Asian American Chamber of Commerce (GDAACC), the U.S. Pan-Asian American Chamber of Commerce—Southwest (USPAACC-SW), and the Tarrant County Asian American Chamber of Commerce (TCAACC).[1] The GDAACC, which boasts on its Web site of being the largest Asian Chamber of Commerce in the United States, emerged in 1986 from an organization called the Asian American Voters Coalition, whose mission was to foster greater political participation among Asians in the DFW region. From this starting point of having a largely political mission the organization moved to having an economic mission—a change instigated by the development of the Asian Trade District in 1995.[2]

According to the executive director (who at the time of our research was of Japanese heritage), the mission of GDAACC is twofold: "to promote business within the Asian American community by providing a place where people can network among themselves and expand their business connections," and "to introduce Asian American business into the 'mainstream.'" Toward these ends, the GDAACC sponsors a job fair to match skilled Asian American workers with employers, a leadership forum to train emerging Asian American leaders, and several "social mixers." The leadership forums cover such topics as Asian American stereotypes and political engagement, as well as facilitate networking between members of the second generation and the city manager, mainstream CEOs, and those employed by multinational companies. "We are interested," the GDAACC executive director said in an interview, "in developing future civic, business, and political leaders."

The chairmanship of the GDAACC board of directors rotates from one national group to another and at least sixteen Asian populations are represented on the board. The approximately 1,200 members are largely businesspeople from across the range of Asian populations in the DFW area. Half of the members are corporations or work for corporations, the other half are small business owners looking for ways to expand their customer base or reach beyond their own communities. The largest groups are Chinese, Koreans, Indians, and Filipinos. One past president of the India Association of North Texas (IANT), a woman, served on the board of the GDAACC in 2006–2007. She was nominated by a Chinese woman who had been serving on the board. Although she admitted that participating in GDAACC events is not a high priority for Indians because there are so many other Indian associations with which to be involved,[3] she said she had agreed to serve because she thought it was an organization that would help extend the community's "mainstream involvement." She viewed the GDAACC as having that concern for Asians in general. She observed that key mainstream community leaders are invited to the four big events that the GDAACC sponsors (the installation of leaders, the Asian Festival, the Education Banquet, and the Awards Banquet), "so that we get press coverage and acceptance." Emphasizing that the real goal is to gain acceptance in the broader community, she observed, "We [Asians] all look different in some way to the whites. That keeps us on the outside. We want to show people that we are not so different. It is an educational effort, and a slow one at that." She went on to note that the GDAACC meets once a year with members of the Hispanic and African American chambers of commerce. They are the two largest minorities in the area, she observed, and "we want to learn from them, how they learned to cope with discrimination in business and in the community. We do feel a sense of attachment with them. I guess we are all 'not white.'"

The executive director of the GDAACC noted that the Vietnamese, despite their size in the Dallas area, are not as active in this chamber, although they do attend the Asian Festival that the GDAACC sponsors. The Vietnamese in Tarrant County are, however, very active in the two Asian chambers of commerce located there—the USPAACC-SW and the TCAACC. The USPAACC-SW is headed by a Vietnamese Chinese businesswoman who had previously held office in the GDAACC and aims to help promote Asian American-owned businesses. The USPAACC-SW was founded in 2001 and serves 1,300 businesses. It is a regional affiliate of the national USPAACC, founded in 1994 and based in Washington, D.C. The USPAACC-SW is based in Arlington. It holds an annual Asian Business Expo and hosts the Asian American Women's Business Roundtable to enhance leadership development and networking among women. One of its major roles is to help Asian-owned businesses get certified as such in order to procure corporate and government contracts aimed at minority businesses.

The TCAACC has a longer history. It was founded by a former Vietnamese refugee in 1990. Its offices are in the Fort Worth International Center in downtown Fort Worth. At the time of our research, its president was a successful Philippine-born businessman. Previous presidents have been natives of India, Laos, Vietnam, and the Philippines. Although a range of ethnic origins are represented on the executive board, the leadership has historically been dominated by Filipinos and Vietnamese. Although there is Indian involvement, there is far less East Asian (Chinese, Taiwanese, Korean) participation in the TCAACC than in the GDAACC—most likely a function of the residential settlement patterns of these various Asian populations. According to one former officer of the TCAACC, its bylaws stipulate that in order to keep a good balance among the diverse Asians involved, no one ethnic group can have more than 25 percent representation on the executive board. In recent years, officers of the Vietnamese American Community (VAC) of Tarrant County have also held office in the TCAACC, and there are close ties between the two associations (as there are between the IANT and the GDAACC). They work together each fall on the Asian Arts Egg Roll Festival and Health Fair, which provides free health screening and medical support to the community. In 2006 this event was held at the large Vietnamese Catholic Church in Arlington. It later moved, as did the Tet Festival, to Traders Village. The president of the TCAACC was a familiar figure at most activities of the VAC. According to 2005 figures, there are approximately three hundred members of TCAACC, which views its mission as offering business support, community education, economic development, civic responsibility, and cultural education. In addition to the health fair, the TCAACC holds an annual Asian Recognition and Scholarship Awards banquet.

One former member of the TCAACC's executive board (who is not ethnically Vietnamese) described the mission of the group as being like the "three legs of a stool—business, culture, and education." In his comments on the TCAACC's two dominant ethnic groups, he mentioned that "Filipinos are classically known for blending in" and attributed this to the fact that the Philippines was once a territory of the United States. The Vietnamese, in contrast, "don't blend in as well, maybe by choice." He also felt that politically they were "a force to reckon with" and that their ability to work together on activities like the Tet Festival was "amazing." "No politician can ignore them," he said. On the basis of his observations while working in the TCAACC's pan-Asian setting, this college-educated professional felt strongly that "Asian Americans have to put aside their differences and come together or they will be marginalized." He had viewed, however, the barriers to this at close range and noted that "Asian Americans don't trust other [Asian] ethnic groups; they tend to work together, so that it is difficult to get Chinese, Japanese, and Filipinos, for example, to work together." When asked why a person would join an Asian American chamber of commerce, he replied that there were two models: corporations joined "to fulfill a diversity goal and also to get a pool for talent in Asian businesses," and individuals joined to network and to take advantage of funding opportunities (grants and scholarships) offered by the TCAACC. He noted that the computer lab in the VAC community center was funded by a grant from the TCAACC.

Our research on the role that these organizations play in the lives of Asian Americans in DFW, including Vietnamese and Indian leaders, reinforces the findings of previous researchers that pan-Asian organizations often emerge to address matters of mutual concern, including job discrimination, media stereotypes, and broader economic and political interests (Vo 1996). They act as "mobilizing structures" that also provide services for group members and hence "strengthen communities by increasing self-sufficiency and education" (Okamoto 2006: 3). It is in this latter capacity that organizations like the business chambers of commerce we have discussed here serve as communities of practice providing Asian newcomers with the skills and opportunities to engage the broader public sphere while also enhancing their economic power. They are both similar to and distinct from the religious and ethnic associations discussed earlier in this book. All of these organizations offer opportunities for civic engagement, but the chambers of commerce more forthrightly emphasize that they are teaching future civic, business, and political leaders. As such, they reflect the growing recognition among immigrant leaders that more emphasis on the development of civic and leadership skills is necessary for Asian Americans to gain greater economic and political power as individuals and as a group. The teaching of such skills is also apparent in the multitude of leadership forums aimed at Asian adults and youth that are sponsored by various DFW-area organizations.

Learning to Lead: The Asian American Leadership Institute

The increasing number of leadership forums, many of which we attended to conduct ethnographic research, suggests how important the phenomenon of "learning to lead" is to new immigrants. One example that illustrates leadership training in the context of pan-Asian networking at the national level is the Asian American Leadership Institute, first held at a DFW-area community college in 2001. It has been held on area college campuses each year since then.[4]

The Asian American Leadership Institute is sponsored by the Asian American Forum, a nonprofit organization whose goal is "to have more, better trained Asian American leaders and stronger Asian American organizations in the political, community and professional arenas of Dallas/Fort Worth."[5] The Asian American Forum's founder and president is a Japanese American businessman who is also a retired development officer from a local public university and a community leader active in local politics. The Forum's board of directors has included Chinese, Korean, Filipino, Indian, and Vietnamese members. In addition to local corporate sponsors—including, over the years, Texas Instruments, State Farm Insurance, and Raytheon—one of the major sponsors of this event is LEAP—Leadership Education for Asian Pacifics.[6] LEAP is a nonprofit organization based in Los Angeles that provides leadership and civic participation workshops and forums for corporations, nonprofits, and universities, as well as for Asian American organizations specifically. It was founded in 1982 by J. D. Hokoyama, who runs two workshops at the Asian American Leadership Institute—one called Understanding Your Core Values, the other called The 21st Century Leader.[7]

The Asian American Leadership Institute is a day-long event, generally held on a Saturday. The registration fee is modest, and free tickets are sent to Asian student organizations. The officers of the Vietnamese Student Association of a local public university attended as a group in 2005. Most of the attendees are professional employees of local companies (such as Texas Instruments and Raytheon) who were encouraged to attend by their employers. In the two years that we attended, the Institute's morning schedule consisted of one large general session followed by four concurrent workshops. Another general session was followed by three more concurrent afternoon sessions, then a networking reception with some light refreshments in the lobby. The Institute followed a corporate training model and provided participants in each session with a Certificate of Completion to verify their attendance.

In 2004, the first speaker of the day was a South Korean immigrant who came to DFW with his parents as a child. He became a three-term elected member of his town's school board. The title of his speech was "Leadership in Elective Office." He spoke of his own experiences, his core values, and of the issues he had dealt with in his position on the school board. He told the audience that leadership is a "learned behavior" that can be acquired by stepping into roles and studying others who have learned to lead. Everyone, he suggested, has the potential "to be the greatest general." The talk was intended to inspire more involvement in both Asian organizations and the wider community. This presenter ended by telling his audience that if they wanted to be heard they needed to get involved.

The luncheon keynote speaker that day was the executive director of the Japanese American Citizens League in San Francisco. His talk was titled "Asian Americans: The Road Ahead." He started by tracing the history of struggles against discrimination among Japanese and Chinese immigrants. He reinforced the need for pan-Asian organizing and discussed the changing demographics of Asians in the United States, noting that Texas has one of the highest populations of Asians.

A former Vietnamese refugee and leadership consultant based in Houston who arrived in the United States as a child was another presenter. During the 2004 and 2005 Institutes he did workshops on business etiquette and on both public presentations and interpersonal conversations at work. In one session he told the assembled participants that those he called "APs" (Asian Pacifics) tend to be shy. In his workshop, participants were encouraged to work in groups and practice the exercises he presented. Electronic "clickers," which are becoming increasingly common in college classrooms, were used in one session to gauge participants' knowledge of proper etiquette.[8] The presenter stressed the importance of making eye contact and shaking hands, and had participants practice this with one another. There was a whole lesson on handshaking that included the admonition to have a handshake "that is firm, but painless; supersize it with a smile and eye contact; it starts and stops crisply, lasts no longer than two to three seconds, no more than two to three pumps."

In his session called Understanding Your Cultural Values, the founder of LEAP stressed, as had other speakers, that "leaders are made" and that "people can develop skills; it is not talent but choice." The workshop aimed to, as he put it, help participants learn to be "comfortable as Asian, to be comfortable in the community." Participants were divided into groups and given a large sheet of paper and a marker to use to brainstorm various elements of cultural values. Topics included what it means to be comfortable with yourself, perceptions of Asians, and the origins of these perceptions. The groups also generated lists of early messages they had received from their parents, including respect for elders, work before play, don't embarrass your family, be helpful, save money, be humble, and don't waste your rice—a comment that was met with laughter but also recognition. Here we see *rice* as a metaphor binding together the participants from different Asian groups. The leader of the workshop shared the philosophy "keep your values but learn new skills." He suggested that understanding the values of one's culture and how one's behaviors are perceived by others allows for intervention so that Asians can, as he put it, "help others understand APA [Asian Pacific American] values" and "develop new skills to be more effective in the mainstream."

Other sessions focused on fostering collaboration and on media access. The audience was told that, in comparison with Hispanics and African Americans, Asians have been silent. They need to learn to speak out, to say, "Look at me," one speaker suggested. In 2005, a session on networking offered by an Indian American member of the Network Centric Systems North Texas Engineering Leadership Team emphasized the power of connections, of doing more than just meeting expectations, of keeping values but changing perceptions, and of personal branding. This presenter spoke about the need to overcome passivity (the tendency to not want to disagree) and move out of an Asian comfort zone of "sticking with the technical." Management, he argued, "has breadth."

Participants in the Asian American Leadership Institute engage in a community of practice in which Asian immigrants, including some Vietnamese and Indians, teach and learn civic skills and confront ways to negotiate cultural barriers to successful leadership in the American public sphere. Whereas the other spaces for citizenship practices that we discuss in this book do not have the overt intention of teaching these skills, forums such as this one do. Adults are encouraged to develop leadership abilities so that they can serve their communities better as advocates and organizers, as well as pursue their own personal career advancement and break through barriers for Asians interested in moving into management positions (Fernandez 2001).[9] They are also encouraged to confront cultural difference, to learn about American approaches to leadership and management, and to serve as role models for their own children. The decision to hold the Asian American Leadership Institute on various college and university campuses rather than in commercial spaces (hotels, convention centers) may be a cost-saving measure, but it also underscores—indeed symbolizes quite powerfully—the desire of Asian Americans to learn about and acquire the skills that will move them into leadership positions in their communities, at their places of employment, and in the larger civic sphere. The location also speaks to the importance of outreach to college-age youth.

From Beauty Pageants to Spelling Bees: Formal and Informal Spheres for Youth Participation

The communities of practice presented so far offer activities oriented toward adults, but there are also communities of practice specifically aimed at youth, where a *teaching curriculum* is emphasized. An example is the Asian American Leadership and Education Conference for high school students of Asian background that is held each year on a local college campus. Such activities, however, are not always organized for those of pan-Asian ethnicity. The Vietnamese in particular have organized many youth leadership programs for Vietnamese youth. One of these is the Vietnamese Culture and Science Association's annual youth leadership summer camp, where high school- and college-age youth are exposed to panel discussions on leadership; presentations by prominent Vietnamese figures in business, the arts, and politics; and team-building activities. Such a route to broader participation emphasizes the specific culture and heritage of the Vietnamese as a way to instill self-confidence in youth who, it is hoped, will go on to participate in wider spheres. This approach indicates that pathways toward wider participation are not always based on a pan-Asian model.

The children of immigrants also learn to engage with the wider civic sphere through cultural activities based on teaching curricula that take them in new directions. In addition to engaging in formal school settings, in which youth are exposed to explicit teaching about American government and public life and to implicit learning through their peers, many youth are also involved in cultural activities that provide alternative pathways to participation in the broader

American society. Although youth leadership forums are perhaps the settings in which participatory citizenship is most explicitly taught, the cultural landscapes of Vietnamese and Indians include several other important event-based sites for engagement in the civic sphere that are not explicitly connected to politics or formal organizations. There is, for example, a Vietnamese youth song and dance troupe (whose leader, Binh, is profiled later in this chapter) called Kids Help Kids that performs at major ethnic festivals and banquets and emphasizes volunteer work and civic engagement.

Another example of the growing civic presence of Vietnamese in the DFW region is beauty pageants. The daughter of Vietnamese refugees recently held the title National American Miss Texas Teen, a competition in which the vast majority of contestants are Anglo Americans, with African American and Hispanic girls following. At the summer 2008 pageant, held at a major conference hotel in the northern suburbs of Dallas, this Vietnamese American girl and her Anglo co-queen (two girls, representing two divisions, are chosen each year) were at the end of their reign and ready to confer the title on two new girls. Each girl presented a video of her reigning year. The Anglo girl spoke of her Christian faith and her missionary work in Canada. The Vietnamese girl, the child of refugees and a Buddhist, did not mention her religion but did speak of her volunteer work in the Vietnamese community. (An image of the freedom and heritage flag was shown briefly in one shot.) She plans a career in media and sees CNN reporter Betty Nguyen (originally from Arlington, Texas) as an important role model. She explained to us that her involvement in beauty pageants is a way to get scholarship money and learn composure on public stages.

There are a host of classical dance schools to which Indian parents send their children, particularly their daughters. These schools have become lucrative businesses for those who run them. The dancers perform at various Indian functions throughout the city, including India Nite and an annual Indian festival in downtown Dallas, co-sponsored by the Crow Collection for Asian Art, as well as at international functions such as the international festivals sponsored by local suburban communities or by the citywide organization DFW International Community Alliance. Although we ourselves have never witnessed the daughter of a local Indian family participating in a beauty pageant,[10] an Asian Indian youth won the 2003 Scripps National Spelling Bee at age thirteen, and a second, at age nine, tied for third place the same year.[11] Both boys were honored at the annual banquet of the Indian American Friendship Council and received monetary prizes to recognize their academic excellence. The younger boy is the only son of two immigrants from Gujarat. His mother homeschools her son and is his full partner in his quest to win spelling bees. The success that Indian students have had in this particular arena is reported in the pages of newspapers such as *India Abroad* but also in the "mainstream" press. Garnering this kind of recognition is another way to claim civic space on both the local and national stages. As one Indian tellingly commented to a reporter, it is "a matter of pride to see if one of our own can win this quintessential American competition" (Pais 2006). Beauty pageants and spelling bees are communities of practice that facilitate learning and visible engagement in the public sphere on the part of the children of immigrants. In addition, they are arenas where youth can participate in spheres beyond the family and in the cultural and religious institutions that are associated with immigrant ethnic identities. In this way, they provide pathways to wider civic engagement.

Civic Engagement Narratives

At many public events of Indians and Vietnamese immigrants, as we have discussed, particular individuals are set up as role models for attendees. These individuals often share their stories of how they entered the public sphere and become more engaged in American civic life. In the final section of this chapter we focus on four individuals—two Vietnamese Americans and two Indian immigrants—who have found ways to participate in spheres beyond their own ethnic group or to make the leap toward formal political engagement. Collectively, these stories illustrate various points of entry to active involvement in the American civic sphere, as well as the different opportunities and interests that are pursued. Each person demonstrates a strong desire to contribute to the local community or to the broader society. Two men and two women are profiled; three are first-generation immigrants and one is the son of Vietnamese refugees and hence a member of the second generation.

Binh N.

Some newcomers use their ethnic base as a foundation on which to build connections to institutions beyond their own immigrant group. A good example of this is Binh N., an Amerasian woman who through her own community service helps younger people to learn about civic engagement—and in some sense launch her own teaching curriculum. Binh was born in 1974 and arrived in the United States with her mother and three siblings in 1991 when she was seventeen years old. She completed high school in the United States. Her mother and Vietnamese stepfather now live with her and her husband in a spacious contemporary home in Tarrant County. As a child, she grew up on a farm in a rural area of South Vietnam. She always loved to sing. "I would sing," she said, "as I was working in the fields cutting rice." After high school, she intended to become a teacher and did some university work toward a degree. Dynamic, attractive, and a talented performer, she got involved in beauty pageants and in 1994 won an Asian pageant in Texas. She has been singing and performing locally since 1994. Binh speaks fluent English with a slight Texas accent. She says that given her looks (her father was Caucasian) she is often mistaken for a Latina by those who do not know she is Vietnamese. She is aware that she "always looks different" and she has always wanted to fit in.

Binh and her husband are part of a well-known musical act in the DFW region. They perform at weddings and other events. Binh is Roman Catholic and her husband is Buddhist. She considers herself "very open-minded about religion." She and her husband perform at both churches and temples, and she teaches Vietnamese classes at both institutions. They have a young son, a toddler at the time of our interview with her. Binh works at two jobs, one in a bank and one in real estate, in addition to their performance work; her husband works in engineering and is also pursuing a graduate degree in management sciences. On top of this, Binh sponsors a song and dance troupe for Vietnamese youth that performs at various festivals and other events. The troupe is a non-profit organization dedicated to community service and to leadership training for the youth who are involved.

Binh is very knowledgeable about traditional Vietnamese folk and popular music and about the music that appeals to the younger generation of Vietnamese youth born in the United States. She sees her youth performance group as a means of building a vital bridge between the generations through the medium of music. The goals of the group, as she articulated them, are "to enrich our culture, to encourage the youth to value higher education, and to help unfortunate children." The group was founded in 2004 and is composed of youth ages seventeen to twenty-four. Binh and her husband compose routines for the performers that combine traditional Vietnamese folk music with remixes and hip-hop. She sees these routines as "two cultures combined." Binh also sees the group as serving "kids born here [in the United States] and those born over there [in Vietnam]. We try to bring them together, to blend them."

There are several interesting features of the structure of this organization that promote community service and leadership skills. Binh has a strict policy mandating that those who are in the group must meet certain standards of school achievement (grade point average) and perform community service. Each person must go through a one-year trial period before becoming a member of the group. It should be considered a privilege to be part of this group, she feels. The youth also help to raise funds for the group by soliciting sponsorship from local businesses. They must volunteer at least twenty hours a year at charity organizations such as Habitat for Humanity, the Red Cross, the local women's shelter, the local homeless shelter, and so on. The group raised funds for Hurricane Katrina victims. In addition, when needs are brought to her attention, Binh mobilizes her group to help. For example, they have helped move an older African American couple whose house was condemned, and a family with a handicapped child. The troupe also sponsors "forgotten angels" on the Christmas tree at the Vietnamese community center. (Forgotten angels are angel-shaped paper ornaments on which are listed the presents that particular poor children wish to receive. Each child's age is included. Several American charity groups, including the Salvation Army, use these ornaments to elicit donations of these presents.) The group also works with Toys for Tots to donate toys to poor Vietnamese families. Binh said that the group "is not limited in who it helps by race or color, but our focus is on children as the priority."

The group recently received the President's Volunteer Service Award from the President's Council on Service and Civic Participation, established by President George W. Bush in 2003. According to Binh, her troupe was the first Vietnamese group to receive this award. They had learned about it through the company for whom her husband works.

Binh feels strongly that it is important to help the younger generation— "you need to move them." During her training as a teacher, she noticed a difference between teachers in the United States and those in Vietnam. In Vietnam, teachers were "equals to or even more important than parents," whereas in the United States, according to Binh, teachers tend to keep their distance from students. Binh wanted a role that was different from each of these—to be close to her young mentees but to encourage them to develop their own leadership skills through participation in the dance troupe. The troupe is coordinated by a board composed of youth from the troupe. Although Binh serves as the troupe's president, the members vote yes or no on all initiatives.

Binh considers herself to be part of the bridging generation between those of the first generation and those who were born in the United States, and she referred to the "gap" between them. Binh connects with both Buddhists and Catholics; she moves easily between boundaries and labels. She is also interested in bridging cultures, an interest that she sees as connected to her status as an Amerasian woman. Her work as a youth mentor is a key example of the contributions that Vietnamese immigrants are making, in a way that serves both the ethnic group—by developing leadership skills among its youth and help-ing to keep the musical traditions of Vietnam alive by providing entertainment for members of the population—and the host society—by offering it services provided by volunteers and by exposing to new hybrid musical performances.

Tho V.

Many of the 1.5- and second-generation Vietnamese American youth we in-terviewed for our research participate in ethnically based associations, such as Vietnamese student organizations and youth groups at their church or temple. Several of the Vietnamese American youth we interviewed are involved in the Rotaract chapter on the campus of a large public university. Rotaract is the young-adult (ages eighteen to thirty) branch of Rotary International. Tho V. is one of those students. When he was interviewed, he was serving both as vice president of Rotaract and as president of the Asian Students Association (ASA) at his university. Tho has been active in civic activities and associations since he was a high school student. Born in the United States to refugee parents who had fled Saigon in 1975, Tho was twenty-two years old and majoring in electri-cal engineering when he was interviewed. His family settled first in Louisiana, where he was born, but moved to the DFW region in 1998. He comes from a large extended family and is the youngest of ten children. As the youngest, Tho benefits from the support of this large family and the economic resources they have acquired. He also feels a great deal of obligation to them. Although he might have liked to attend university elsewhere, Tho decided to attend a school near his home and live with his parents and a sister who is a single mother so he could help his parents, who still struggle with language barriers and have long depended on their children for translation help in their daily lives. Tho's father, now retired, worked in construction; his mother still works in a small textile factory. One married sister, who lives in Louisiana, has become wealthy through ownership of a gas station and has purchased land both in the United States and in Vietnam. She has assisted others in the family and bought Tho a new car as a high school graduation gift. He is aware that she may still be paying off the loan for that car.

There were several influences on Tho's involvement with clubs and civic activities. In high school, he said, he got "bored with just academics." A Viet-namese teacher of calculus and algebra played a significant role in encouraging his involvement. As Tho explained, he and the teacher "shared the experience" of being Vietnamese, so the teacher encouraged him. In high school, Tho be-came a member of the National Honor Society, the French Club, the Academic

Decathlon, and Quiz League. He also became involved in Interact (the high school branch of the Rotary Club) and through that activity got to know an adult member of the Rotary Club, who became a mentor to him. This man is Mexican American and owns a local business. He eventually hired Tho to work at his store, which he did for a while.

Through his involvement in Interact, Tho was led to attend a leadership training program called the Rotary Youth Leadership Awards (RYLA). According to Rotary International's Web site, "RYLA emphasizes leadership, citizenship, and personal growth."[12] The leadership program was a sleepover camp held for one week in Fort Worth. Tho received a scholarship to attend it. There were about fifty students at the camp, and with the exception of Tho, one other Asian student, and one African American student, "the rest were Caucasian." The camp experience encouraged Tho and taught him about leadership. He feels he has grown as a leader since that time. As he said, "I took a personality test and learned that I get things done, but quietly—not the one to be standing up and telling people what to do." Now, he continued, "I'd be the one motivating the group."

When Tho arrived for college in the fall of 2002, he got involved in the ASA after he was approached by someone at the fall activities fair. "I wanted to be involved right away in some activity," Tho explained, because he had been active in clubs in high school. He did not identify himself as Asian, he said, until he entered college. During his earlier years he had associated mostly with other Vietnamese youth, at the Catholic Church and in school. Tho felt he had been drawn into the Asian American identity primarily through his participation in associations, starting with Interact and then through the ASA. Few of his high school peers were attending the local university, so the ASA was a way to meet people and "get involved." According to Tho, the ASA is "mostly a social group, with not much community service; it is a break from studying." The ASA at that time was, as reported by Tho, composed primarily of Chinese and Vietnamese students, but also included students with Korean, Taiwanese, and Japanese immigrant backgrounds. Tho was very aware of the geographic distribution of different Asian ethnic groups. He explained that whereas the Chinese students were from Plano, the Vietnamese students were primarily from Arlington, the Laotians were mostly from Fort Worth, and the Koreans were from Flower Mound. When asked about Asian Indians, Tho said there were none in the ASA, that "most [Indians on his campus] are international students," and they get more involved in the Indian Student Association.

Tho's involvement with the ASA led him to make some interesting observations about pan-Asian involvement. Not only was it "fun" to socialize with other Asian students but, he said, "Vietnamese is more limited, for politics or government issues. Also there are scholarships for Asians, but you never see a scholarship just for Vietnamese students." He attended a conference on Asian American issues at the university that convinced him that adopting an "Asian American" identity was a good strategic move. He felt that Vietnamese American youth could make better use of the Asian American identity than they currently do. He also observed that Vietnamese students who were what he called "Americanized" were more apt than students who joined the VSA to take part in the ASA. For Tho, taking on the Asian American identity was a symbol of being more Americanized than those who identified only as Vietnamese or even as Vietnamese American.

In contrast to the ASA, Rotaract is mainly a service organization. When Tho was vice president of Rotaract, the president also was Vietnamese. As Tho explained, Rotaract is sponsored by the Arlington Great Southwest Rotary Club, which meets at a local bank. At the time of our interview with Tho this Rotaract chapter was composed primarily of Vietnamese students. When asked if Vietnamese adults were involved in the Rotary Club, Tho said no and that although the Rotary members had approached him about starting one for Vietnamese adults, there was not enough interest to do so.[13] Rotaract does community service with the Rotary Club. For example, students will go to a nursing home to help celebrate residents' birthdays. Rotaract also became involved in relief for Hurricanes Katrina and Rita. At one point they were involved in raising money for a dental clinic in India, through an Indian student whose father was involved in that effort, but the student left the club, so they transferred the funds they had raised for the clinic to the hurricane relief effort.

Tho's experience demonstrates an interesting network of ties between student associations, such as ASA and VSA, on campus. It also shows the ways in which students in those associations, through their contacts with one another, engage in a dialogue about ethnic identity and develop forms of participatory citizenship. When asked if he was involved in the VSA, Tho said, not at all. He explained, "there has been dissention. Most of the ASA members who are Vietnamese were born here and are more Americanized, while the VSA members are more traditional. . . . It is my goal to try to mend the relationship between ASA and VSA."[14] The VSA, he felt, is more involved in activities related to the Vietnamese community, and although its membership has been shifting, many of its members were born in Vietnam. Just as Tho was a member of both Rotaract and the ASA, there were ties between the ASA and the VSA, because the vice president of the VSA at the time was also a member of the ASA. This has led to ties between the Vietnamese members and leaders of the VSA, the ASA, and Rotaract. Tho was involved in a joint project between Rotaract and the VSA in which UNICEF boxes for donations were taken door to door at Halloween. The students planned to visit different neighborhoods and to take along younger siblings who would go trick or treating. This collaboration was initiated by the president of VSA.

Perhaps due to his association with Rotary International, a business-oriented service organization, Tho sees clearly that "you need to network to make it in the business world. And this means going beyond the Vietnamese community." He plans to acquire a master's in business administration and eventually get business experience. For Tho, community involvement is important for "personal growth." As he put it, "in business, you need to have public speaking skills and know how to get contacts." Tho has also learned through being mentored himself that it is important to motivate other students to get involved in associations and activities. "I would want to stress that community involvement depends on your background. If there are people to push and promote them, then people will get involved. I try to encourage kids. I hear people complain and I ask them if they are in an organization. And if not, then they should get involved." In addition to his other activities, Tho has served as a mentor to a Chinese university student.

It is significant that Tho does not cite Vietnamese American leaders as instrumental in his development, and when asked he could identify no Vietnamese role models. He had just recently become aware, he said, of Texas State Representative Hubert Vo but was not involved much in politics (either domestic or homeland). His parents participate in the wider social sphere through the Catholic Church and, like many of the former refugees of the first generation who were interviewed for this study, do not get involved in ethnic associations beyond the religious sphere. As for political involvement and interest in events in Vietnam, Tho said, "It depends on how you were raised. My parents did not raise me to be focused on that, but they taught me moral issues, how to interact, how to behave." When asked about politics, Tho responded, "I steer away from choosing political parties. I want to remain open-minded." He is not active in politics but "would consider it" if someone approached him and encouraged him.

Tho is a young man living his life at the intersection of his origins as the child of Vietnamese refugees who still have little command of English and have devoted their lives to scraping together an income in working-class jobs to support their large family, and his current involvement with his studies in engineering and his association activities, influenced by both a Vietnamese and a non-Asian adult mentor, and by other students (non-Asian, Vietnamese, and from other

Asian backgrounds). At the time of the interview he had recently attended the Vietnamese American Society Conference Year One (VASCON), a forum held in Austin that emphasizes youth leadership. As had his experience at the RYLA camp in high school, VASCON provided important lessons in leadership for Tho, because he was exposed to other Vietnamese students who encouraged one another "to be more vocal, talk about opinions," and "spread the word" about issues. At his own university he had felt a bit isolated as a Vietnamese student who wanted to be civically engaged, and it was not easy to keep the momentum going in the campus clubs and associations. Tho attributed this inertia to a trend by which "a lot of the Vietnamese students are aiming at medical careers, and focused on getting into medical school, and leaving [campus] eventually." At VASCON Tho felt part of a larger group (which we could label a community of practice) of other students who shared his commitment and his experience as a second-generation Vietnamese youth. Tho's story shows the ways in which Vietnamese youth are participating in American civic life as they negotiate and try to make sense of issues of identity, sociality, and family origins. The role in Tho's life of two key mentors while he was in high school—one a Vietnamese teacher and one a Mexican American small business owner—highlights the importance of guidance and support to students who are otherwise primed to contribute to society.

Tho is an example of a second-generation youth born to refugee parents who has become involved in both pan-Asian student activities and a broader organization—Rotaract. We also found some members of the first generation who entered the public sphere through such organizations. One such organization is the PTA.[15] Mai, the first-generation Vietnamese refugee profiled at the beginning of Chapter 1, was involved in the PTA when her children were in elementary school. Ngo, profiled in Chapter 4, was also involved. They are exceptions, however, among first-generation Vietnamese parents in the region. By contrast, first-generation Indian women—many of whom are stay-at-home mothers, have a good command of English, and are college educated—demonstrate a much higher level of engagement with the PTA.[16] Neela D. is a good example of an Indian PTA mother.

Neela D.

Neela was born in India, in the city of Bombay (now Mumbai). She grew up in Pune and then in Bangalore. She pursued a bachelor of science degree and then a master of arts degree in the social sciences, both in India. After working for a few years in India she decided to come to the United States to pursue a master's degree in business administration. She arrived in 1989 to study at an American university, and it is there that she met her husband, another India-born student who had come to the United States from Bombay. They were married in India in 1992. Although both she and her husband wanted to remain in the city where they received their advanced degrees after graduation, there were few job opportunities. Her husband was finally offered a position in the Dallas area, to which they relocated in 1993.

When Neela moved to the Dallas area, she was not employed, so she volunteered at a local women's shelter—drawing, as she put it, on her social science background. No other volunteers at the time were foreign born. Eventually—at about the time her and her husband's green cards were about to come through as a result of applications filed by her husband's employer—she found a job with the company for which she still works. Both she and her husband are now naturalized U.S. citizens. Her current employer allows her a good deal of flexibility (her work is project based), including the option to work from her home when her son was small.

Neela was involved in volunteer work in India, including at an organization that emphasized equal opportunities for disabled people. It was founded by a dynamic woman who also had disabilities. Married to the police commissioner, this woman was a role model for Neela, who volunteered for this organization while she was working in Bangalore for an information technology company. Despite her own activities, Neela observed that volunteering and doing community work were not as common in India as they are in the United States and she was probably attracted to it more than others because of her social science degree. She noted that in India there is a fine line between charity work and advocacy work, and that married women (but rarely single women, she noted) with spare time do the former but not the latter. (Advocacy work has to do with helping people to help themselves and working at the system level.) Neela thinks that things are changing now in India, however. She added that her parents had served as leadership models—her father especially was unconventional and would pursue issues and "do a lot for the community." Neela said, "When he died people came up and commented on how much my parents had helped them. I had no idea!"

Neela's son was born in 1999. For two-and-a-half years he attended a Montessori preschool, first for just a few hours and later for the full school day. When he was young, Neela worked half-time, but once he was in school full-time, she worked more, although in a job with flexible hours. When her son was in kindergarten she began to volunteer for several activities, and it is in this context that she met people who were involved with the PTA and she liked working with them. She mentioned that her "child-centered focus" determines what she does with her spare time. She noted that she and her husband are the only couple involved in the PTA, and they do it because they are interested and want to learn from others. There is one other man involved—a man whom Neela described as "a mainstream American." She suggested that the DFW-area suburb where they live is very conservative, with traditional families and many stay-at-home mothers. Neela is one of a handful of women on the PTA who works. "Both of us are unique," she said, "my husband in the PTA and me working, and the fact we are both foreign born." In other words, Neela and her husband are busy, but she stressed that they share an outlook about being involved. But they have to coordinate things carefully. Her husband, who is active in the community in other ways as well, including serving as president of a local Indian organization, has launched an effort to start a dads club to involve more fathers. Neela described her husband as another role model—"he is unconventional and thinks about these kinds of things".

Neela sometimes spends five hours a week on PTA activities. She volunteers for the bike rodeo, which she says her son loves, and for the math games once or twice each month. But her most responsible position is as chair of the cultural diversity committee. Each November this committee sponsors a diversity day, with country booths and international costumes. Her company gives her five weeks of vacation and she takes one week of it to organize this event. She said that she also works a bit on the PTA newsletter. Neela is not a member of the PTA board and therefore does not attend those meetings, but she does attend the general meetings. At her son's school these meetings have been scheduled on the same nights as other events—"the kids are safe in the gym in some activity and then they can have a meeting."

Neela observed that there are not that many foreign-born parents involved in the PTA, and those who participate do so because they want to be involved in their children's lives. But interest is growing. (As an aside, she wondered if there were really any differences among mainstream parents in terms of level of involvement. She brought up a neighbor who is or was a teacher who does not attend PTA meetings.) Sometimes foreign-born parents are not involved because they have a lot of work to do and little time, or because they feel intimidated by organizations like the PTA. If they are involved, they do not necessarily assume leadership roles, and often they are taking their children to five or six activities a week and emphasizing academic extracurricular activities. Neela is not active in other Indian organizations in the area, although she attends events sponsored by the organization her husband serves as president. "That is a good group for my own networking," she commented. Last year her company was one of the sponsors of the annual conference of her husband's organization. She also participated in one of the annual fundraising banquets for the transnational Indian organization Pratham USA (see Chapter 4) because she thinks "they do good work and focus on empowerment." She said she will continue her PTA work in her son's school for several years and then maybe continue in middle and high school. "I cannot imagine not being involved because I learn so much." The educational system is not familiar to her, so she learns how it works. "And my son also gets more because I am involved." She observed that her husband also attends the school board meetings and learns a lot about the system that way. She seemed to be stressing that being active was a good way to acquire civic knowledge.

Neela said she is not sure that the concept of being a "good citizen" exists in India. "Maybe the idea of a good person, good son, good student. But here it is important to be involved." She talks to her son a lot about it and noted that he has a good idea of the importance of "sharing, listening, lending understanding, and being respectful of processes." When asked about other forms of citizenship, such as politics, Neela noted that people do not come to the United States with much interest in politics, because in India there is a general belief that one's vote does not really matter. "There are so many people there, and that one person does not count. Some are just jaded while others rise above it." She continued, however: "They come to the U.S. and realize that there are opportunities to make a difference and so some get quite active." This participation may begin with activities that involve their children, but then some people move on to other arenas. Neela's interest developed during the 2004 election, the first time she voted as a U.S. citizen. She emphasized the responsibilities dimension of citizenship rather than the rights dimension, stressing that she had not really encountered discrimination and that to her the rights of someone with a green card seemed similar to those of a citizen.

Historically, the PTA has often served as an entry point for civic and sometimes political participation; for some individuals it can be a springboard to involvement with the local school board, because the PTA often fields candidates.[17] Although during our fieldwork we did not encounter anyone who followed such a path, we did identify two Indian fathers who decided to run for their respective local school boards. One of them was Naman V.

Naman V.

Naman V. was born in central India and came to the United States in 1985. He has been in the DFW area since 1994. He lives in an inner-ring suburb of Dallas. His parents, who were missionaries, live in another nearby suburb. Naman's brother, who is a pastor at a local Baptist church, and his sister also live in the area. Naman works in information technology and his wife is employed as a nurse.

Naman first became interested in politics when he was in college in India and some friends encouraged him to run for a place on the city council in his hometown. He was not for any party but he was contemplating running on the Communist Party ticket—in a Congress Party area. A Congress Party official came to see him, asked why he was running and what he wanted, and discouraged him from running. He decided to withdraw, but after he did so things in his neighborhood were fixed, including the street in front of his parents' house. His parents did not know about his running until he withdrew, but they would have been opposed to it. Naman described his parents as "prominent people" in their neighborhood "and people of a certain class and education in India are disdainful of politicians. Everything in India works by bribery and a kind of mafia system."

Naman began his involvement in the U.S. civic sphere by serving on the board of his homeowners association, as a school volunteer, as a delegate to the PTA council, and on an advisory committee for his local school district. Naman said he made the decision to run for office, first for a position on his local city council and then for a position on the school board, because someone at city hall had commented that minorities come to the United States and just want to make money; they take but they do not want to give back. "That really made an impression on me." His wife and his parents were opposed to his decision, wondering why he bothered and suggesting that there was no benefit. His wife, he said, insisted that he put none of their own money into his campaigns. But, he said, running for the city council and then for the school board were his way of "giving back to the community." Naman expressed disappointment at the lack of diversity on various local governing bodies. He reported that there was a list of about eighty minority names proposed for various local planning commissions, but they are never included, and if there is one person on a commission, "they think that is enough. But the more liberal Anglos realize that they need this kind of diversity to solve problems."

Naman said he was directed toward running for the school board by his interest in community issues and by the fact that others had told him that this is where people who were interested in politics often got their start. Naman developed a platform based on his own ideas for the schools. He participated in a series of debates just prior to the election in which he outlined some of his concerns. He said he supported better pay for teachers and giving them more authority to make decisions about what is best for students. He suggested that administrators should support teachers so as not to undermine their credibility with parents and students. Naman suggested in one public forum that he was representing a so-far-unrepresented but fast-growing segment of the population, and that he could bring new ideas based on his experience with the educational system of another country. His goals, as he outlined them during his campaign, were to improve academic standards, introduce more accountability and discipline in the schools, work toward long-term solutions for the financial shortfalls, and put teacher salaries and benefits on par with those in other districts.

Naman described the education he had received as a result of running for office, claiming that he had learned a lot about the U.S. political system and political process. "There is a good deal of patronage and corruption even in the United States," he observed. He talked about working for the congressional campaign of Democrat Martin Frost and finding "some goods" on Frost's Republican opponent, Pete Sessions—on a public Web site—that he shared with someone working on the Frost campaign. But it was too close to the election to use it. Although he did not succeed at either of his races, he said that if he runs again he will do more mail-outs and work more with community leaders. He now has a list of Indians that he got from a local radio station and he will work to verify their contact information. He can target Asians the next time he runs. He does not have a lot of help and his wife works as a nurse so they have to coordinate the care of their children. Naman expressed some concern, however, about uniting Asians behind a single candidate. Muslims might not vote for him because they can tell by his name that he is not Muslim. An Anglo, learning that he was running, might try to convince someone in the Chinese community to run, in order to divide and conquer the Asian vote. In short, he said, "the Asians do not necessarily see another Asian representing them because of all the lines of division. Asians come here and sometimes they cannot forget the divides of back home." As a result, he said, he had learned that he needs to operate through community leaders; if he can get them behind him, the rest of the community might come along. He also talked about what he had learned about mobilizing a base by going to churches and organizations and securing the support of leaders, who would then talk about him to their communities.

Naman also talked about what he had learned about party positions. "Although school board positions are not supposed to be party aligned," he observed, "people can find out how you vote by checking on what primaries you participate in." He said he had been advised by party people to register Republican. "People ask if you are liberal or conservative, Republican or Democrat."

He reported being told that because he is against abortion and for the teaching of creationism in the schools, to many Democrats he is a Republican—even though he worked for the Frost campaign.

Naman thought that local communities needed to reach out to newcomers and provide them with information on the schools and on how to become involved. He wanted more Asians to become involved and his message was to point out to them that it is the school board that sets property taxes—and this should motivate them. He also talked about people's tendency to stay in their own communities. He went on to suggest, however, that although churches and other ethnic organizations within Asian communities are often inward looking, they can also help Asian immigrants to be outward looking.

Emerging Forms of Civic Engagement for "New" Immigrants

In the pan-Asian associations discussed in both Chapter 5 and this chapter, we see communities of practice that draw together people from different national backgrounds to work together on the basis of shared Asian ethnicity. Even though a relatively small number of Vietnamese and Indian newcomers participate directly in such associations, these groups and their activities affect the civic presence of these two immigrant groups and bring the benefits of greater political clout to a broad spectrum of Asian individuals. Unlike other ethnically based associations that emphasize cultural events, charitable activities, and the promotion of group-specific interests, pan-Asian associations often direct their attention to the more formal development of leadership and business skills through "teaching curricula," and to forging social networks and forms of cooperation across Asian groups. However, informal learning also takes place. The Vietnamese and Filipino leaders of the TCAACC have learned from each other how to organize banquets, scholarships, and other events to benefit their own ethnic groups, as well as to raise broader awareness of their efforts. In pan-Asian associations, immigrant newcomers also learn how to exercise their rights of fair treatment and equal access to opportunity—certainly important dimensions of civic participation. The Indian woman quoted earlier who is involved in the GDAACC stated that she hopes to learn from Hispanic and African American chambers of commerce more about how to deal with discrimination, and she sees the GDAACC as a vehicle for gaining greater acceptance in the wider society for Asian businesses and for Asians in general.

Most of our research suggests that there is not much direct contact between Indian and Vietnamese immigrants in the DFW region, and that they participate in the civic sphere most often with co-ethnics (through associations or religious assemblies) and occasionally with other ethnic groups (such as Vietnamese interacting with Filipinos and Latinos in Tarrant County, and Indians interacting with Chinese and Koreans through organizations in Dallas and Collin Counties). In pan-Asian contexts such as the DFW Asian-American Citizens Council banquet (discussed in Chapter 5) and in the cases discussed in this chapter, however, we see Indians and Vietnamese participating together in the same spheres of civic life. As we have previously suggested, the Indian and Vietnamese populations are not as visible in these pan-Asian efforts as are the older Asian immigrant groups, such as the Chinese, Koreans, and Japanese. We do, however, see evidence of their growing participation in these efforts, and of their awareness of the benefits of pan-ethnic collaboration at particular times and for particular purposes. Of note is the fact that the Vietnamese are especially active in the TCAACC but not very active in the GDAACC. We believe that this reflects in part the complexities of immigrant settlement patterns in a big metropolitan area such as DFW. In Tarrant County, the Vietnamese are one of the larger Asian populations, while in Dallas and Collin Counties the Chinese, Koreans, and Indians are more numerous and have a very forceful business presence.

The number of Indians involved in the pan-Asian contexts we have discussed here remains low by comparison with other Asian populations. We think this may be not only the result of their own ambivalence about being categorized as Asian, but also because phenotypically they are not considered Asian by outsiders as frequently as people of East Asian or Southeast Asian backgrounds. Further, the cultural stereotypes that were emphasized in the Asian American Leadership Institute (shyness, lack of assertiveness, and so on) do not necessarily resonate with DFW-area Indians as much as they might with individuals who are members of other Asian immigrant populations in DFW. Indians in the United States, including those who have settled in DFW, generally have a good command of the English language, as well has high levels of education. These advantages may facilitate their more direct entry into wider arenas. Nevertheless, as this chapter demonstrates, we do see Indian leaders engaged in pan-Asian contexts for strategic purposes, and they do recognize that there are political skills they can gain from these interactions.

Our research also led us to identify some of the ways in which immigrants and their children develop links to and even enter into broader civic organizations and into activities that do not involve pan-Asian ethnicity. Their participation in such events as beauty pageants and spelling bees for Vietnamese and Indian youth, respectively, provides evidence of this. In this chapter's narratives drawn from the experiences of four adults, we see even more clearly the paths that individuals can take and the ways they learn about wider participation. Although she was still rooted in her ethnic community and focusing on Vietnamese youth in her volunteer activities, the Amerasian woman Binh also enhanced her knowledge of how to participate in American society through her education and work here, as well as through her experiences in U.S. beauty pageants. In addition, she was encouraged in her volunteerism and her civic engagement with those she mentors by former President George W. Bush's initiative that rewards such service. The second-generation Vietnamese youth Tho built on his experience in high school and campus organizations to become involved in Rotaract, an organization linked to Rotary International. The Indian mother Neela became and intends to remain an active participant in the PTA, an archetypal American organization for civic engagement. And then there is Naman, who stepped more directly into the political arena by deciding to run for a mainstream elective office.

Some individuals do not acquire their skills of civic engagement in the United States but arrive here with an orientation toward civic engagement that can be applied in ways that respond to how they come to understand "good citizenship" in a new environment. Naman, who ran for office (albeit briefly) in his hometown in India, brought some of his leadership skills, as well as a general interest in politics, with him. So did other individuals whose narratives we have presented in this book (such as Cao, profiled in Chapter 4), and certainly several of them also talked about family members (or culture heroes) who served as role models for public service while they were growing up. Telling in this regard is Neela's observation that the idea of being a "good citizen" is not marked in India, but you can be a good person, a good son, or a good student.

Despite having a preexisting orientation to get involved, Naman also claims to have learned a good deal about the political process as he ran for a place on his local school board in the United States. Along similar lines, Binh suggested that she draws on her own skills—on her singing and on the confidence she gained by having a marginal identity, first as an Amerasian in Vietnam and then as an immigrant to the United States—but she also has learned new leadership skills in the communities of practice with which she has become involved. Because he has directly engaged the political sphere by running for political office, Naman demonstrates a grasp of the broader issues that reach across ethnic groups—issues that must be addressed if one is to be successful in the political process. What is perhaps most interesting about his narrative of civic engagement is his admission that it was a remark from a native-born American about minorities who do not give back or participate that motivated him to become more involved, thus setting himself up as role model and as someone who might change attitudes about first-generation immigrants.

The civic engagement narratives in this chapter illustrate both the situated learning and the social agency of immigrants in the process of acquiring and enhancing civic skills.[18] Individuals pursue quite diverse pathways to civic engagement. They can be involved in multiple communities of practice simultaneously, and they may participate in associations based on shared ethnicity or national origin, as well as in pan-Asian or mainstream associations. Immigrant participation in civic and political behaviors is a fluid and dynamic process, and the role of national origin in the types of activities engaged in may vary across Asian populations. In general, due to language barriers and to their strongly anticommunist sentiment, many first-generation Vietnamese are heavily involved in homeland politics and, compared to Indian immigrants, less involved with broader American associative life. However, as Tho's narrative illustrates, this is not the case for the children of immigrants and refugees—a point that reinforces the claim made by both Vietnamese and Indian parents that their children would be the ones to raise the level of broader civic and political participation by the Indian and Vietnamese populations in the United States. Our research shows that both a teaching curriculum and a learning curriculum are part of the communities of practice through which immigrants become civically engaged.

Conclusion

THIS IS A BOOK ABOUT how Vietnamese and Indian immigrants in the DFW region of Texas become civically engaged. We have found it analytically useful to think of immigrant newcomers as peripheral to the communities of practice that make up the civic sphere in the United States, but moving ever closer toward the center, and as social actors carving out new communities of practice through participation in various kinds of activities. Although this research builds on other recent analyses of civic engagement (especially Chavez 2008; Bloemraad 2006; Detroit Arab American Study Team 2009), the special contribution of our approach, beyond the detailed ethnography on Vietnamese and Indian immigrants, is to explore how these two groups acquire civic skills and thus learn forms of civic engagement within communities of practice. We define *civic engagement* (which we use interchangeably with the term *participatory citizenship*) as the process by which individuals enter into and act within civic spaces to address issues of public concern. Civic engagement includes knowledge about how to participate, as well as a sense of belonging that motivates participation. Our formulation of civic engagement includes both formal political activities and more everyday or vernacular forms of cultural and social citizenship. To frame our discussion of the myriad spaces for civic engagement, we draw on the concept of cultural citizenship, because it emphasizes "people's own experiences and interpretations of their own political, cultural, and economic position in the United States" (Coll 2010: 8). We also address the connections between activities in civic spaces and matters of identity; that is, how do members of these two populations define what it means to be an American citizen, as well as a Vietnamese, Indian, Asian, or Asian American in America?

194

We chose to focus on Indians and Vietnamese not only because they are both among the top five foreign-born populations (in total numbers) in DFW, but also because they provide significant contrasts while also practicing similar forms of civic engagement. In the first chapter of the book we discussed the cultural landscapes and social spaces that have been constructed by Vietnamese and Indian immigrants. These are part of the "emplacement" of these populations—spaces for the expression of cultural citizenship as a mode of belonging and participation that draw on the nuanced cultural and ethnic identities we discussed in Chapter 2. In Chapters 3 and 4 we discussed the religious assemblies and ethnic associations that form part of this landscape and contribute to the emplacement, or "the orienting of self" (Narayan 2002: 425), of these two immigrant groups. Along with the festivals, banquets, and pan-Asian as well as broader organizations (such as the PTA and Rotaract) discussed in Chapters 5 and 6, these are communities of practice where immigrant newcomers can engage in social practices that are enactments of the legal status of "citizen." In Chapter 6 we included examples of business contexts for civic learning, a particularly salient arena in the DFW region due to its expanding population and economic growth.

The community of practice model (Lave and Wenger 1991), although not previously applied to the study of immigrants and civic engagement, draws attention to situated learning through participation, emphasizing both process and social agency. We illustrate these dimensions of agency with personal narratives, showing how immigrants themselves construct their own understandings of citizenship and meaningfully put them into operation to claim civic presence. These issues of agency have not received sufficient attention in the literature on civic engagement in the sense of highlighting how individuals learn about the possibilities for entering the public sphere, as well as the decisions they make about their own participation. It is important to emphasize that our interest throughout this book has been on citizenship not simply as a "legal status" but as "desirable activity," a notion highlighting "the quality of one's citizenship as a function of one's participation in that community" (Kymlicka and Norman 1994: 353).

The Civic Participation of Refugees Versus Immigrants

Our work shows that there are intriguing similarities in the processes by which the two populations we studied learn civic skills and engage the public sphere in the United States, but there are also significant differences in civic participation related to the distinction between immigrants and refugees. The auspices, or circumstances, of migration for Vietnamese and Indians have been quite distinct, with the first group coming primarily as a refugee population and the second as economic migrants. Their overall social class positions, as indicated by levels of education and income, also differ—at least for the first generation. Whereas individuals in both populations become naturalized citizens at high rates and recognize the benefits of U.S. citizenship, the Vietnamese participants in our research placed somewhat more emphasis on rights and on "democracy as freedom" than did Indians. We suggest that this difference has to do with their prior experiences: Indians moved from a country with a democratic form of government, whereas the Vietnamese fled a homeland that has been ruled by a communist regime ever since the fall of Saigon. Fleeing Vietnam was a political act. The diasporic identity of former Vietnamese refugees, which is constructed in opposition to the communist regime in Vietnam, shapes their greater interest, compared with Indian immigrants, in influencing homeland politics through organizational structures in the United States. Among the majority of first-generation Vietnamese, homeland politics (in the form of anticommunism) helps to unite the population and mobilize them to engage in protests and other activities related to this cause, even though there can be sharp divisions resulting from suspicions about communist sympathizers among the population or moral claims about the "proper" stance toward the current regime in Vietnam.[1] Several of the Vietnamese ethnic associations discussed in this study have combined the preservation of cultural traditions and language with engagement in voluntary and other civic activities and explicit political participation—some of it related to homeland issues and some to domestic ones.

By contrast, Indian associations in DFW forthrightly avoid political issues unless they were expressly founded for such a purpose—as was the Indian American Friendship Council, though in this particular case the goal was to promote India as a player among the world democracies rather than to influence how politics operates in India. Homeland politics is potentially divisive for Indians in America, and although it has mobilized Indians in other U.S. cities, such as Los Angeles and the New York-New Jersey area, in DFW, where the Indian population is smaller and perhaps less diverse in terms of social class, such activities are more muted. As mentioned in Chapter 1, even the ethnic media avoid political controversy. Efforts among Indians to build a Hindu temple that encompasses the regional diversity in forms of Hindu worship, or to maintain the India Association of North Texas as an organization representative of Indians of all faiths, castes or classes, and regional backgrounds, reflect an awareness that in order to be effective within the broader American society, it is beneficial to leave homeland differences and divisiveness behind, to work together, and to manage an image of collaboration. This attitude is clearly present among Indians who declare themselves Democrats and yet make financial contributions to India-born or Indian-ancestry Republican political candidates (such as Bobby Jindal or Nikki Haley). The identification of ethnic spaces as places for the expression of unity or diversity merits further consideration in relation to the process by which immigrant newcomers enter the public sphere and become active civic and political citizens.

Another difference between our two groups is that civic engagement and local political participation, at least for the first generation, are sometimes constrained by lack of facility with the English language. On the one hand, their command of English makes Indians more comfortable, by comparison with the Vietnamese, in their initial forays into the public sphere, particularly in the local context. Through their voluntary and religious organizations, Indians partner on particular projects with what they consider to be mainstream organizations, and we see that they organize ethnicity-based Lions Clubs that nevertheless interact with other local clubs as well as with the national and international dimensions of this global organization. Those with time and interest express little linguistic insecurity about participating in organizations like the PTA or on a local citizens' council. For many in the first generation of Vietnamese refugees, on the other hand, language barriers are paramount and often cited by research participants as an important issue. Very few Vietnamese refugees arrive with fluent English language skills, and for the first generation this can prohibit participation in such civic spaces as schools, local government, or other institutions. It also affects employment opportunities. Language is, however, less of a problem for the growing 1.5 and second generation, who are increasingly assuming leadership roles.

The Vietnamese population, as a refugee group, has benefited in some ways from the long-standing historical involvement between Vietnam and the United States due to the Vietnam War, and from the special circumstances of having been a refugee population that arrived under the direct auspices of the State Department and other official agencies. Many first-wave Vietnamese refugee leaders in the United States were highly educated and fluent in English and had strong ties to military and government officials. Special legislation regarding Vietnamese refugees has long received input from such leaders. Therefore, although Vietnamese Americans are a refugee population, some institutional structures for ethnic organization were set up on a national scale by the elite members of this first wave, primarily in California and in the Washington, D.C., area, which helped shape subsequent forms of civic engagement in other areas of the country such as Texas.

By carrying out this comparison of Indians and Vietnamese, our work contributes to debates about the analytical utility of the category *refugee* as a "naturally self-delimiting domain of anthropological knowledge" (Malkki 1995: 496),[2] but not in any obvious way. Vietnamese interactions with the state and the experience of sudden rupture and displacement impact both their subjective experiences of being in America and the platform from which they engage the American public sphere. However, our research has demonstrated that despite the linguistic and economic advantages that many Indian economic migrants bring with them, Vietnamese engage in similar kinds of civic activities and work through similar institutional spheres to establish and articulate their right to belong. Thus we suggest that the category *refugee* is certainly significant for some dimensions of analysis and has some enduring subjective characteristics for those who have lived this experience, but being a refugee does not permanently differentiate some populations from others. All migrants experience a form of displacement and all strive toward emplacement in the country to which they have moved.

Voluntary Associations and Civic Engagement

In contrast to much previous work on voluntary associations and civic engagement, we have not relied primarily on the framework of social capital. Rather, we have found it instructive to add a new dimension to the study of associative life among immigrants—a focus on social learning about civic participation. This social learning not only comes from the new surroundings but also can be grounded in the moral values and previous experiences of the respective immigrant groups. We see this in both religious institutions and secular ethnic associations.

Both the Indian and Vietnamese immigrant populations support charitable works through their religious and ethnic associations and express a strong sense of social responsibility, articulated among the Vietnamese as "doing good" and among Indians as "giving back." Indeed, we have found it significant to identify how Hindus adapt ideas of social responsibility embedded in the concept of *seva* to their charitable work, while the Vietnamese invoke the concept of *trach nhiem*. Both populations are drawing on values that they brought with them and applying them to what they have learned to identify as being a "good citizen." This response suggests that the process of civic incorporation does not mean abandoning who you are but building on it to find your own path to engagement in the public sphere.

In this regard, we have been particularly struck by the capacity of both Indian and Vietnamese immigrants to "talk the talk" of civic engagement—that is, to learn the rhetoric of "team work," "good neighborship," "giving back to the community," and entering "the mainstream," and then to shape their actions accordingly. Gerard Delanty (2003: 603) has recently emphasized that an "important dimension of citizenship concerns the language . . . that people use to make sense of their society, interpret their place in it, and construct courses of action." Our research substantiates this observation, but we would suggest further that adopting the language or rhetoric of civic engagement also involves a process of making claims. Whereas Indian participants were more comfortable than Vietnamese participants with much of the rhetoric just quoted, and used it more frequently—a reflection no doubt of their better English skills, higher levels of education, and social class position—there certainly were contexts in which the Vietnamese used the rhetoric of civic engagement that is prevalent in the United States today.

The religious assemblies of both Vietnamese and Indian immigrants have changed to accommodate a different lifestyle in the United States. They have developed not only a more congregational and membership format (in the case of Hindus, Buddhists, and Muslims), but also a system of governance that has itself become an important arena for learning about civic life in the United States. Our research identified subtle differences between Indians and Vietnamese in the dimensions of civic engagement that characterize their religious assemblies. One was in the goals of and target populations for charitable work. Such activities that reach beyond the ethnic community are more extensive within Indian religious assemblies than within Vietnamese religious assemblies. Indians, many of whom are health care professionals or engineers, have skills that can be donated within the public sphere for the greater good, and they are often generous with them. Vietnamese medical professionals also volunteer their skills—both in Vietnam, through the charitable work done by groups who travel there, such as the Vietnamese Professional Society; and at the local level, at such venues as the Asian Health Fair and Eggroll Festival sponsored by the Fort Worth Asian American Chamber of Commerce (aimed at various Asian groups and not just at Vietnamese). Also, Vietnamese engineers participate in leadership conferences, helping to mentor the younger generation. The main difference between Indian and Vietnamese activities is that the Vietnamese focus primarily on their own ethnic group, which is perceived as having many newly arrived families who are still struggling financially and otherwise, or on the need for charity back home in Vietnam, whereas Indian professionals attempt to reach out beyond Indian concerns and the Indian population while also taking care of their own as the need arises. Among the Vietnamese, the relationship between civic engagement and religion is primarily based not on direct civic engagement with the American public sphere but rather on the leadership skills and organizational networks fostered in these contexts, which facilitate mobilized civic action in other arenas.

Among both Indians and Vietnamese, religious assemblies are contexts within which civic learning takes place, organizational skills are fostered, and the lessons learned are then transported into other communities of practice that may have greater civic and political presence than the religious assemblies. Our research therefore offers an alternative perspective to those who have argued that "joining a religious or ethnic association may be more a matter of withdrawing from the mainstream of society than of learning how to participate in it" (Kymlicka and Norman 1994: 364).[3] We suggest that by framing these religious organizations as communities of practice we are able to highlight their role as "training grounds" for civic engagement and participatory democracy (Eck 2001:336), and as arenas in which immigrants can "become American" in the sense of feeling that they belong.[4]

We make the same argument for ethnic associations, which, for both Vietnamese and Indians, bind individuals together in a common purpose (as defined by the organization) and allow them to express themselves not only as Indians or Vietnamese, but also as American. Further, we suggest that such processes are equally characteristic of a host of other civic spheres within the cultural landscape of immigrant communities in urban contexts—festivals, banquets, leadership training seminars, beauty pageants, and spelling bees. Documenting how our research participants come together to enjoy and share a cultural performance or to engage in other emotionally salient aspects of cultural expression at banquets and festivals draws attention to those forms of engagement in the civic sphere that go beyond narrow views of political participation. Attending leadership conferences helped us see the active role taken by Asian immigrants in fostering political and civic engagement, a role that underscores their recognition of the advantages that greater participation will afford their co-ethnics. Our interviews with Vietnamese and Indian leaders of various generations provide a unique perspective on the wealth of experience and knowledge that these individuals possess, and on the diverse trajectories that led all of them to greater participation.

By viewing voluntary associations as places where people learn new forms of social participation, we do not mean to emphasize solely the *adaptive* functions of these associations. They are also sites for competition, for the acquisition of power and prestige within the ethnic community and beyond, and they are arenas in which the divisions within immigrant populations are displayed. However, we suggest that for immigrants, part of learning about civic engagement is strategically downplaying divisions or points of conflict in order to provide a united and collective front when interacting with what is often referred to as mainstream society. Our research reveals that those Vietnamese and Indian immigrants who are involved in ethnic organizations, particularly those who have taken a leadership role, have become aware that civic and political power reside in constructive and strategic collaboration. Our research also indicates that, despite their differences, both Indians and Vietnamese immigrants understand the importance of building bridges to elected officials as part of the process by which newcomers become more active and visible in the civic sphere and hence establish their political presence. The Vietnamese American Community (VAC), like various Indian organizations, regularly invites local and state officials to their events.

Lave and Wenger (1991) have stressed the collective empowerment that can emerge through communities of practice. This empowerment is important to the process of civic and political incorporation and we see it taking place within the range of civic spheres discussed in this book. In these arenas, Asian Indians and Vietnamese "come out" as social and cultural citizens, asserting their right to belong and be recognized (that is, their civic and political presence) through social practice and cultural autonomy. As we have stressed, cultural and social citizenship are both important dimensions of participatory citizenship, which we argue must be evaluated alongside the more formal parameters of citizenship if we are to understand fully the process by which immigrant newcomers become incorporated into the civic polity. We also argue, however, that in relation to fourth-wave immigrants such as the Indians and Vietnamese, civic engagement and civic incorporation must be broadly defined rather than limited to being active in politics or being a member of a political party or union.

Pan-Asian Ethnicity and Participatory Citizenship

This book contributes to debates on *pan-ethnicity*, which is "the development of bridging organizations and identities among subgroups of ethnic collectivities that are often seen as homogeneous by outsiders" (Espiritu and Lopez 1990:

198). Scholars have explored the likelihood that such identities and organizations will emerge, and have asked in what contexts, for what purposes, and with what implications for the process of incorporation into American society.[5] Our interviews with parents and college-age youth were instructive on these points and led to some interesting findings about identity. Although our ethnographic fieldwork revealed that Indian and Vietnamese immigrants are building bridges through a form of pan-ethnicity and across differences within their populations (based on such factors as regional origins, ethnicity, religion, and language), we found discomfort with pan-Asian and Asian American categories among many first-generation men and women in both populations. Participants in the parent interviews also expressed skepticism about the possibilities for political mobilization based on these categories. As South Asians and Southeast Asians, respectively, our Indian and Vietnamese research participants expressed their feelings of being located somewhat on the periphery of pan-Asian organizations that can be dominated, especially in the Dallas area, by a category of people that is viewed, particularly by Indian immigrants, as "oriental." Nevertheless, certain Indian American and Vietnamese American individuals, especially those who are most active in ethnic associations, recognize the strategic importance of collective Asian action, and a growing number of them participate in business organizations and leadership conferences that are based on pan-Asian identities. We found such organizations to have a particular resonance within the entrepreneurial and business environment of the DFW metropolitan area.

First-generation Indians and Vietnamese both acknowledge that their children may hold different views of the Asian identity, and some observed that youth are already participating in Asian American and South Asian organizations on college campuses, which our own field research substantiated. In our group interviews with college-age youth from both populations, we encountered young adults who were struggling to balance their ethnic and American identities and to negotiate the racialized concepts of whiteness and brownness or yellowness that have implications for their sense of belonging as well as for the right to belong that is extended to them by the broader American society. Whether the pan-Asian activities of the second generation will endure into their adulthood and shape how they engage the public sphere and participate in the political process is an empirical question worthy of further exploration, although some scholars have already suggested that Asian youth share a unique second-generation experience in the context of U.S. society that cuts across the lines of national origin as well as social class.[6]

For both populations and across both generations identities are fluid. Among those of the first generation who were interviewed there are clear differences between being American and acting American, although perhaps more so for the Vietnamese than for Indians. These meaningful differences do not, however, affect political and civic participation, and they underscore the importance of distinguishing between cultural belonging and political belonging. Immigrant newcomers can, we suggest, enter the public sphere from a platform of difference and be effective citizens. This is precisely why the concept of cultural citizenship is so critical to understanding the processes of civic engagement, and why a community-of-practice approach that identifies paths from peripheral or marginal to broader forms of participation is so illuminating.

Looking to the Future:
From Civic Engagement to Political Voice

In this book we have explored the ways in which Vietnamese and Indians who have settled in the Dallas-Arlington-Fort Worth metropolitan region learn about, understand, and demonstrate aspects of civic engagement through their participation in various communities of practice where they acquire civic knowledge and practice what they define as "good" citizenship. In the process, they may teach the wider society something about citizenship even as they are learning new skills themselves. We are left, however, with the question of what all this means for the future and for the political potential of these two populations, both locally and nationally, in a more formal sense.

In the United States, claiming a place in the polity is based not only on American citizenship but often also on identity politics. Indeed, much of U.S. politics is a "politics of recognition" (Taylor 1992), with ethnic categories used to build constituencies, to secure limited resources, and to facilitate "electing one's own" in local districts that have frequently been redrawn in the aftermath of the Voting Rights Act of 1965 (Wolfinger 1965; Litt 1970). In the United States, ethnicity has become a way to enter into and participate in the public sphere. The mobilization of the Latino ethnic vote is well known and often discussed. By contrast, some scholars have suggested that Asian Americans have not reached their full potential as political actors given their high levels of education.[7] Observers note that the fragmentation of Asian immigrants "along lines of national origin and language," as well as their greater residential dispersion in comparison with Latinos, makes them less a target "for mobilization by national political parties" (Jones-Correa 2007: 195). It could equally be observed that residential dispersion makes it more difficult for Asians to "elect their own" at the local level. Despite this fragmentation and dispersal, however, recent scholarship demonstrates that Asian Americans of various national origins are increasingly becoming involved in electoral politics and other forms of political activity (Lien 2001; Lien, Conway, and Wong 2004; Aoki and Takeda 2008).

Our research among Indians and Vietnamese suggests that first-generation newcomers value the right to vote and approach it as a responsibility, although some individuals, especially Indians, have developed a more jaded approach that many have described as characteristic of the American population in general. Within both populations, more men than women express interest in politics. Although our formal interviews and informal conversations with Indian immigrants yielded more examples of involvement in local political issues than did our interviews with Vietnamese, the Vietnamese certainly indicated that national elections draw their attention, and our participant-observation research among both populations revealed extensive cases of interaction with local and regional elected officials, particularly as mediated by ethnic associations. First-generation immigrants from both populations think about their political activity in the United States in relation to their respective homelands, but in different ways. Indians draw direct comparisons between what democratic processes and activity are like in India and what they are like in the United States, whereas the Vietnamese, as indicated earlier, express more concern about how they can influence homeland politics in order to restore what they perceive to have been a democratic government in South Vietnam before the Vietnam War, and to influence U.S. policy toward the communist regime. Among both Vietnamese Americans and Indians there are also those who indicated during interviews that they do not follow homeland politics, and for the same reason—because the United States is now their home. Similarly, individuals in both populations indicated that it is important to follow U.S. politics because of the global impact of the United States. However, many first-generation Vietnamese are constrained by language in acquiring the political knowledge they need. Although members of both populations mentioned discrimination as an issue of concern, the Vietnamese participants were more vocal about this matter than the Indians, a difference that undoubtedly has something to do with class position as well as with the legacy of the Vietnam War.

As pointed out earlier in this book, both Indian and Vietnamese first-generation immigrants think their children will be more active in the political sphere and in the broader American society than they have been. They see their generation concentrated in particular professions—engineers, health professionals, and small business owners who work long hours—but their children are branching out into legal, business, media, and other careers, including politics. They see their children growing up with more knowledge of the system and with a greater "vested interest" in America. A Hindu business executive in his early fifties who entered the United States in 1975 and participated in the parent interviews put it this way:

> [First-generation Indians] recognize that they are financially powerful but politically impotent and that this balance has to change. But it is understand-able. The first people who came needed to establish themselves. Now that they are established they can turn to things beyond just making a livelihood. This is what the next generation will do.

The Vietnamese were also confident that their children's generation would become more active. For them, Representative Hubert Vo, as a fellow Texan and Vietnamese American, is an important symbol of the potential for more politi-cal participation. Whereas the first generation struggled with language barri-ers and economic survival, their children are better educated; and as expressed by one parent, "because the younger generation is more American, they will pursue this." As one male research participant observed, "Before, we did not understand American life. People like me have suffered a lot. Ten years in war, fifteen years in jail. Mentally and physically we are exhausted. Then we need to feed our families. But the younger generation is different."

Because refugees came to the United States for political reasons, there is a strong political consciousness in many of those we interviewed, and a keen interest in greater involvement. An interest in politics was explained by one person in terms of the Vietnamese refugee experience: "These are people who fled from the country because of political reasons; those people will encour-age their children to join into U.S. politics." Both Vietnamese and Indian im-migrant parents see evidence that their political influence will grow with the next generation.

In this study, gender is an equally salient topic alongside generation. Whereas we found that most of the leadership positions in the ethnic associations and religious organizations of Indians and Vietnamese Americans were held by first-generation men rather than women, there were several arenas in which women participated. One of these was the pan-ethnic associations. Vietnamese women in particular have held leadership positions in both the DFW Asian American Citizens Council and the Tarrant County Asian American Cham-ber of Commerce, and a few Indian women have held leadership positions in the Greater Dallas Asian American Chamber of Commerce. Second-generation

Vietnamese and Indian women are also taking leadership roles, in associations on college campuses and in associations aimed at younger generations (such as the Vietnamese Professionals Society). First-generation Indian women have become heavily involved in such associations as the PTA, and some of them are active board or committee members within ethnic and religious associations, as well as in transnational associations such as Pratham USA. Indian women in Dallas have founded their own Lions Club, as well as their own organization to deal with domestic violence.

The participation of Indians and Vietnamese in the public sphere is extensive and complex, and we had to be selective about what from the vast array of observations and interviews we amassed during our fieldwork could be included in this book. Our portrait here is thus, of necessity, only a partial glimpse into a realm that is dynamic and ongoing. We can illustrate this dynamism with two examples from the Vietnamese associations profiled in Chapter 4. Since this research ended and during the period in which this book has been written, the Dallas chapter of the Vietnamese Professionals Society has become inactive. This group was very active in the years immediately prior to and during our fieldwork. Eventually it became difficult to find individuals with the time to invest in its activities. This group of young professionals with busy lives, starting families, and involved in other pursuits simply could not recruit enough people to carry on the work of the society. This deactivation, however, does not undermine our argument about associations as communities of practice for civic engagement. The last president of the group, a first-generation refugee who arrived in the 1990s, is now working and going to law school part-time, hoping to gain the skills that will open up a political career. In contrast, the VAC of Tarrant County is being energized by the political position of its former president, Andy Nguyen, who ran for election as one of four Tarrant County commissioners and first won the Republican primary for this office in April 2010 after a tough race against the incumbent, an Anglo woman. He went on to win the general election in November 2010 against no credible Democratic challenger in this highly Republican county and state. He mobilized his base of support among the Vietnamese population and beyond, and built on contacts with elected officials that the VAC had developed in recent years. Nguyen's campaign Web site indicated that he was running as a former "U.S. Army officer, a successful businessman, and a community servant leader." Although he served as a primarily ethnicity-based community leader for several years, this former refugee, who arrived in the United States as a teenager, is moving from the periphery to the center of American public life after honing *general assertion* [handwritten margin annotation]

his skills in communities of practice that were based in Vietnamese and pan-Asian identities.

The successful candidacy of Andy Nguyen reflects the growing interest among Indians and Vietnamese in running for elected office. This interest was illustrated in the story of Naman V., the Indian man profiled in Chapter 6 who ran for a school board position. In another recent case, Raj Narayanan, born in India and the owner of an aerospace consulting firm, put himself on the ballot in the fall of 2008 to represent District 13 on the Dallas City Council. In the suburban community of Sunnyvale, India-born Saji George, an engineer with degrees from Texas Tech University and Southern Methodist University and an active member of St. Paul Mar Thoma Church in Mesquite, was elected to the city council in the spring of 2010. Another individual, Raj Menon, cofounder and former president of the Indian Institute of Technology Alumni Association in the DFW area and a member of his son's elementary school PTA, ran for a position on the Plano Independent School District's board of trustees during the spring of 2010. And the previous spring, as mentioned in Chapter 5, former Vietnamese refugee and lawyer Sandra VuLe ran for the Texas State Legislature as a Democrat, demonstrating the growing political presence of Vietnamese women. Narayanan lost to an Anglo woman who raised a lot of money for her campaign. Menon also lost to an Anglo candidate, but had he won he would have been the first non-native-born citizen to serve on the hundred-year-old school board. VuLe lost to a female Chinese opponent. But significant to the argument we make in this book is evidence that several of these candidates are using skills developed in ethnicity-based communities of practice to launch themselves into the arena of local and state-level politics.

Final Thoughts

The members of the Indian American Friendship Council who made a significant donation in order to rub shoulders with a U.S. senator at an exclusive dinner have certainly learned what it takes to be at the influence-buying epicenter of the political process in the United States. The members of the VAC who can effectively mobilize a protest against the display of a flag they do not feel represents them have clearly learned about grassroots political action that can produce outcomes. The members of the DFW Indian Lions Club who recognize the community service of outsiders to their associations, who make donations to mainstream associations, who rally their members to collect goods and money for the victims of natural disasters in America or to engage in charity work in the home country are communicating their understanding of what it means to be a good citizen. And the children of Vietnamese and Indian immigrants who compete successfully in such archetypal American events as beauty pageants and spelling bees or who earn their places as class salutorians and valedictorians are establishing their right to recognition and belonging in the American public sphere.

Our research suggests that the civic engagements of immigrant newcomers build on ethnic identity and prior experiences in the homeland. Increasingly, policymakers are placing emphasis on finding mechanisms that would enhance the process of what they often frame as the *assimilation, incorporation,* or *integration* of new Americans. We are concerned about the connotations of these words, and about any policy that imposes a unitary model of outcomes on individuals or sets a standard of how citizenship should be expressed and experienced. Our exploration of the implications of the concept of communities of practice for civic engagement indicates that it is not necessarily the case that a top-down approach is needed to bring immigrants into full participation in the civic sphere, although the structures of opportunity and organization within which they operate are, as political sociologist Irene Bloemraad (2006) suggests, important. Within immigrant communities themselves there are spaces and places that are already operating as viable arenas for "becoming American" and being a responsible American citizen. Any program aimed at enhancing the "incorporation" of immigrants into American public life must, we argue, be mindful of and maintain respect for cultural differences and for the myriad ways in which immigrants are paving their own paths to citizenship and belonging.

Reference Matter

Notes

Introduction

1. Vo was reelected in 2006 and in 2008.

2. In this book we use the terms *Indian* and *Vietnamese,* and sometimes *Vietnamese American* because this phrase is commonly used by members of this group, whereas Indian American was viewed with more ambivalence by Indians involved in our research. We also use the category *Asian* for broad descriptive purposes. However, as we discuss in Chapter 2, these labels are fluid and understood in complex ways by our research participants.

3. This is the first book-length ethnography of Vietnamese in the DFW region, and the second such book dealing with Indians (see Dhingra 2007). See Brady (2004) and Tang (2007) for overviews of Asian immigrants in Texas.

4. Bayly (2007) also pairs Indians and Vietnamese to explore the postcolonial experiences of cosmopolitan members of these two nations.

5. Other recent work on immigrant civic engagement in the United States includes Wong (2006), Kniss and Numrich (2007), Chavez (2008), Somers (2008), Ramakrishnan and Bloemraad (2008a), Reed-Danahay and Brettell (2008a), and Stepick, Rey, and Mahler (2009). On concepts of assimilation in the context of civic engagement, see Waters (2008). For more general discussions of civic engagement, see Verba, Schlozman, and Brady (1995); Skocpol and Fiorina (1999); and Zukin et al. (2006). Civic engagement among youth is a topic growing in importance (Sherrod, Torney-Purta, and Flanagan 2010); on immigrant youth see Jensen and Flanagan (2008).

6. Bloemraad (2000, 2006) also uses *participatory citizenship.*

7. Our approach differs from that of Ramakrishnan and Bloemraad (2008b), who distinguish between what they call *civic engagement* and *political engagement.* We view both formal political participation and less formal ways of engaging with the civic sphere as modes of civic engagement.

8. Another recent volume on comparative political incorporation is Hochschild and Mollenkopf (2009). For approaches within the disciplines of political science and sociology, see, for example, DeSipio (1996), Jones-Correa (1998), Gerstle and Mollenkopf (2001), Leal (2002), Barreto (2005), and Bloemraad (2006).

9. Several writers have offered nuanced views of citizenship. See, for example, Kymlicka and Norman (1994) and Castles and Davidson (2000). We review much of this literature in Reed-Danahay and Brettell (2008b).

10. See also Rosaldo (1997).

11. Baker and Shryock (2009) explore what they term the *rights theme* and the *multiculturalism theme* in the literature on citizenship.

12. For discussions of social citizenship see Dwyer (2004) and Faist (1995). For discussion of Marshall and his critics, see Isin and Wood (1999).

13. Other notions of citizenship recently introduced in the literature include flexible citizenship (Ong 1999; 2003), long-distance nationalism (Anderson 1992; Glick Schiller and Fouron 2001), transborder citizenship (Smith and Bakker 2008), extraterritorial citizenship (Fitzgerald 2000), diasporic citizenship (Laguerre 1998; Siu 2005), and semi-citizenship (Cohen 2009).

14. See also Ngai (2004). Race-based immigration laws, many of them directed against Asians, date back to the nineteenth century and include the 1875 Page Act and the 1882 Chinese Exclusion Act. Examples of local discriminatory ordinances include the Sidewalk Ordinance of 1870 and the Pigtail Ordinance of 1873 in San Francisco, both directed against Chinese immigrants (Wong 1998).

15. The legal citizenship of immigrant women was particularly limited. For further discussion, see Volpp (2001) and Gardner (2005).

16. For further discussion, see Waters (1990), Reed-Danahay (1991; 1996), and Hall (2002).

17. For studies of naturalization among Salvadoran immigrants, see Coutin (1998; 2003a; 2003b). On the relationship between citizenship laws and political participation, see, for example, Brubaker (1989), Soysal (1994), Joppke (1999), Castles and Davidson (2000), and Joppke and Morawska (2003). On the pragmatics of naturalization, see Gilbertson and Singer (2003).

18. Wong and Pantoja's model uses the variables of "political interest, religiosity, member of a community organization, and strong partisan" (2009: 266) to measure level of civic engagement.

19. See, for example, Panagakos (1998), Karpathakis (1999), Itzigsohn (2000), and Chavez (2008). Graham (2001: 89) refers to this phenomenon as "simultaneous political incorporation." See Collet and Lien (2009) for work on the transnational politics of Asian Americans.

20. http://www.state.gov/g/prm

21. We do not, however, use the term *immigrant* to refer to the second generation—children born to immigrants in the United States.

22. For further discussion of the concept of diaspora in relation to Asian immigrants, see Parreñas and Siu (2007).

23. We acknowledge that many refugees and immigrants experience forms of social suffering due to the logics of capitalism, but our approach differs somewhat from that of Aihwa Ong (1999; 2003), who emphasizes diasporic transnationalism and the mobility of immigrants and refugees as new economic actors in global neoliberal economies. Ong (2003) emphasizes the zones of contact between refugees and governmental agencies and nongovernmental organizations (NGOs) that seek to transform their subjectivities and instill forms of economic individualism. We focus instead on the ways that immigrants and refugees are social actors who negotiate spaces of civic engagement that they help to create.

24. The phrase "the cultural production of" has been variously applied to studies of education (Levinson, Foley, and Holland 1996) and ethnicity and immigration (Hall 2002).

25. See Hughes, Jewson, and Unwin (2007) for a recent collection of essays on communities of practice.

26. Robert Putnam (2000) has argued that civic engagement declined in the United States during the latter part of the twentieth century because Americans, instead of coming together in formal and informal organizations (such as bowling leagues), are increasingly "bowling alone." As a consequence, their social capital, which he defines as "social networks and the associated norms of reciprocity and trustworthiness" (2007: 137), has also declined. Many studies engage Putnam's ideas (Maloney, Smith, and Stoker 2000; and Paxton 2002). For critical evaluations of Putnam's argument, see Evers (2003). See also the brief discussion in Ramakrishnan and Bloemraad (2008b). Putnam and Feldstein (2003) offer a more positive (compared to the argument in *Bowling Alone*) portrait of civic engagement in the United States.

27. See, for example, Zhou and Bankston (1994); Min and Kim (2002); Jacobs, Phalet, and Swyngedouw (2004); Tillie (2004); Stepick (2005); Vermeulen and Berger (2008); Lorentzen et al. (2009); and Stepick, Rey, and Mahler (2009).

28. Other scholars (Foley and Hoge 2007) draw on Pierre Bourdieu's resource-based notion of social capital (1986).

29. Portes (1998) raises this issue of the "dark side" (see also Fiorina 1999). For critical analysis of the concept of social capital, see Baron, Field, and Schuller (2000). Thiess-Morse and Hibbing (2005), while not addressing immigrant organizations, criticize the social capital approach to voluntary associations and civic engagement and suggest that voluntary associations can work against democratic values in many cases.

30. These are also the criticisms against forms of ethnic association that have been prevalent in European contexts, especially France (Schnapper 1998).

31. See also Ramakrishnan and Bloemraad (2008c: 49), who differentiate between *mainstream organizations* and *ethnic organizations*" on the basis of whether or not the group makes "reference to national origin groups or racial-ethnic categories in the organization's title and mission." They further point out that so-called mainstream organizations are in general predominately "white," making the unmarked ethnic category *white* the mainstream.

32. For an earlier study that examined modes of immigrant accommodation to the United States in the context of schooling and families and demonstrated a rejection of "assimilation" by Punjabi Sikhs without a rejection of the idea of participating in civic or organizational life, see Gibson (1988).

33. See Das Gupta's ethnography (2006) of activist South Asian women's organizations in the northeastern United States.

34. The appointment of Sonal Shah (a woman) as an advisor to the process of assembling Obama's White House team in the aftermath of the election generated excitement but also concern because Shah was rumored to be an active member of Vishwa Hindu Parishad of America (VHPA), a Hindu extremist group. Shah denied the rumors.

35. See Do (1999: 110) and Gold (1992).

36. See also Reed-Danahay (2008).

37. Commander Le was profiled in the *New York Times* (Mydans 2009) when the naval destroyer he commands made a formal port call in Vietnam in the fall of 2009. It was the first time he had returned to his natal country since leaving with his family in 1975.

38. The full roster of members was listed on the transition team's Web site: http://change.gov/learn/obama_biden_transition_agency_review_teams (accessed October 20, 2010).

39. Cao is the first Vietnamese American member of Congress. He made national headlines in November 2009 for being the sole Republican in the U.S. House of Representatives to vote for the health care reform that passed by a narrow margin (Herszenhorn 2009).

40. See Junn et al. (2008).

41. Reed-Danahay conducted most of her interviews with Vietnamese parents in their homes, often with the assistance of a trained research assistant-translator. Brettell conducted the majority of her parent interviews in Indian homes, although a few were done at places of business.

Chapter 1

1. There are seven Indian Institutes of Technology (IIT). The first was founded in 1951 in West Bengal. Developed to train scientists and engineers, these institutes have become the premiere institutions of higher education in India. Admission is by means of a highly competitive entrance examination, although seats have been reserved for "scheduled castes" since 1973. IIT alumni are scattered throughout the world.

2. Several recent histories of Dallas provide good background (Hill 1996; Fairbanks 1998; Payne 2000; Phillips 2006; Graff 2008). There is no comparable material on Fort Worth and Tarrant County. See Roark (2003) for a study of Tarrant County that deals primarily with historic preservation. See also Kemper (2005), Brettell (2008a; 2008b), and the Texas Handbook Online, http://www.tshaonline.org/handbook/online (accessed October 20, 2010).

3. The Fort Worth Convention & Visitors Bureau touts Fort Worth as the "City of Cowboys and Culture," http://www.fortworth.com, whereas the Dallas Convention & Visitors Bureau proclaims "Live Large, Think Big," http://www.visitdallas.com (accessed October 20, 2010).

4. According to U.S. Census 2000, the ethnic breakdown in the Dallas Primary Metropolitan Statistical Area (PMSA) was 56.2 percent white/non-Hispanic, 15.1 percent black/African American, and 23 percent Latino (all races). The Fort Worth-Arlington PMSA had a higher concentration in the category of white/non-Hispanic (65.6 percent) and fewer black/African Americans (11.2 percent) and Latinos (18.2 percent). The percentage of Asians was similar in both regions: Dallas, 4 percent, and Fort Worth-Arlington, 3.2 percent.

5. The DFW International Airport is the busiest in Texas and ranks seventh in the world for volume of passenger traffic.

6. According to the Dallas Regional Chamber, 760,000 new jobs were created.

7. See Batheja (2010). The Barnett Shale is a geological formation located in the area surrounding Fort Worth and containing vast natural gas reserves. Vietnamese families who have permitted drilling on their property are, along with other residents, earning revenue from this new effort, and Vietnamese individuals have also been employed by the companies that are exploiting this resource in order to recruit families to permit drilling on their land. The environmental impact of this recent push to drill for gas has been hotly contested in these cities.

8. The top employers in DFW are Lockheed Martin (FW), American Airlines (DFW International Airport and FW), Naval Air Station Fort Worth Joint Reserve Base (FW), Texas Instruments (Dallas), Parkland Health & Hospital System (Dallas), University of Texas Southwestern Medical Center (Dallas), University of North Texas (Denton), Baylor University Medical Center (Dallas), and the University of Texas at Arlington. http://www.nctcog.org/ris/demographics/majemp.asp (accessed October 20, 2010).

9. http://www.fortworthchamber.com/eco/business_charts.html#2 (accessed October 20, 2010).

10. See, however, Graff's recent (2008) critique of what he calls the "Dallas Myth."

11. The Texas governor's office was held by Democrats between 1874 and 1979, when William ("Bill") Clements Jr., a Republican, was elected. He was succeeded by Democrat Mark White in 1983, but Clements won again in 1987. He was succeeded by Ann Richards, a Democrat, in 1991, and she was in turn succeeded by George W. Bush in 1995.

12. Montcrief was elected in 2003 and reelected in 2007.

13. Elzie Odom, an African American, was mayor of Arlington from 1997 to 2003. He was succeeded by Republican Robert Cluck.

14. The recent budget crisis in California, however, has led to cuts in services that will have significant consequences for immigrants, refugees, and, more broadly, low-income citizens. See "California Budget Crisis." http://topics.nytimes.com/topics/news/national/usstatesterritoriesandpossessions/california/budget_crisis_2008_09/index.html (accessed October 20, 2010).

15. http://ext.nazarene.org/rcms/073.html (accessed October 20, 2010).

16. Jerry Falwell's "Moral Majority" movement of the late 1970s and early 1980s was heavily fueled by support from a Dallas-based First Baptist Church (Phillips 2006: 2).

17. Recent studies of the Arab community in Detroit (Abraham and Shryock 2000; Detroit Arab American Study Team 2009) offer an interesting comparison. Arab populations have been in Detroit since the 1920s and hence have provided a foundation for new migrations to a city that was not prospering economically during the 1980s and 1990s, as was the DFW region.

18. For previous studies of Mexicans in Dallas, see Achor (1978) and Adler (2007). See Cueller (2003) on Mexicans in Fort Worth. Previous studies of Asian immigration in Dallas include Dhingra (2007) and Um (1996). We are not aware of any earlier work on Asian immigration in Tarrant County and Fort Worth.

19. These figures, from American Community Survey (ACS) data of the United States Census Bureau for 2005, are estimates but nevertheless suggest that during the first half of the first decade of the twenty-first century, Indians and Vietnamese continued to settle in Texas and DFW.

20. See information at http://www.hhsc.state.tex.us/program/refugees/index.html (accessed October 20, 2010) and the Office of Refugee Resettlement (2007).

21. Since then, more work has focused on suburban immigrant incorporation (Singer, Hardwick, and Brettell 2008). See also Jones (2008).

22. The Immigration Act of 1924 limited the number of immigrants from any country who could be admitted to the United States to 2 percent of the number of people from that country who were living in the United States in 1890, based on the 1890 U.S. Census, and excluded Asian immigration. The Immigration and Nationality Act of 1965 abolished these national-origin quotas.

23. The H1B visa is a work visa issued to skilled international professionals. It is a "dual intent" visa that makes it possible for an individual to apply through an employer for a "green card" (legal permanent residence) while in the United States. In 2007, just over 65,000 Indians were granted legal permanent resident status in the United States; of these, 44 percent were employment-sponsored, 28 percent were close relatives of U.S. citizens, 24 percent were family-sponsored, and 4 percent were refugees or asylum seekers (Terrazas 2008a).

24. According to 2006 ACS estimates, nationwide 74 percent of India-born adults aged twenty-five and older had bachelor's or higher degrees, and 63 percent of those aged five or older reported speaking English "very well." In 2006, the median household income of Indians (measured in inflation-adjusted dollars) in the United States was $78,315 (compared with a national average of $48,451) and the median family income was $87,484 (compared with a national average of $58,526).

25. In 2006, at about the time we were conducting our interviews, 20 percent of Indian males and 15.3 percent of Indian females sixteen and older in the civilian labor force nationwide were in management, business, and finance; 27.4 percent of males and 13.1 percent of females were in information technology; 11.2 percent of males and 6.2 percent of females were in other sciences and engineering; and 7.1 percent of males and 20.5 percent of females were in health care (as physicians, registered nurses, or other health professionals. See footnote 33 for comparable data on the Vietnamese.

26. Emigration from Kerala has often been led by women who are active in the nursing profession and hence are recruited by hospitals across the developed world. The Indian families in Mesquite were some of the earliest to arrive in Dallas and, because they are South Indians and often of darker complexion than North Indians, they often faced discrimination, which made it more difficult for them to settle in the more white northern suburbs.

27. See Kelly (1977), Montero (1979), Rutledge (1992), Kibria (1993), and Freeman (1995). Between 1975 and 1977, 175,000 Vietnamese refugees arrived in the United States. The earliest camps set up to receive these refugees were Camp Pendleton (near San Diego, California), Fort Chaffee (in Arkansas), Elgin Air Force Base (Pensacola, Florida), and Fort Indiantown Gap (in Pennsylvania).

28. In 2007, close to 29,000 Vietnamese were granted legal permanent residence in the United States. This number had peaked at almost 80,000 in 1992. Of these, 49 percent were immediate relatives of U.S. citizens, 43 percent were family-sponsored immigrants, and only 6 percent had arrived as refugees or asylum seekers. The number of Vietnamese refugees admitted to the United States in 2007 was 1,500, down significantly from the 1990 figure of 27,378 (Terrazas 2008b). Between 1983 and 2007, 470,709 Vietnamese refugees were settled in the United States and 46,000 of them were initially settled in Texas (Office of Refugee Resettlement 2007), although many refugees moved to Texas after initial settlement elsewhere.

29. See, for example, Gold (1992), Hein (1995), Freeman (1995), and Do (1999).

30. The experience of Amerasians in Vietnam and after coming to the United States has been chronicled in various genres, including film (*Mother Tongue, Fatherland* 2005), autobiography (Nguyen 2001), and oral history (DeBonis 1995).The term *Amerasian* is used to refer to children born to Vietnamese women who became pregnant during the Vietnam War by American soldiers, many of whom returned to the United States and had no further contact with the children or their mothers. Such offspring of "the enemy," many of whom physically resembled their fathers, were mistreated after the war.

31. Refugee resettlement in the United States since 1980 has been shaped by State Department programs permitting entry by Vietnamese. The McCain Amendment of 2004 extended initial policies permitting settlement by a spouse and the unmarried children of a former detainee to adults whose parents had been detainees. Vietnamese Amerasians are permitted to migrate to the United States under the 1987 Amerasian Homecoming Act, which was passed by Congress in 1988 and implemented in 1989. There have been various structural changes in the policies and laws dealing with Vietnamese refugees. The Orderly Departure Program (ODP), established in 1980, was closed in 1999. The Humanitarian Resettlement (HR) Initiative of the State Department is expected to process all remaining applicants under the ODP by the end of 2009. http://www.state.gov/g/prm/rls/117280.htm (accessed October 20, 2010).

32. In 2006, according to ACS data, 24 percent of Vietnamese aged twenty-five and older had a bachelor's degree or higher, and just over a quarter (26 percent) reported speaking English very well. Nationwide, 27 percent of adults have a bachelor's degree, and in Texas, the percentage is 25.1 percent. With a median household income of $52,408 in 2006 (higher than the national average) and a median family income of $56,186 (lower than the national average), Vietnamese immigrants make significantly less than Indians. Nationwide, 9.7 percent of Vietnamese males and 9.9 percent of Vietnamese females sixteen and older in the civilian labor force were in management, business, and finance; 6.0 percent of males and 2.81 percent of females were in information technology; 8.9 percent of males and 3.4 percent of females were in other sciences and engineering; 4.4 percent of males and 3.1 percent of females were in health care (as physicians, registered nurses, or other health professions); 17.2 percent of males and 30.9 percent of females were in services and 27.3 percent of males and 18 percent of females were in manufacturing, installation, and repair. The comparable nationwide figures for Indians for the latter two categories were 3.3 percent of males and 5.8 percent of females, and 4.4 percent of males and 4.7 percent of females, respectively.

33. Viswanath and Lee (2007) offer a brief discussion of the history of Asian American media.

34. Viswanath and Lee (2007: 208–209) identify five "typical functions" of ethnic media: cultural transmission, community boosting, surveillance, assimilation, and the dissemination of information.

35. See Bloemraad (2006) for additional discussion of the role of ethnic media in the process of political incorporation.

36. Other scholars have also identified modes of place-making among Vietnamese Americans in various locations in the United States (Bankston 1998; Mazumdar et al. 2000; Shelley 2001; Airriess 2002; and Aguilar-San Juan 2009).

37. Schrock 2008.

38. See also Wood (1997) and Meyers (2006).

39. See, for example, Lessinger (1995), Waghorne (1999), Bubinas (2003, 2005), and Skop (forthcoming).

40. For other models of commercial spaces, see Lessinger (1995) and Rangaswamy (2000). In early 2010 a part of southwest Houston was officially renamed Mahatma Gandhi District to recognize the high concentration of South Asian shops and restaurants. See http://www.hindu.com/2010/01/27/stories/2010012754661800.htm (accessed October 20, 2010).

41. See further discussion in Brettell (2008c).

42. Brettell (2005b).

43. This service was discontinued in 2007 because it became easier to access application forms on the Internet.

44. For further discussion, see Brettell (2005b).

45. See Brettell (2008a) for further discussion.

Chapter 2

1. This is in contrast to other nations, such as France (see Silverstein 2008), where republican traditions have historically minimized ethnicity, at least at the level of national discourse.

2. According to 2006 ACS data, 42 percent of foreign-born Indians in the United States had been naturalized (see Terrazas 2008a). The rate of naturalization in our research was higher than these national rates because the interviews were conducted among individuals who had been in the United States for a longer period of time and had children in U.S. schools, colleges, or universities.

3. Observations like these—and there were others—clearly essentialize Americans, but they also suggest the characteristics of the "other," relative to which first-generation Indian immigrants define themselves.

4. Kurien (2003; 2006; 2007) suggests that Indians in the United States have begun to mobilize as Hindus. She argues that this is a consequence not only of "pre-existing cultural commonalities but also of emergent identities" (2003: 283).

5. Espiritu (2001) finds a similar equation of *American* with *white* among Filipinos in the United States. The discussion of the Vietnamese in this chapter suggests that this idea is also meaningful to them, although they often include African Americans in their understanding of *American*.

6. O'Brien (2008: 129ff) refers to this as the "Where are you from? No, where are you from?" dance. It is a common experience among Latinos and Asians.

7. See also Dang (2005) on the "cultural work of anticommunism" among Vietnamese Americans in California.

8. A recent report (Terrazas 2008b) that drew on 2006 ACS data indicates that 72.8 percent of Vietnamese in the United States had become naturalized citizens. This rate is much higher than the rate for Indians (see note 2), but the data indicate that only 14.1 percent of Vietnamese arrived in the United States in 2000 or later, compared with just over a third of Indians. In general, Vietnamese in the United States move rather quickly from refugee status to legal permanent resident status and then to U.S. citizenship. The path to U.S. citizenship for the Vietnamese was facilitated by the 1975 Indochina Migration and Refugee Assistance Act, which set forth the conditions for resettlement. Under the Refugee Act of 1980, Vietnamese with refugee status could become permanent residents within one year of arrival and then become naturalized citizens after an additional four years.

9. This response is not common among Indians, many of whom observe dietary restrictions guided by their religious faith. Food is hence fundamental to their non-American cultural identity.

10. Of course under British colonial rule a "class" of Anglo-Indians—generally the result of partnerships between British men and Indian women—developed.

11. See Reed-Danahay (2010) for more discussion of the embodied aspects of identity among Vietnamese Americans.

12. See also Espiritu (1992).

13. See, for example, Maira (2002), Khandelwal (2002), Kurien (2003), Purkayastha (2005), and Shankar (2008). Many 1.5 and second-generation Indians find their way back to being Indian (and maybe South Asian or *desi*) when they go to college. For a recent study of South Asian Muslim youth and issues of citizenship and identity, see Maira (2009).

14. Dhingra (2007: 116) notes that after 9/11 many Indian Americans avoided the term *South Asian* in order to differentiate themselves from Muslim Americans. Kurien (2003), however, suggests that some Indian Americans are entering the public sphere by mobilizing around this term, which she suggests means "made in America." The difference here may be related to the pragmatic aspects of setting up organizations with broader appeal.

15. See Das Gupta (2006) for further discussion of the census classification debates. South Asians have been classified over the last century as Hindu, white, other,

and Asian (Lee 1993). In 1970, Asian Indians were counted as white and hence denied minority status. This was reversed in the 1980 census. Leonard (2007b: 460) points out that 93 percent of Indians identified themselves as racially "Asian" on the 2000 census. Mohapatra et al. (2003), in a survey conducted after 9/11, found that Asian Indian was the ethnic label preferred by many. See Jensen (1988) and Mazumdar (1989) for other discussions of race and whiteness among Asian Indians and South Asians, respectively.

16. See also Koshy (2002).

17. See Portes and Rumbaut (2001) for a consideration of younger immigrant youth and the influence of their family's human and social capital on their adaptation to life in the United States. Stepick, Stepick, and Labissiere (2002) argue that civic engagement among immigrant youth is not incompatible with a strong ethnic identification.

18. See also Reed-Danahay (2005).

19. The term *Americanized* is a negative one for many first-generation refugees and leads to a process of what Zhou and Bankston (1998: 224–227) call "selective Americanization."

20. This distinction is similar to the one common in France, between *l'état* (the nation and government) and *la patrie* or *le pays* (the country). It explains how those who fled South Vietnam can have such a strong nationalistic attachment to that country, because they fled the regime of communist North Vietnam, not their homeland.

21. The label *international student* is used to distinguish between students who are studying in the U.S. but plan to return home to Vietnam after completing their studies, and "domestic" students, who are Vietnamese Americans who live in the United States. The students in our group interviews were all Vietnamese American and these remarks from the international student were from a separate interview with Deborah Reed-Danahay about the student's leadership roles on campus and at home.

22. See Rudrappa (2004) and Subramanian (2007) for further discussion.

23. The different attitudes toward race that first- and second-generation Indians in the United States have has been noted by other scholars (Visweswaran 1997; Prasad 2000; Koshy 2002; Dhingra 2003; Kurien 2005; Bhatia 2007; Subramanian 2007; Shankar 2008). Morning (2001) concludes that respondents who are more acculturated to U.S. society are more likely than those who are less familiar with the United States to accept the black/white classification. For a discussion of the impact of 9/11 on the concept of race among Indian immigrants, see Bhatia (2008). For broader discussions of Asian immigrants, see Lowe (1996) and Lott (1998); on brownness, see O'Brien (2008).

24. Bhatia (2007: 171) suggests that many Indians in the United States acknowledge discrimination at work but tend to blame it more on themselves than on the system. Other scholars (Rangaswamy 2000) have noted that the rejection of a racial identity may also have to do with the ambiguity of where to place Indians racially. This uncertainty dates back to early twentieth-century debates in the United States over the Cau-

casian status of Indians, and to a broad tendency in America to treat them more as an ethnic group than as a racial group. Certainly the discomfort with "being Asian" that was articulated by participants in this research aligns with this conception. They felt no affinity with either the racial or cultural attributes of that classification.

25. For further discussion, see Brettell and Nibbs (2009).

26. Lisa Lowe (1996: 10) has observed that the state "legally transforms an Asian alien into an Asian-American citizen." See Espiritu (1992) and Gee et al. (1976) for more discussion of these imposed categories for Asian immigrants. See Oboler (1995) on Latin American migrants, for whom the category *Latino* or *Hispanic* becomes relevant only in the U.S. context.

27. Where political mobilization around a South Asian platform has occurred in the United States, the individuals involved have overwhelmingly been Indian Americans, and sometimes it is a *pan-Hindu* or *Indic* identity that emerges as the basis for mobilization in relation to homeland issues (Kurien 2004: 262). Such activities were not identified among Indians in the DFW area—a smaller and more uniformly professional population than the populations found in larger centers of Indian settlement on the East and West coasts. For additional discussion of West Coast mobilization of Indian immigrants see Kurien 2001a.

28. There are several recent studies of the impact of American institutions and popular culture on Asian American youth (Zhou and Bankston 1998; Kibria 2002; Min 2002; Park, Goodwin, and Lee 2003; Davé, Nishime, and Oren 2005; Lee and Zhou 2004). For collections of narratives of college students from Asian immigrant backgrounds in the United States, see Dublin (1996) and Chan (2006). See also Min and Kim (1999). Lam (2005) and Pham (1999, 2008) are examples of autoethnographic writing that deals with issues of identity from the perspective of 1.5-generation Vietnamese Americans. On racialized notions of American identity among Asian youth, see Junn and Masuoka (2008) and Zhou (2004).

29. Discussions that began to appear early in 2010 regarding the "whitening" of the official portrait of Governor Bobby Jindal, by comparison with more informal photographs, are particularly interesting in this regard (Aravosis 2010).

Chapter 3

1. An increasing focus on the religious practices of post-1965 immigrants remedies what sociologist R. Stephen Warner (1998: 6) described more than a decade ago as the "nearly complete neglect of their burgeoning religious institutions by researchers and the public." For earlier work, see Haddad and Lummis (1987), Williams (1988), Min (1992), and Numrich (1996). For more recent work, see Ebaugh and Chafetz (2000), Chen (2002), Min and Kim (2002), Carnes and Yang (2004a), Leonard et al. (2005), Ecklund (2006), Joshi (2006), Leong et al.(2007), Levitt (2007), Foley and Hoge (2007), Hondagneu-Sotelo (2007), Kniss and Numrich (2007), Foner and Alba (2008), and Stepick,

Rey, and Mahler (2009). For survey research on Asian immigrants and religious participation, see Klineberg (2004); Lien, Conway, and Wong (2004); and Lien (2007).

2. See also Eck 2007.

3. Warner's use of the term *congregation* is distinct from that of Ebaugh and
Chafetz (2000: 347), who draw on the more formal definition of a particular kind of
religious organization patterned on Western Christian denominations.

4. An earlier estimation set the proportion of Catholics at 40 percent of all first-
wave refugees from Vietnam (Kelly 1986: 141). For an overview of religion in Vietnam, see Condominas (1987). For other U.S.-based studies of Vietnamese religious
participation, see Rutledge (1992), Bankston and Zhou (1995, 1996), Nguyen and Barber (1998), McLellan (1999), and Phan (2005).

5. It is primarily Vietnamese of the 1.5 and second generations who are involved
in Protestant religious groups, and these individuals were not captured in the parent
interviews, which drew only from the first generation. No parent respondents mentioned Cao Dai or any other Vietnamese sect, even though some members of the first
generation do participate in such religions.

6. Our use of Vietnamese terms here is intended to provide cultural background
for concepts and ideas expressed by our research participants, to indicate where "native" terms exist and what they mean, and not for the purposes of linguistic analysis.
Therefore, we do not include the correct diacritical marks for these terms.

7. Trevino (2006: 71–72) also notes the importance of Catholic youth organizations that "fostered a sense of social responsibility through community service"
among Mexican Catholics.

8. The Catholic Church does, however, communicate an antiabortion stance in
publications that reach parishioners. There are significant political implications for
this position among the most devout, especially in terms of voting for those who share
their views.

9. Other scholars (Rutledge 1992; Numrich 1996, 1998; Prebish 1999) have noted
that the dominant form of Buddhism in Vietnam is the Mahayana tradition, car-
ried over from China. The Theravada tradition came directly from India and is more
prevalent in South Vietnam and in Southeast Asia more generally. DFW informants
explained that the presence of Theravada in the DFW area is due to the many Vietnamese who migrated from the central region and the city of Hue, where Theravada
is more common. No research participant mentioned the "engaged Buddhism" that
has become prevalent among Buddhists worldwide, including among the followers
of Vietnamese monk Thich Nhat Hanh, who is based in France. As Thomson (2007:
115) points out, this movement is associated more with Western converts to Buddhism
than with Asian immigrant temples.

10. In an earlier study of Vietnamese refugees in Oklahoma City, Paul Rutledge
(1985: 15) suggests that in this "portion of the solid South Bible Belt, a visibly prom-

inent and most acceptable category of the host society is its religious institutions. Therefore, as a strategy for adaptation, the Vietnamese have employed their religions as avenues of acceptability." Rutledge reports, for example, that the Buddhists referred to their temple as a "church" and to their monk as a "priest," and that classes for children on Sunday were called "Sunday school." The temple was also set up with pews. The differences between Vietnamese Buddhists in Oklahoma City in 1981 and those in the DFW region in 2006–2008 may reflect historical changes in the reception of refugees and immigrants.

11. Reed-Danahay thanks Linh Le for her assistance in the cultural translation of this phrase and concept.

12. Although Rydström associates this concept primarily with values of femininity, Chi (2009: 323) sees it in terms of male roles in the family. This variety suggests that it is perhaps a value that cuts across genders.

13. See Brettell (2005a) for further discussion of religious participation based on a larger survey of 102 Indian immigrants in DFW. Several authors (Rangaswamy 2000, Purkayastha 2005) emphasize that Hindus in particular are periodic rather than regular attendees at their temples, largely because they are also involved in home-based rituals. Throughout the United States, Indian Hindu homes usually have a small corner (maybe a closet) where sacred images are displayed and where they can pray (see Jacob and Thakur 2000). Such altars also exist in Buddhist Vietnamese homes.

14. See, for example, Leonard (1997; 2006), Waghorne (1999), Purkayastha (2005), and Eck (2007). Hirschman (2004) views the adaptation to weekly and weekend services as one measure of Americanization.

15. See Lessinger (1995), Levitt (2000), Khandelwal (2002), and Kurien (2002).

16. See Brettell (2005b) for discussion of the development of the DFW Hindu Temple.

17. See Jones (1990) and Beckerlegge (2006).

18. Brettell is grateful to Steven Lindquist for his bibliographical suggestions regarding *seva*, and to B. B. Ghate for further clarification. Beckerlegge (2006) specifically addresses the question of whether *seva* (as organized philanthropy) was rooted deeply in Hindu tradition or emerged in the context of India's encounter with the West.

19. Compared to Hindu temples in other cities in the United States, the DFW Hindu Temple appears to be stronger in its focus on civic engagement. Jacob and Thakur (2000: 156) claim that in Houston social service provision is more informal because many members of the Hindu temple there argue that the temple is "for worship while society is for services." These authors found that their informants consider social service provision to be a Western idea and not part of Hindu tradition. Nevertheless, temple members in Houston have participated in a blood drive for someone in need of a bone marrow transplant.

20. Swaminarayan (1781–1830) established a movement that has considerable importance in India and to Indians, particularly to Gujaratis spread throughout the world. Its founder, Sahajanand, encouraged care for the poor and the building of hospitals. He was opposed to the Hindu practice of *sati* (bride burning) and instead encouraged the remarriage of young widows. He also taught that the wealthy should be generous with their wealth. The Chinmaya Mission was founded in 1953 by devotees of Swami Chinmayananda. It emphasizes the wisdom of Vedanta, a spiritual tradition within Hinduism that focuses on self-realization and higher inquiry. *Veda* means knowledge. In India, Chinmaya Mission is active in school sponsorship.

21. Jains strongly adhere to the principle of *ahimsa* or nonviolence. Jainism includes the Hindu concepts of karma, *moksha* (release from the cycle of death and rebirth), and reincarnation. Jains worship some Hindu gods and goddesses, follow many of the same customs and traditions as Hindus, and often intermarry with Hindus. Jains in India support a number of charitable trusts.

22. Although not writing about the Mar Thoma Church, George (2005) offers an interesting analysis of how a more orthodox Indian Christian church becomes a space for empowerment for Indian men from Kerala who follow their wives to the United States.

23. See Neill (1984).

24. The Patriarch of Babylon is the leader of the Assyrian Church of the East. The Syriac liturgy, also known as the Assyro-Chaldean liturgy, is one of the most ancient traditions of Christian worship and emphasizes the divine nature of Christ.

25. See Abraham and Shryock (2000) and Leonard (2003).

26. Several anti-Muslim incidents occurred in the DFW area in the aftermath of 9/11. A mosque in the suburb of Irving was vandalized two days after 9/11 when six bullets shattered windows, causing more than $3,000 worth of damage. Another mosque, in suburban Carrollton, was also shattered by bullets, and a firebomb was hurled into a mosque in Denton. A Pakistani Muslim was killed at his grocery store in Pleasant Grove.

27. Indian Muslims, of course, may interact with non-Indians in mosques that draw a more ethnically diverse membership.

28. Our work supports Ecklund and Park's recent (2005) observations that religious participation among Asian Americans in general can lead to greater civic participation, especially defined as "volunteerism."

29. This issue has also been addressed by Foley and Hoge (2007) and Becker (1999).

30. Carnes and Yang (2004b: 13) observe that religions such as Islam, Buddhism, and Hinduism do not have well-developed traditions of providing organized social services in home-country religious institutions, but they may develop them in the United States.

31. See, for example, the role that Mary Queen of Vietnam Catholic Church in New Orleans played in rebuilding the community after Hurricane Katrina (Leong et al. 2007).

32. See Reed-Danahay (2008) for a profile of a Vietnam-born convert to fundamentalist Christianity who was heavily involved in Texas politics.

33. Prominent politicians Bobby Jindal, governor of Louisiana, and Nikki Haley, governor of South Carolina, both converted to Christianity, from Hinduism and Sikhism, respectively. These conversions have been controversial and much discussed within the U.S. Indian immigrant population.

34. Religion has historically been polarizing in Vietnam too, with Catholics being persecuted because of their link to colonial regimes. However, among the diaspora population this history is viewed primarily in terms of anticolonial and nationalist movements rather than as a Buddhist versus Catholic split. Buddhists and Catholics in the United States unite in criticizing the lack of religious freedom in Vietnam.

35. In this approach, they operate in similar fashion to their fellow nationals in the Chicago area, where Hindus and Muslims "coexist peaceably," leading "somewhat separate social and religious lives" but "sharing a commercial center" and viewing themselves "as a minority with common interests in a larger, white-dominated world" (Rangaswamy 2000: 30). Of course in many Hindu temples in the United States, people bridge regional religious differences as well as linguistic differences in order to work together.

36. Although the DFW Indian community has not been identified in our research as being involved in such activities, in California, Indian immigrants have been active in the Hindu Nationalist movement, as well as in activities related to how Hinduism and Indian history are represented in sixth grade school text books. These activities have been proposed by organizations such as the Hindu Education Foundation and the Vedic Foundation, both of which are affiliated with militant Hindu nationalist ideology and linked to the World Association for Vedic Studies, a Hindu nationalist organization. Similarly, Khandelwal (2002) writes about Hindu fundamentalist and Hindu nationalist activities within the Hindu community in New York City. She observes, however, that "Hindu nationalist versus secularist struggles were not waged openly, but rather smoldered in certain organizations" (90). For more discussion, see Rajagopal (2000).

37. See Reed-Danahay (2008).

38. See Brettell (2005b) and Darling (2008).

Chapter 4

Portions of this chapter were adapted from Brettell and Reed-Danahay (2008) and reprinted with permission. (c) 2008 Russell Sage Foundation, 112 East 64th Street, New York, NY 10065.

1. See, for example, Okamura (1983), Markowitz (1992), Gold (1995), Liu (1998), Gamm and Putnam (1999), Soyer (2001, 2006), Moya (2005), Avenarius (2007), Ramakrishnan and Bloemraad (2008a).

2. Some of this work has been comparative across several immigrant populations in the United States (Sassen-Koob 1979; Min 1998; Dhingra 2003); other work has traced phases in the growth of voluntary associations within a single population—for example, from traditional associations to service organizations to political action coalitions (Kuo 1977). Scholars have also explored whether participation in homeland politics through association activities enhances or hinders the process of political incorporation in the country of immigration (Pantoja 2005; Landolt 2008). At least one author (Orozco 2004) points to the development of civic participation skills within homeland associations, while another (Breton 1991) looks at the political dimensions of community organization, emphasizing how ethnic communities govern themselves, formulate collective goals, and mobilize support. For comparable work on the political dimensions of immigrant associations in Europe, see, for example, Werbner (1985), Bousquet (1991), Fennema and Tillie (1999), Hamidi (2003), and Caponio (2005).

3. Political sociologist Irene Bloemraad (2006) has, for example, drawn attention to the role of governments in extending support to such associations by contrasting the Canadian context of extensive support, which derives from Canada's multiculturalist immigration policy, with the U.S. context, where such support is virtually absent.

4. For discussions of association life among Indians elsewhere in the United States, see Bacon (1996), Abraham (2000), Rangaswamy (2000), Khandelwal (2002), Rudrappa (2004), and Das Gupta (2006).

5. For further analysis based on another research sample, see Brettell (2005a).

6. For previous discussions of association life among Vietnamese in the United States and Canada, see Dorais (1992, 2007), Kibria (1993), and Bloemraad (2006).

7. Dr. Reddy attended the Texas Chapter banquets in 2004, 2005, and 2006.

8. In the summer of 2009, Raj Goyle announced his bid for a seat in the United States Congress. In the fall of 2009 and again in the fall of 2010, Nikki Haley returned to Dallas as a candidate for governor of South Carolina and spoke to members of the IAFC, several of whom made contributions to her campaign. Haley traveled across the United States to visit various Indian communities and referred to all Indian immigrants in the country as her political base.

9. On October 29, 2007, the U.S. House of Representatives also recognized Diwali as an important festival.

10. See Reed-Danahay (2010) for a cultural analysis of this parade.

11. See Reed-Danahay (2008) for further discussion of this protest.

12. See Ong and Meyer (2008).

13. This was an ethnographic question asked to elicit how Indians themselves think about the meaning of citizenship. The question contained no a priori assumption about either the legal or participatory dimensions, nor about rights versus duties. Thus, what is most interesting is how individuals responded and what they chose to emphasize.

14. Several members of this Club were born in Africa (Zambia, Uganda)—evidence of the importance of networks in building an organization.

15. Some of the factors surrounding the change from active to inactive are discussed in the conclusion to this book.

16. This aspect of Vietnam's relationship with China came up more recently in China's claim to the Spratly and Paracel islands in the South China Sea, which was the focus of a display during the 2008 Tet festival (discussed further in Chapter 5). This dispute was also a concern of Cao P's. A land treaty regarding the Sino-Vietnamese border was signed by the two governments in 1999 (see Thao 2000), but the controversy over the border continues to fuel discussion among Vietnamese Americans. The dispute over sovereignty of the Spratly and Paracel Islands continues unresolved. Secretary of State Hillary Clinton warned China about its activities in these islands during an official state visit in summer 2010 (see Jacobs 2010).

17. These strong female role models also included Lady Trieu, a somewhat mythic figure and important general in about 225 A.D. One female leader mentioned that her role model was a late nineteenth-century emperor of the Nguyen dynasty who as a teenager fought against French colonialism.

18. To the extent that all such organizations fill a vacuum to which the Indian government does not attend, there is a political dimension to their missions.

19. Pratham has developed a unique model to address illiteracy in India. They hire women who have completed at least the tenth grade who are from the same poor neighborhoods and villages as the children to be teachers. Each teacher has her own school and about twenty children in her charge. As the women gain experience they can move up into the management of several schools. Pratham has built a network of global support, and in 2010 it won the Henry R. Kravis Prize in Leadership—an extraordinary recognition for an Indian transnational charitable organization.

20. See, for example, Ebaugh and Chafetz (1999) and Marquardt (2005).

21. Dorais (2007: 91) observes that among the Vietnamese in Montreal there is a lack of strong leadership, partly due to division within the population, partly due to the lack of interest among educated professionals in getting too involved in ethnic associations.

22. Elsewhere Brettell (2003: 184–190) has described this character as the "cultural ethos" of a city. This ethos may impact immigration flows as well as settlement patterns and processes of incorporation. See Rutheiser (1996; 1999) for discussion of the messages and images that a city projects.

Chapter 5

1. See also Bankston and Henry (2000), McAloon (1984), Beeman (1993), and Procter (2004). Our use of *spectacle* is different from that of Guy Debord (1994), who focuses on aspects of authenticity, representation, and alienation in cultural forms. We employ *spectacle* in a looser sense, to refer to various cultural performances and rituals connected to political symbolism.

2. Flores and Benmayor (1997: 1, 7); see also Rosaldo (1997).

3. On political symbolism, see also Cohen (1979), Handelman (1990), and Harrison (2000). On secular symbolism, see Gusfield and Michalowicz (1984).

4. See, for example, Orsi (1985); Meagher (1985); Conzen (1989); Schneider (1990); Bodnar (1992); Moss (1995); Heideking, Fabre, and Dreisbach (2001); Graden (2003); Sterne (2004); Greene (2005).

5. See also Waters 1990.

6. For other examples, see Baumann (1996) and Davila (2001).

7. See Avieli (2005) on the role of Tet in national identity in Vietnam, through a discussion of food symbolism.

8. The accounts that follow are based on ethnographic fieldwork conducted at the festivals and on informal interviews of organizers and attendees. Reed-Danahay attended the DFW Tet Festival for three successive years (2006, 2007, and 2008), working the second two years as a volunteer. Brettell attended India Nite five times between 2002 and 2008.

9. Many studies of Vietnamese in other regions of the country mention the importance of Tet festivals. See, for example, Meyers (2006), Rutledge (1992), and Mazumdar et al. (2000).

10. The festival was held there again in 2009, 2010, and 2011.

11. See http://www.tradersvillage.com/en/about

12. See also Davila (2001) and Comaroff and Comaroff (2009).

13. The 2008 festival at Traders Village was also connected to festivities and the sale of Tet-related items at the newly renovated shopping mall, Asia Times Square, mentioned in Chapter 1. People went to both locations, but few non-Vietnamese were seen at the mall events. Inside the grocery store in the mall, Lion Dancers performed in the aisles and danced on top of the checkout conveyer belts, to the glee of watching children, as they had done in previous years at an older shopping center.

14. See the discussion of this in Chapter 4.

15. See Reed-Danahay 2008.

16. The Horseshoe Casino is not just a site for gambling. It also hosts important musical acts that draw audiences because of the quality of their performance of both traditional and popular Vietnamese music and dance. Although concerns about excessive gambling and about strong marketing to Asian populations on the part of casinos are expressed in the national media (see Smith 2006), criticism of the Horseshoe

Casino's sponsorship of the festival was not observed during fieldwork at Tet or in any coverage of it in the local media.

17. The format of the event is similar each year, although the specific content, including what guests are honored, varies. This routine is what lends the evening its ritualistic dimension.

18. The Congressional Caucus on India and Indian Americans is the largest country caucus in the United States. Its mission is to push the agenda of the Indian American community on Capitol Hill.

19. As mentioned earlier, as an umbrella organization, IANT emphasizes that it is not overtly political. Homeland politics are left to other organizations with specifically Hindu or Muslim identities. See Kurien (2001b) for a discussion of two such organizations in the California context.

20. We both attended this banquet.

21. For broad discussions, see Wiessnert and Schiefenhovel (1996), Dietler and Hayden (2001), Mintz and Du Bois (2002). Examples include displays of status and prestige in the Kwakiutl potlatch (Jonaitis 1991) and at feasts among the prehistoric Maya (Count 2001: 940).

22. On the Web site for DFW AACC (http://www.dfwaacc.org/dfwaacc/about-us; accessed February 1, 2011), the logo for the organization is described as follows: "The logo has a flat bottom line suggesting a solid foundation. The round shape/curve line of name suggests a smiling face. The whole logo looks like an Asian bowl of rice; its seven stars mean Texas with luck."

23. Chow, who as of 2010 was still serving as mayor of Addison, came to the United States in 1979. He has a master's in business administration and owns a successful restaurant as well as an Allstate Insurance agency (advertised in the 2005 banquet program). He is also involved in real estate. For several years Addison has hosted the annual international festival sponsored by DFW International Community Alliance.

24. Duranti (2006: 492) usefully looks at how politicians use "linguistic resources to construct the kind of person that they want voters to know and believe in," but his study of rhetorical strategies does not include those of immigrant politicians.

Chapter 6

1. There is also the Greater Dallas Indo-American Chamber of Commerce, founded in 1999, which is extremely active. Its mission is to promote and foster local commerce and trade and to encourage and facilitate trade between the United States and India. At the tenth anniversary banquet of this organization, the Indian Ambassador to the United States was the keynote speaker. The existence of this chamber in itself suggests the ambivalence about Asianness that exists among the DFW-area Indian population.

2. This district, located near Harry Hines and Royal Lane, west of downtown Dallas, has more than two hundred wholesale and retail enterprises, the majority owned by Koreans. For further discussion, see Panchuk (2001).

3. Only 18 percent of individuals involved in the Indian parent interviews indicated that they participated in a pan-Asian organization.

4. We both attended this forum in 2004 and 2005.

5. http://www.asianamericanforum.org/Mission.htm (accessed October 20, 2010).

6. http://www.leap.org

7. LEAP has recently published an electronic public policy report, "The State of Asian America: Trajectory of Civic and Political Engagement" (Ong 2008).

8. Clickers are handheld audience-response devices that allow students or others participating in a public event such as a lecture to provide instant feedback to questions from the teacher or speaker.

9. In the fall of 2009, DFW International Community Alliance, an organization whose mission is to bring together all the immigrant communities in the North Texas region for various activities and events as well as to promote the increasing diversity of the area, sponsored its own leadership institute. The program included seminars and workshops designed to "enhance skills and cultivate leadership talents through training for more efficient and effective practices in the traditional American style of conducting business." Workshop topics included nonprofit management, communication, organizing events, fundraising, accessing the city council and the mayor's office, and running for civic office. This is another example of a teaching curriculum.

10. Of course this does occur, as evidenced in the film *Miss India Georgia* (1998).

11. Between 1999 and 2005, five children of Indian ancestry won the Spelling Bee, and in 2005 the top four finalists were of Indian ancestry. The film *Spellbound* (2002) captured this craze among Indian Americans. See Berger (2005).

12. http://www.rotary.org/EN/STUDENTSANDYOUTH/YOUTHPROGRAMS/ ROTARYYOUTNGOEADERSHIPAWARDS(RYLA)/Pages/ridefault.aspx (accessed October 20, 2010) has information about Interact, Rotaract, and RYLA. Interact is a service organization and branch of Rotary International for youth ages fourteen to eighteen. Community service is a vital component of Interact, as it is for Rotary Club in general.

13. Although there is no Rotary Club composed of Vietnamese American adults, there is increasing participation in Rotary Clubs by Vietnamese Americans as their civic participation in general increases. There are no Rotary Clubs in Vietnam, although several humanitarian projects in Vietnam were organized by U.S. Rotary Club chapters. See http://www.rotary.org/EN/ABOUTUS/SITETOOLS/CLUBLOCATOR (accessed October 20, 2010).

14. Over the course of our research, membership between the two associations shifted, especially after a controversy on the campus (see Reed-Danahay 2008) over

the display of the Vietnamese flag provoked division among students over how active Vietnamese American students should be in anticommunist activities orchestrated by the older generation. Just as Vietnamese immigrants in general experience fragmentation within and between their associations (see Chapter 4), it seems that students also exit groups and form alliances in other associations in order to voice their dissent to one another. There is also, however, mobility and flexibility in this process.

15. Putnam (2000) notes that the PTA was one of the most common community organizations in the middle of the twentieth century, although membership has waxed and waned since 1945. To our knowledge, no one has ever explored the extent to which Asian immigrant parents are involved in the PTA, although there has been some discussion of Latino participation (Hero et al. 2000; Segura, Pachon, and Woods 2003).

16. Participation in the PTA can be difficult even for working mothers who are native-born U.S. citizens, which Reed-Danahay found when the PTA meetings at her children's elementary school in Texas were scheduled during morning hours, when she was teaching and neither she nor her husband could attend. When the PTA is organized primarily by stay-at-home mothers, any mothers who work outside the home are less able to participate, and this is a barrier for immigrant parents who are unable to take off time from work for such participation.

17. See Just (1980) and Tsai (2000), who discusses "accidental" candidates who may move from involvement in organizations like the PTA to running for political office.

18. See Reed-Danahay (2008) for additional examples of immigrant leadership using a communities of practice approach.

Conclusion

1. This potential for division was brought into clear focus in 1999 in Westminster, California, when a protest erupted over the display of a communist Vietnamese flag in a storefront (Tran and Warren 1999); it was also evident in the struggle over the proper flag to display on a university campus in 2006 (Reed-Danahay 2008), and on a smaller scale in the example of the disagreement discussed in Chapter 6 over labeling a map of Vietnam at the Tet festival with Saigon or Ho Chi Minh city.

2. See also Hansen and Oliver-Smith 1982, Richmond 1988, Hein 1993, Harrell-Bond 1999, Colson 2003, Peteet 2005.

3. See also Rutledge (1985).

4. Recent work on religious assemblies (Stepick 2005; Foley and Hoge 2007; Foner and Alba 2008) has tended to emphasize the latter view more.

5. See, for example, Waters (1996), Itzigsohn and Dore-Cabral (2000), Otis (2001), and Lien, Conway, and Wong (2004).

6. See, for example, Lee and Zhou (2004).

7. See, however, Moon (1984).

Bibliography

Abraham, Margaret. 2000. *Speaking the Unspeakable: Marital Violence Among South Asian Immigrants in the United States.* New Brunswick, NJ: Rutgers University Press.

Abraham, Sameer Y., and Andrew Shryock. 2000. *Arab Detroit: From Margin to Mainstream.* Detroit: Wayne State University Press.

Achor, Shirley. 1978. *Mexican-Americans in a Dallas Barrio.* Tucson: University of Arizona Press.

Adler, Rachel H. 2007. *Yucatecans in Dallas, Texas: Breaching the Border, Bridging the Distance.* 2nd edition. Boston: Allyn and Bacon.

Aguilar-San Juan, Karen. 2009. *Little Saigons: Staying Vietnamese in America.* Minneapolis: University of Minnesota Press.

Airriess, Christopher A. 2002. "Creating Vietnamese Landscapes and Place in New Orleans." In *Geographical Identities of Ethnic America: Race, Space, and Place,* edited by Kate A. Berry and Martha L.Henderson, 228–253. Las Vegas: University of Nevada Press.

Alba, Richard, and Victor Nee. 2003. *Remaking the American Mainstream: Assimilation and Contemporary Immigration.* Cambridge, MA: Harvard University Press.

Alexander, George P. 2004. *New Americans: The Progress of Asian Indians in America.* 2nd edition. Columbia, MO: South Asia Books.

Anderson, Benedict. 1991. *Imagined Communities: Reflections on the Origins and Spread of Nationalism.* Revised edition. London: Verso.

———. 1992. *Long-Distance Nationalism: World Capitalism and the Rise of Identity Politics. The Wertheim Lecture.* Amsterdam, Netherlands: CASA.

Anderson, Wanni W., and Robert G. Lee. 2005. "Asian American Displacements." In *Displacements and Diasporas: Asians in the Americas,* edited by Wanni W. Anderson and Robert G. Lee, 1–22. New Brunswick, NJ: Rutgers University Press.

Aoki, Andrew L., and Okiyoshi Takeda. 2008. *Asian American Politics*. Malden, MA: Polity Press.

Appadurai, Arjun. 1996. *Modernity at Large: Cultural Dimensions of Globalization*. Minneapolis: University of Minnesota Press.

Aravosis, John. 2010. "A Tale of Two Jindals." http://www.americablog.com/2010/01/tale -of-two-jindals.html (accessed July 15, 2010).

Avenarius, Christine. 2007. "Cooperation, Conflict and Integration Among Sub-Ethnic Immigrant Groups from Taiwan." *Population, Space and Place* 13: 95–112.

Avieli, Nir. 2005. "Vietnamese New Year Rice Cakes: Iconic Festive Dishes and Contested National Identity." *Ethnology* 44: 167–187.

Bacon, Jean. 1996. *Life Lines: Community, Family, and Assimilation Among Asian Indian Immigrants*. New York: Oxford University Press.

Baker, Wayne, and Andrew Shryock. 2009. "Citizenship and Crisis." In *Citizenship and Crisis: Arab Detroit After 9/11*, edited by Detroit Arab American Study Team, 3–32. New York: Russell Sage Foundation.

Balibar, Étienne. 1988. "Propositions on Citizenship." *Ethics* 98: 723–730.

Bammer, Angelika, ed. 1994. *Displacements: Cultural Identities in Question*. Bloomington: Indiana University Press.

Bankston, Carl L., III. 1998. "Versailles Village: The History and Structure of a Vietnamese Community in New Orleans." *Free Inquiry in Creative Sociology* 26: 79–89.

Bankston, Carl L. III, and Jacques Henry. 2000. "Spectacles of Ethnicity: Festivals and the Commodification of Ethnic Culture Among Louisiana Cajuns." *Sociological Spectrum* 20: 377–407.

Bankston, Carl L., III, and Min Zhou. 1995. "Religious Participation, Ethnic Identification, and the Adaptation of Vietnamese Adolescents in an Immigrant Community." *Sociological Quarterly* 36: 523–534.

———. 1996. "The Ethnic Church, Ethnic Identification, and the Social Adjustment of Vietnamese Adolescents." *Review of Religious Research* 38: 18–37.

Baron, Stephen, John Field, and Tom Schuller. 2000. *Social Capital: Critical Perspectives*. Oxford, UK: Oxford University Press.

Barreto, Matt A. 2005. "Latino Immigrants at the Polls: Foreign-Born Voter Turnout in the 2002 Election." *Political Research Quarterly* 58: 79–86.

Barth, Fredrik. 1969. *Ethnic Groups and Boundaries: The Social Organization of Culture Difference*. Boston: Little, Brown.

Batheja, Aman. 2010. "More D-FW Cities Tapping into Natural Gas Drilling Revenue to Help Ease Budget Woes." *Fort Worth Star-Telegram*, August 29: B.

Baumann, Gerd. 1996. *Contesting Culture: Discourses of Identity in Multi-Ethnic London*. Cambridge, UK: Cambridge University Press.

Bayly, Susan. 2007. *Asian Voices in a Postcolonial Age: Vietnam, India, and Beyond*. Cambridge, UK: Cambridge University Press.

Becker, Penny Edgell. 1999. *Congregations in Conflict: Cultural Models of Local Religious Life*. New York: Cambridge University Press.

Beckerlegge, Gwilym. 2006. *Swami Vivekananda's Legacy of Service: A Study of the Ramakrishna Math and Mission*. New Delhi, India: Oxford University Press.

Beeman, William O. 1993. The Anthropology of Theater and Spectacle, *Annual Review of Anthropology* 22: 369–393.

Berger, Joseph. 2005. "Striving in America, and in the Spelling Bee." *New York Times*, June 5. www.nytimes.com/2005/06/05/weekinreview/05berger.html (accessed September 30, 2008).

Bhalla, Vibha. 2006. "The New Indians: Reconstructing Indian Identity in the United States." *American Behavioral Scientists* 50: 118–136.

Bhatia, Sunil. 2007. *American Karma: Race, Culture, and Identity in the Indian Diaspora*. New York: New York University Press.

———. 2008. "9/11 and the Indian Diaspora: Narratives of Race, Place and Immigrant Identity." *Journal of Intercultural Studies* 29: 21–39.

Billett, Stephen. 2007. "Including the Missing Subject: Placing the Personal Within the Community." In *Communities of Practice: Critical Perspectives*, edited by Jason Hughes, Nick Jewson, and Lorna Unwin, 55–67. New York: Routledge.

Bloemraad, Irene. 2000. "Citizenship and Immigration: A Current Review." *Journal of International Migration and Integration* 1: 9–37.

———. 2006. *Becoming a Citizen: Incorporating Immigrants and Refugees in the United States and Canada*. Berkeley: University of California Press.

Bodnar, John. 1992. *Remaking America: Public Memory, Commemoration, and Patriotism in the Twentieth Century*. Princeton, NJ: Princeton University Press.

Bourdieu, Pierre. 1986. "The Forms of Capital." In *Handbook of Theory and Research in the Sociology of Education*, edited by John G. Richardson, 241–258. New York: Greenwood Press.

———. 2004. *Equisse pour une auto-analyse*. Paris: Editions Raisons d'Agir.

Bousquet, Gisele L. 1991. *Behind the Bamboo Hedge: The Impact of Homeland Politics in the Parisian Vietnamese Community*. Ann Arbor: University of Michigan Press.

Brady, Marilyn Dell. 2004. *The Asian Texans*. San Antonio: University of Texas Institute of Texan Cultures.

Bramadat, Paul A. 2001. "Shows, Selves, and Solidarity: Ethnic Identity and Cultural Spectacles in Canada." *Canadian Ethnic Studies Journal* 33: 78–100.

Breton, Raymond. 1991. "The Political Dimension of Ethnic Community Organization." In *Ethnicity, Structured Inequality, and the State in Canada and the Federal Republic of Germany*, edited by Robin Ostow, Jurgen Fijalkowski, Y. Michael Bodemann, and Hans Merkens, 157–165. New York: Peter Lang.

Brettell, Caroline B. 2003. "Bringing the City Back In: Cities as Contexts for Immigrant Incorporation." In *American Arrivals: Anthropology Engages the New Immigration*, edited by Nancy Foner, 163–195. Santa Fe, NM: School of American Research.

———. 2005a. "The Spatial, Social, and Political Incorporation of Asian Indians in Dallas, Texas." *Urban Anthropology* 34: 247–280.

———. 2005b. "Voluntary Organizations, Social Capital, and the Social Incorporation of Asian Indian Immigrants in the Dallas-Fort Worth Metroplex." *Anthropological Quarterly* 78: 821–851.

———. 2008a. "Immigrants in a Sunbelt Metropolis: The Transformation of an Urban Place and the Construction of Community." In *Immigraton and Integration in Urban Communities: Renegotiating the City*, edited by Lisa M. Hanley, Blair A. Ruble, and Allison M. Garland, 143–175. Washington, DC, and Baltimore: Woodrow Wilson Center Press and Johns Hopkins University Press.

———. 2008b. "Big D: Incorporating New Immigrants in a Sunbelt Metropolis." In *Twenty-First Century Gateways: Immigrant Incorporation in Suburban America*, edited by Audrey Singer, Susan Hardwick, and Caroline B. Brettell, 53–86. Washington, DC: Brookings Institution.

———. 2008c. "Immigrants as Netizens: Political Mobilization in Cyberspace." In *Citizenship, Political Engagement, and Belonging: Immigrants in Europe and the United States*, edited by Deborah Reed-Danahay and Caroline B. Brettell, 226–243. New Brunswick, NJ: Rutgers University Press.

Brettell, Caroline B., and Faith Nibbs. 2009. "Lived Hybridity: Second-Generation Identity Construction Through College Festival." *Identities: Global Studies in Culture and Power* 16: 678–699.

———. 2011. "Immigrant Suburban Settlement and the 'Threat' to Middle Class Status and Identity: The Case of Farmers Branch, Texas." *International Migration* 49 (1): 1–30.

Brettell, Caroline B., and Deborah Reed-Danahay. 2008. "'Communities of Practice' for Civic and Political Engagement: Asian Indian and Vietnamese Immigrant Organizations in a Southwest Metropolis." In *Civic Hopes and Political Realities: Immigrants, Community Organizations, and Political Engagement*, edited by S. Karthick Ramakrishnan and Irene Bloemraad, 195–221. New York: Russell Sage Foundation.

Brubaker, William Rogers, ed. 1989. *Immigration and the Politics of Citizenship in Europe and North America*. Lanham, MD: University Press of America.

Bubinas, Kathleen. 2003. "The Commodification of Ethnicity in an Asian Indian Economy in Chicago." *City and Society* 15: 195–223.

———. 2005. "The Social Construction and Production of an Ethnic Economy in Chicago." *City and Society* 17: 161–179.

Cadaval, Olivia. 1998. *Creating a Latino Identity in the Nation's Capital: The Latino Festival*. New York: Garland.

Caponio, Tiziana. 2005. "Policy Networks and Immigrants' Associations in Italy: The Cases of Milan, Bologna and Naples." *Journal of Ethnic and Migration Studies* 31: 931–950.

Carnes, Tony, and Fenggang Yang, eds. 2004a. *Asian American Religions: The Making and Remaking of Borders and Boundaries*. New York: New York University Press.

———. 2004b. "Introduction." In *Asian American Religions: The Making and Remaking of Borders and Boundaries*, edited by Tony Carnes and Fenggang Yang, 1–37. New York: New York University Press.

Castles, Stephen, and Alastair Davidson. 2000. *Citizenship and Migration: Globalization and the Politics of Belonging*. New York: Routledge.

Chan, Sucheng, ed. 2006. *The Vietnamese American 1.5 Generation*. Philadelphia: Temple University Press.

Chavez, Leo R. 2008. *The Latino Threat: Constructing Immigrants, Citizens, and the Nation*. Stanford, CA: Stanford University Press.

Chen, Carolyn. 2002. "The Religious Varieties of Ethnic Presence: A Comparison Between a Taiwanese Immigrant Buddhist Temple and an Evangelical Christian Church." *Sociology of Religion* 63: 215–238.

Chi, Truong Huyen. 2009. "A Home Divided: Work, Body, and Emotions in the Post-Doi Moi Family." In *Reconfiguring Families in Contemporary Vietnam*, edited by Daniele Belanger and Megalie Barbieri, 298–328. Stanford, CA: Stanford University Press.

Chow, Esther Ngan-Ling. 1987. "The Development of Feminist Consciousness Among Asian American Women." *Gender and Society* 1: 284–299.

Cohen, Abner. 1979. "Political Symbolism." *Annual Review of Anthropology* 8: 87–113.

Cohen, Anthony P. 1982. *Belonging: Identity and Social Organization in British Rural Cultures*. Manchester, UK: Manchester University Press.

Cohen, Elizabeth F. 2009. *Semi-Citizenship in Democratic Politics*. Cambridge, UK: Cambridge University Press.

Coll, Kathleen. 2010. *Remaking Citizenship: Latina Immigrants and New American Politics*. Stanford, CA: Stanford University Press.

Collet, Christian, and Hiroko Furuya. 2005. "Transnationalism and Immigrant Incorporation: Considering the Protest-to-Politics Model in a Vietnamese American Community." Paper presented at annual meeting of the Western Political Science Association, Oakland, CA, March 17–19, 2005.

Collet, Christian, and Pei-Te Lien. 2009. *The Transnational Politics of Asian Americans*. Philadelphia: Temple University Press.

Colson, Elizabeth. 2003. "Forced Migration and the Anthropological Response." *Journal of Refugee Studies* 16: 1–18.

Comaroff, John L., and Jean Comaroff. 2009. *Ethnicity, Inc.* Chicago: University of Chicago Press.

Condominas, Georges. 1987. "Vietnamese Religion." In *The Encyclopedia of Religion*, edited by Mircea Eliade, translated by Maria Pilar Luna-Magannon, 256–260. New York: Macmillan.

Conzen, Kathleen. 1989. "Ethnicity as Festive Culture: Nineteenth-Century German America on Parade." In *The Invention of Ethnicity*, edited by Werner Sollors, 44–76. New York: Oxford University Press.

Count, Lisa J. 2001. "Like Water for Chocolate: Feasting and Political Ritual Among the Late Classic Maya at Xunantunich, Belize." *American Anthropologist* 103: 935–953.

Coutin, Susan Bibler. 1998. "From Refugees to Immigrants: The Legalization Strategies of Salvadoran Immigrants and Activists." *International Migration Review* 32: 901–925.

———. 2003a. *Legalizing Moves: Salvadoran Immigrants' Struggle for U.S. Residency.* Ann Arbor: University of Michigan Press.

———. 2003b. "Cultural Logics of Belonging and Movement: Transnationalism, Naturalization, and U.S. Immigration Politics." *American Anthropologist* 30: 508–526.

Cueller, Carlos. 2003. *Stories from the Barrio: A History of Mexican Fort Worth.* Fort Worth: Texas Christian University Press.

Dang, Thuy Vo. 2005. "The Cultural Work of Anticommunism in the San Diego Vietnamese American Community." *Amerasia Journal* 31: 64–86.

Darling, Carl. 2008. *North Texas Leads the Way in Bringing "Desi" Culture to a Wider Audience.* http://www.vscconsulting.com/vsc/article/4891 (accessed February 1, 2011).

Das Gupta, Monisha. 2006. *Unruly Immigrants: Rights, Activism, and Transnational South Asian Politics in the United States.* Durham, NC: Duke University Press.

Davé, Shilpa, LeiLani Nishime, and Tasha G. Oren, eds. 2005. *East Main Street: Asian American Popular Culture.* New York: New York University Press.

Davila, Arlene. 2001. *Latinos, Inc.: The Marketing and Making of a People.* Berkeley: University of California Press.

DeBonis, Steven. 1995. *Children of the Enemy: Oral Histories of Vietnamese Americans and Their Mothers.* Jefferson, NC: McFarland.

Debord, Guy. 1994. *The Society of the Spectacle.* New York: Zone Books.

Delanty, Gerard. 2002. "Two Conceptions of Cultural Citizenship: A Review of Recent Literature on Culture and Citizenship." *Global Review of Ethnopolitics* 1: 60–66.

———. 2003. "Citizenship as a Learning Process: Disciplinary Citizenship Versus Cultural Citizenship. *International Journal of Lifelong Education* 22: 597–605.

DeSipio, Louis. 1996. "Making Citizens or Good Citizens? Naturalization as a Predictor of Organizational and Electoral Behavior Among Latino Immigrants." *Hispanic Journal of Behavioral Sciences* 18: 194–213.

———. 2001. "Building American, One Person at a Time: Naturalization and Political Behavior of the Naturalized in Contemporary American Politics." In *E Pluribus Unum: Contemporary and Historical Perspectives of Immigrant Political Incorporation*, edited by Gary Gerstle and John Mollenkopf, 67–106. New York: Russell Sage Foundation.

Detroit Arab American Study Team. 2009. *Citizenship and Crisis: Arab Detroit After 9/11.* New York: Russell Sage Foundation.

Dhingra, Pawan. 2003. "The Second Generation in 'Big D': Korean American and Indian American Organizations in Dallas, TX." *Sociological Spectrum* 23: 247–278.

———. 2007. *Managing Multicultural Lives: Asian American Professionals and the Challenge of Multiple Identities.* Stanford, CA: Stanford University Press.

Dietler, Michael, and Brian Hayden. 2001. *Feasts: Archaeologial and Ethnological Perspectives on Food, Politics and Power.* Washington, DC: Smithsonian Press.

Do, Hien Duc. 1999. *The Vietnamese Americans.* Westport, CT: Greenwood Press.

Dorais, Louis-Jacques. 1992. "Les Associations Vietnamiennes à Montréal." *Canadian Ethnic Studies* 24: 79–95.

———. 2007. *Les Vietnamiens de Montréal.* Montréal: Les Presses de l'Université de Montréal.

Dublin, Thomas, ed. 1996. *Becoming American, Becoming Ethnic: College Students Explore Their Roots.* Philadelphia: Temple University Press.

Dufoix, Stéphane. 2008. *Diasporas.* Translated by William Rodarmor. Berkeley: University of California Press.

Dunbabin, Katherine M. D. 2003. *The Roman Banquet: Images of Conviviality.* Cambridge, UK: Cambridge University Press.

Duranti, Alessandro. 2006. "Narrating the Political Self in a Campaign for U.S. Congress." *Language in Society* 35: 467–497.

Dwyer, Peter. 2004. *Understanding Social Citizenship.* Bristol, UK: Policy Press.

Ebaugh, Helen Rose, and Janet Saltzman Chafetz. 1999. "Agents for Cultural Reproduction and Structural Change: The Ironic Role of Women in Religious Institutions." *Social Forces* 78: 585–612.

Ebaugh, Helen Rose, and Janet Saltzman Chafetz, eds. 2000. *Religion and the New Immigrants: Continuities and Adaptations in Immigrant Congregations.* Walnut Creek, CA: AltaMira Press.

Eck, Diana L. 2001. *A New Religious America: How a "Christian" Country Has Become the World's Most Religiously Diverse Nation.* San Francisco: HarperSanFrancisco.

———. 2007. "Religion." In *The New Americans: A Guide to Immigration Since 1965*, edited by Mary C. Waters and Reed Ueda, 214–227. Cambridge, MA: Harvard University Press.

Ecklund, Elaine Howard. 2006. *Korean American Evangelicals: New Models for Civic Life.* Oxford, UK: Oxford University Press.

Ecklund, Elaine Howard, and Jerry Z. Park. 2005. "Asian American Community Participation and Religion: Civic Model Minorities?" *Journal of Asian American Studies* 8: 1–21.

Espiritu, Yen Le. 1992. *Asian American Panethnicity: Bridging Institutions and Identities.* Philadelphia: Temple University Press.

———. 2001. "'We Don't Sleep Around Like White Girls Do': Family, Culture, and Gender in Filipina American Lives." *Signs: Journal of Women in Culture and Society* 26: 415–440.

Espiritu, Yen-Le, and David Lopez. 1990. "Panethnicity in the United States: A Theoretical Framework." *Ethnic and Racial Studies* 13: 198–224.

Evers, Adalbert. 2003. "Social Capital and Civic Commitment: On Putnam's Way of Understanding." *Social Policy and Society* 2: 13–21.

Fabre, Genevieve, and Jurgen Heideking. 2001."Introduction." In *Celebrating Ethnicity and Nation: American Festive Culture from the Revolution to the Early 20th Century*, edited by Jurgen Heideking, Genevieve Fabre, and Kai Dreisbach, 1–24. New York: Bergahn Books.

Fairbanks, Robert. 1998. *For the City as a Whole: Planning, Politics and the Public Interest in Dallas, Texas, 1900–1965*. Columbus: Ohio State University Press.

Faist, Thomas. 1995. *Social Citizenship for Whom?* Brookfield, VT: Ashgate.

Farber, Carole. 1983. "High, Healthy, and Happy: Ontario Mythology on Parade." In *The Celebration of Society: Perspectives on Contemporary Performance*, edited by Frank E. Manning, 33–50. Bowling Green, OH: Bowling Green State University Popular Press.

Fennema, Meindert, and Jean Tillie. 1999. "Political Participation and Political Trust in Amsterdam: Civic Communities and Ethnic Networks." *Journal of Ethnic and Migration Studies* 25: 703–726.

Fernandez, Marilyn. 2001. "Asian Indian Americans in the Bay Area and the Glass Ceiling." In *Race and Ethnicity: Critical Concepts in Sociology*, Vol. 4, edited by Harry Gouldbourne, 121–149. New York: Routledge.

Fiorina, Morris P. 1999. "Extreme Voice: The Dark Side of Civic Engagement." In *Civic Engagement in American Democracy*, edited by Theda Skocpol and Morris P. Fiorina, 395–426. Washington, DC: Brookings Institution.

Fitzgerald, David. 2000. *Negotiating Extra-Territorial Citizenship: Mexican Migration and the Transnational Politics of Community*. La Jolla: Center for Comparative Immigration Studies, University of California, San Diego.

Flores, William V. 2003. "New Citizens, New Rights: Undocumented Immigrants and Latino Cultural Citizenship." *Latin American Perspectives* 30: 87–100.

Flores, William V., and Rina Benmayor. 1997."Constructing Cultural Citizenship." In *Latino Cultural Citizenship: Claiming Identity, Space, and Rights*, edited by William V. Flores and Rina Benmayor, 1–23. Boston: Beacon Press.

Foley, Michael W., and Dean R. Hoge. 2007. *Religion and the New Immigrants: How Faith Communities Form Our Newest Citizens*. Oxford: Oxford University Press.

Foner, Nancy, and Richard Alba. 2008. "Immigrant Religion in the U.S. and Western Europe: Bridge or Barrier to Inclusion?" *International Migration Review* 42: 360–392.

Fortier, Anne-Marie. 2000. *Migrant Belongings: Memory, Space, Identity*. New York: Berg.

Freeman, James M. 1995. *Changing Identities: Vietnamese Americans, 1975–1995*. Boston: Allyn and Bacon.

Gamm, Gerald, and Robert D. Putnam. 1999. "The Growth of Voluntary Associations in America, 1840–1940." *Journal of Interdisciplinary History* 29: 511–557.

Gans, Herbert. 1979. "Symbolic Ethnicity: The Future of Ethnic Groups and Cultures in America." *Ethnic and Racial Studies* 2: 1–20.

Gans, Herbert J. 2007. "Ethnic and Racial Identity." In *The New Americans: A Guide to Immigration Since 1965*, edited by Mary C. Waters and Reed Ueda, 98–109. Cambridge, MA: Harvard University Press.

Gardner, Martha. 2005. *The Qualities of a Citizen: Women, Immigration and Citizenship, 1870–1965*. Princeton, NJ: Princeton University Press.

Gee, Emma, June Okida Kuramoto, Dean S. Toji, and Glen Iwasaki. 1976. *Counterpoint: Perspectives on Asian America*. Los Angeles: Asian American Studies Center, University of California.

Geertz, Clifford. 1962. "The Rotating Credit Association: A Middle Rung in Development." *Economic Development and Cultural Change* 10: 241–263.

Geertz, Clifford. 1973. *The Interpretation of Culture*. New York: Basic Books.

George, Rosemary Marangoly. 1997. "From Expatriate Aristocrat to Immigrant Nobody: South Asian Racial Strategies in the Southern California Context." *Diaspora* 6: 31–60.

George, Sheba. 2005. *When Women Come First: Gender and Class in Transnational Migration*. Berkeley: University of California Press.

Gerstle, Gary. 1999. "Liberty, Coercion, and the Making of Americans." In *The Handbook of Internaitonal Migration: The American Experience*, edited by Charles Hirschman, Philip Kasinitz, and Josh DeWind, 275–293. New York: Russell Sage Foundation.

Gerstle, Gary, and John Mollenkopf. 2001. *E Pluribus Unum? Contemporary and Historical Perspectives on Immigrant Incorporation*. New York: Russell Sage Foundation.

Gibson, Margaret A. 1988. *Accommodation Without Assimilation: Sikh Immigrants in an American High School*. Ithaca, NY: Cornell University Press.

Gilbertson, Greta, and Audrey Singer. 2003. "The Emergence of Protective Citizenship in the USA: Naturalization Among Dominican Immigrants in the Post 1996 Welfare Reform Era." *Ethnic and Racial Studies* 26: 25–51.

Glick Schiller, Nina, and Ayşe Çağlar. 2008. "'And Ye Shall Possess It, and Dwell Therein': Social Citizenship, Global Christianity, and Nonethnic Immigrant Incorporation." In *Citizenship. Political Engagement, and Belonging: Immigrants in Europe and the United States*, edited by Deborah Reed-Danahay and Caroline B. Brettell, 203–225. New Brunswick, NJ: Rutgers University Press.

Glick Schiller, Nina, and Georges E. Fouron. 2001. *Georges Woke Up Laughing: Long-Distance Nationalism and the Search for Home*. Durham, NC: Duke University Press.

Gold, Steven J. 1992. *Refugee Communities: A Comparative Field Study*. Newbury Park, CA: Sage.

———. 1995. *From the Workers' State to the Gold State: Jews from the Former Soviet Union in California*. Boston: Allyn and Bacon.

Goodman, Allen E. 1973. *Politics in War: The Bases of Political Community in South Vietnam*. Cambridge, MA: Harvard University Press.

Graden, Lizette. 2003. *On Parade: Making Heritage in Linsborg, Kansas.* Uppsala, Sweden: Acta Universitas Upsaliensis.

Graff, Harvey. 2008. *The Dallas Myth: The Making and Unmaking of an American City.* Minneapolis: University of Minnesota Press.

Graham, Pamela M. 2001. "Political Incorporation and ReIncorporation: Simultaneity in the Domincan Migrant Experience." In *Migration, Transnationalization, and Race in a Changing New York,* edited by Héctor Cordero-Guzmán, Robert C. Smith, and Ramón Grosfoguel, 87–108. Philadelphia: Temple University Press.

Graszyk, Michael. 2005. "From Saigon to the Texas House." *Dallas Morning News,* January 2: 6A.

Greater Dallas Chamber Statistical Facts. 2008. http://www.dallaschamber.org/research/ DFW Facts.pdf (accessed September 12, 2008).

Greeley, Andrew. 1972. *The Denominational Society: A Sociological Approach to Religion.* Glenview, IL: Scott Foresman.

Greene, Victor. 2005. "Dealing with Diversity." *Journal of Urban History* 31: 820–849.

Gusfield, Joseph R., and Jerzy Michalowicz. 1984. "Secular Symbolism: Studies of Ritual, Ceremony, and the Symbolic Order in Modern Life." *Annual Review of Sociology* 10: 417–435.

Habermas, Jurgen. 1989. *The Structural Transformation of the Public Sphere.* Cambridge, MA: MIT Press.

Haddad, Yvonne Y., and Adair T. Lummis. 1987. *Islamic Values in the United States: A Comparative Study.* New York: Oxford University Press.

Hall, Kathleen. 2002. *Lives in Transition: Sikh Youths as British Citizens.* Philadelphia: University of Pennsylvania Press.

Hamidi, Camille. 2003. "Voluntary Associations of Migrants and Politics: The Case of North African Immigrants in France." *Immigrants and Minorities* 22: 317–322.

Handelman, Don 1990. *Models and Mirrors: Towards an Anthropology of Public Events.* Cambridge, UK: Cambridge University Press.

Hansen, Art, and Anthony Oliver-Smith. 1982. *Involuntary Migration and Resettlement: The Problems and Responses of Dislocated People.* Boulder, CO: Westview Press.

Harrell-Bond, Barbara. 1999. "The Experience of Refugees as Recipients of Aid." In *Refugees: Perspectives on the Experience of Forced Migration,* edited by Alastair Ager, 136–168. New York: Pinter.

Harrison, Henrietta 2000. *The Making of the Republican Citizen: Political Ceremonies and Symbols in China, 1911–1929.* Oxford, UK: Oxford University Press.

Heideking, Jurgen, Genevieve Fabre, and Kai Dreisbach, eds. 2001. *Celebrating Ethnicity and Nation: American Festive Culture from the Revolution to the Early 20th Century.* Oxford, UK: Berghahn Books.

Hein, Jeremy. 1993. "Refugees, Immigrants, and the State." *Annual Review of Sociology* 19: 43–59.

————. 1995. *From Vietnam, Laos, and Cambodia: A Refugee Experience in the United States*. New York: Twayne.

Hero, Rodyne, F. Chris García, John García, and Harry Pachon. 2000. "Latino Participation, Partisanship and Office Holding." *PS: Political Science and Politics* 33: 529–534.

Herszenhorn, David M. 2009 "Louisiana Republican Breaks Ranks on Health Bill," *New York Times*, September 11. http://www.nytimes.com/2009/11/09/us/politics/09cao.html (accessed October 20, 2010).

Herzfeld, Michael. 2005. *Cultural Intimacy: Social Poetics in the Nation-State*. 2nd edition. New York: Routledge.

Hill, Patricia Evridge. 1996. *Dallas: The Making of a Modern City*. Austin: University of Texas Press.

Hirschman, Charles. 2004. "The Role of Religion in the Origins and Adaptation of Immigrant Groups in the United States." *International Migration Review* 38: 1206–1233.

Hobsbawn, Eric, and Terence Ranger, eds. 1983. *The Invention of Tradition*. Cambridge, UK: Cambridge University Press.

Hochschild, Jennifer L., and John H. Mollenkopf, eds. 2009. *Bringing Outsiders In: Transatlantic Perspectives on Immigrant Political Incorporation*. Ithaca, NY: Cornell University Press.

Hondagneu-Sotelo, Pierrette, ed. 2007. *Religion and Social Justice for Immigrants*. New Brunswick, NJ: Rutgers University Press.

Hughes, Jason, Nick Jewson, and Lorna Unwin, eds. 2007. *Communities of Practice: Critical Perspectives*. New York: Routledge.

Huynh, Thuan. 2000. "Center for Vietnamese Buddhism: Recreating Home." In *Religion and the New Immigrants: Continuities and Adaptations in Immigrant Congregations*, edited by Helen Rose Ebaugh and Janet Saltzman Chafetz, 45–66. Walnut Creek, CA: AltaMira Press.

"Indian Americans Score." 2008. *India Post*, November 10. http://www.indiapost.com/article/usnews/4406 (accessed November 10, 2008).

Isin, Engin F., and Patricia K. Wood. 1999. *Citizenship and Identity*. Thousand Oaks, CA: Sage.

Itzigsohn, Jose. 2000. "Immigration and the Boundaries of Citizenship: The Institutions of Immigrants' Political Transnationalism." *International Migration Review* 34: 1126–1154.

Itzigsohn, Jose, and Carole Dore-Cabral. 2000. "Competing Identities? Race, Ethnicity, and Panethnicity Among Dominicans in the United States." *Sociological Forum* 15: 225–247.

Jacob, Simon, and Pallavi Thakur. 2000. "Jyothi Hindu Temple: One Religion, Many Practices." In *Religion and the New Immigration*, edited by Helen Rose Ebaugh and Janet Saltzman, 151–162. Walnut Creek, CA: AltaMira Press.

Jacobs, Andrew. 2010. "China Warns U.S. to Stay Out of Islands Dispute." *New York Times*, July 26. http://www.nytimes.com/2010/07/27/world/asia/27china.html (accessed October 20, 2010).

Jacobs, Dirk, Karen Phalet, and Marc Swyngedouw. 2004. "Associational Membership and Political Involvement Among Ethnic Minority Groups in Brussels." *Journal of Ethnic and Migration Studies* 30: 543–559.

Jensen, Joan M. 1988. *Passage from India.* New Haven, CT: Yale University Press.

Jensen, Lene Arnett, and Constance A. Flanagan. 2008. "Immigrant Civic Engagement: New Translations." *Applied Developmental Science* (Special Issue) 12 :55–56.

Jonaitis, Aldona, ed. 1991. *Chiefly Feasts: The Enduring Kwakiutl Potlatch.* Seattle, WA: University of Seattle Press.

Jones, Kenneth. 1990. *Socio-Religious Reform Movements in British India: The New Cambridge History of India.* Cambridge, UK: Cambridge University Press.

Jones, Richard C. 2008. "Immigrants Transform and Are Transformed by the U.S. Heartland." In *Immigrants Outside Megalopolis: Ethnic Transformation in the Heartland*, edited by Richard C. Jones, 3–24. Lanham, MD: Lexington Books.

Jones-Correa, Michael. 1996. "Reshaping the American Dream: Immigrants, Ethnic Minorities, and the Politics of the New Suburbs." In *The New Suburban History*, edited by Kevin Michael Kruse and Thomas J. Sugrue, 183–204. Chicago: University of Chicago Press.

———. 1998. *Between Two Nations: The Political Predicament of Latinos in New York City.* Ithaca, NY: Cornell University Press.

———. 2007. "Ethnic Politics." In *The New Americans: A Guide to Immigration Since 1965*, edited by Mary C. Waters and Reed Ueda, 189–201. Cambridge, MA: Harvard University Press.

Joppke, Christian. 1999. *Challenges to the Nation-State: Immigration in Western Europe and the United States.* Oxford, UK: Oxford University Press.

Joppke, Christian, and Ewa Morawska. 2003. *Toward Assimilation and Citizenship: Immigrants in Liberal Nation-States.* New York: Palgrave Macmillan.

Joshi, Khati Y. 2006. *New Roots in America's Sacred Ground: Religion, Race, and Ethnicity in Indian America.* Brunswick, NJ: Rutgers University Press.

Junn, Jane, Taeku Lee, S. Karthick Ramakrishnan, and Janelle Wong. 2008. "National Asian American Survey," October 6. http://www.naasurvey.com/assets/NAAS -National-report.pdf (accessed October 15, 2010).

Junn, Jane, and Natalie Masuoka. 2008. "Identities in Context: Politicized Racial Group Consciousness Among Asian American and Latino Youth." *Applied Developmental Science* 12: 93–101.

Just, Anne F. 1980. "Urban School Board Elections: Changes in the Political Environment Between 1950 and 1980." *Education and Urban Society* 12: 421–435.

Karpathakis, Anna. 1999. "Home Society Politics and Immigrant Political Incorporation: The Case of Greek Immigrants in New York." *International Migration Review* 33: 55–84.

Kasinitz, Philip, and Judith Freidenberg. 1987. "The Puerto Rican Parade and West Indian Carnival: Public Celebrations in New York City." In *Caribbean Life in New York City: Sociocultural Dimensions*, edited by Constance Sutton, 327–349. New York: Center for Migration Studies.

Kelly, Gail. 1977. *From Vietnam to America: A Chronicle of Vietnamese Immigration to the United States.* Boulder, CO: Westview Press.

Kelly, Gail P. 1986."Coping with America: Refugees from Vietnam, Cambodia, and Laos in the 1970s and 1980s." *Annals of the American Academy of Political and Social Science* 487: 138–149.

Kemper, Robert V. 2005. "Dallas-Fort Worth: Toward New Models of Urbanization, Community Transformation, and Immigration." *Urban Anthropology* 34: 125–149.

Kerber, Linda. 1997."The Meanings of Citizenship." *Journal of American History* 84: 833–853.

Kertzer, David. 1988. *Ritual, Politics, and Power.* New Haven, CT: Yale University Press.

Khandelwal, Madhulika S. 2002. *Becoming American, Being Indian: An Immigrant Community in New York City.* Ithaca, NY: Cornell University Press.

Kibria, Nazli. 1993. *Family Tightrope: The Changing Lives of Vietnamese Americans.* Princeton, NJ: Princeton University Press.

———. 1998. "The Racial Gap: South Asian American Racial Identity and the Asian American Movement." In *A Part, Yet Apart: South Asians in Asian America*, edited by L. D. Shankar and R. Srikanth, 69–78. Philadelphia: Temple University Press.

———. 2002. *Becoming Asian American: Second-Generation Chinese and Korean American Identities.* Baltimore: Johns Hopkins University Press.

———. 2007. "South Asia." In *The New Americans: A Guide to Immigration Since 1965*, edited by Mary C Waters and Reed Ueda, 612–623. Cambridge, MA: Harvard University Press.

Klineberg, Stephen L. 2004. "Religious Diversity and Social Integration Among Asian Americans in Houston." In *Asian American Religions: The Making and Remaking of Borders and Boundaries*, edited by Tony Carnes and Fenggang Yang, 247–262. New York: New York University Press.

Kniss, Fred, and Paul D. Numrich. 2007. *Sacred Assemblies and Civic Engagement: How Religion Matters for America's Newest Immigrants.* New Brunswick, NJ: Rutgers University Press.

Korac, Maja. 2009. *Remaking Home: Reconstructing Life, Place and Identity in Rome and Amsterdam.* Oxford, UK: Berghahn Books.

Koshy, Susan. 2002. "South Asians and the Complex Interstices of Whiteness: Negotiating Public Sentiment in the United States and Britain." In *White Women in Racialized Spaces: Imaginative Transformation and Ethical Action in Literature*, edited by

Samina Najmi and Rajinia Srikanth, 29–50. Albany: State University of New York Press.

Kuo, Chia-Ling. 1977. *Social and Political Change in New York's Chinatown: The Role of Voluntary Associations*. New York: Praeger.

Kurashige, Lon. 2002. *Japanese American Celebration and Conflict: A History of Ethnic Identity and Festival, 1934–1990*. Berkeley: University of California Press.

Kurien, Prema A. 2001a."Constructing 'Indianness' in Southern California." In *Asian and Latino Immigrants in a Restructuring Economy: The Metamorphosis of Southern California*, edited by Lopez-Garza and David R. Diaz, 289–312. Stanford, CA: Stanford University Press.

———. 2001b. "Religion, Ethnicity and Politics: Hindu and Muslim Immigrants in the U.S." *Ethnic and Racial Studies* 24: 263–293.

———. 2002. "We Are Better Hindus Here: Religion and Ethnicity Among Asian Americans." In *Religions in Asian America: Building Faith Communities*, edited by Pyong Gap Min and Jung Ha Kim, 99–120. Walnut Creek, CA: AltaMira Press.

———. 2003. "To Be or Not to Be South Asian: Contemporary Indian American Politics." *Journal of Asian American Studies* 6: 261–288.

———. 2004. "Christian by Birth or Rebirth? Generation and Difference in an Indian American Christian Church." In *Asian American Religions: The Making and Remaking of Borders and Boundaries*, edited by Tony Carnes and Fenggang Yang, 160–181. New York: New York University Press.

———. 2005. "Being Young, Brown, and Hindu: The Identity Struggles of Second-Generation Indian Americans." *Journal of Contemporary Ethnography* 34: 434–469.

———. 2006. "Multiculturalism and 'American' Religion: The Case of Hindu Indian Americans." *Social Forces* 85: 723–741.

———. 2007. "Who Speaks for Indian Americans? Religion, Ethnicity, and Political Formation." *American Quarterly* 59: 759–783.

Kymlicka, Will, and Wayne Norman. 1994. "Return of the Citizen: A Survey of Recent Work on Citizenship Theory." *Ethics* 104: 352–381.

Laguerre, Michel S. 1998. *Diasporic Citizenship: Haitian Americans in Transnational America*. New York: St. Martin's Press.

Lam, Andrew. 2005. *Perfume Dreams: Reflections on the Vietnamese Diaspora*. Berkeley, CA: Heyday Books.

Landolt, Patricia. 2008. "The Transnational Geographies of Immigrant Politics: Insights from a Comparative Study of Migrant Grassroots Organizing." *Sociological Quarterly* 49: 53–77.

Langton, Elizabeth. 2005. "India Group Rallies to Help Its Devastated Homeland." *Dallas Morning News*, January 2: 1B.

Lave, Jean. 1996. "The Practice of Learning." In *Understanding Practice: Perspectives on Activity and Context*, edited by Seth Chaiklin and Jean Lave, 3–34. Cambridge, UK: Cambridge University Press.

Lave, Jean, and Etienne Wenger. 1991. *Situated Learning: Legimate Peripheral Participation*. Cambridge, UK: Cambridge University Press.

Leal, David L. 2002. "Political Participation by Latino Non-Citizens in the United States." *British Journal of Political Science* 32: 353–370.

Lee, Jennifer, and Min Zhou, eds. 2004. *Asian American Youth*. New York: Routledge.

Lee, S. M. 1993. "Racial Classifications in the U.S. Census, 1880–1990." *Ethnic and Racial Studies* 16: 75–94.

Leonard, Karen Isaksen. 1997. *The South Asian Americans*. Westport, CT: Greenwood Press.

———. 2003. *Muslims in the United States: The State of Research*. New York: Russell Sage Foundation.

———. 2006. "South Asian Religions in the United States: New Contexts and Configurations." In *New Cosmopolitanisms: South Asians in the United States*, edited by Gita Rajan and Shailja Sharma, 91–114. Stanford, CA: Stanford University Press.

———. 2007a. *Locating Home: India's Hyderabadis Abroad*. Stanford, CA: Stanford University Press.

———. 2007b. "India." In *The New Americans: A Guide to Immigration Since 1965*, edited by Mary C. Waters and Wade Ueda, 458–468. Cambridge, MA: Harvard University Press.

Leonard, Karen Isaksen, Alex Stepick, Manuel A Vasquez, and Jennifer Holdaway. 2005. *Immigrant Faiths: Transforming Religious Life in America*. Walnut Creek, CA: AltaMira Press.

Leong, Karen J., Christopher A. Airriess, Wei Li, Angela Chia-Chen Chen, and Verna M. Keith. 2007. "Resilient History and the Rebuilding of a Community: The Vietnamese American Community in New Orleans East." *Journal of American History* 93: 770–779.

Lessinger, Johanna. 1995. *From the Ganges to the Hudson: Indian Immigrants in New York City*. Boston: Allyn and Bacon.

Levinson, Bardley A., Douglas E. Foley, and Dorothy C. Holland, eds. 1996. *The Cultural Production of the Educated Person: Critical Ethnographies of Schooling and Local Practice*. Albany: State University of New York Press.

Levitt, Peggy. 2000. "Migrants Participate Across Borders: Toward an Understanding of Forms and Consequences." In *Immigration Research for a New Century*, edited by Nancy Foner and Ruben Rumbaut, 459–479. New York: Russell Sage Foundation.

———. 2007. *God Needs No Passport: Immigrants and the Changing American Religious Landscape*. New York: New Press.

Lien, Pei-te. 2001. *The Making of Asian America Through Political Participation*. Philadelphia: Temple University Press.

———. 2007. "Religion and Political Adaptation Among Asian Americans: An Empirical Assessment from the Pilot National Asian America Political Survey." In *Asian*

American Religions: The Making and Remaking of Borders and Boundaries, edited by Tony Carnes and Fenggang Yang, 263–284. New York: New York University Press.

Lien, Pei-te, M. Margaret Conway, and Janelle Wong. 2004. *The Politics of Asian Americans: Diversity and Community*. New York: Routledge.

Litt, Edgar. 1970. *Ethnic Politics in America*. Glenview, IL: Scott, Foresman.

Liu, Hong. 1998. "Old Linkages, New Networks: The Globalization of Overseas Chinese Voluntary Associations and Its Implications." *China Quarterly* 155: 582–609.

Lorentzen, Lois Ann, Joaquin Jay Gonzalez III, Kevin M. Chun, and Hien Duc Do, eds. 2009. *Religion at the Corner of Bliss and Nirvana: Politics, Identity, and Faith in New Migrant Communities*. Durham, NC: Duke University Press.

Lott, Juanito Tamayo. 1998. *Asian Americans: From Racial Category to Multiple Identities*. London: Sage.

Lowe, Lisa. 1996. *Immigrant Acts: On Asian American Cultural Politics*. Durham, NC: Duke University Press.

Luong, Dominic M. n.d. "A Historical Sketch About the Vietnamese in the United States." Washington, DC: Asian and Pacific Island Affairs, United States Conference of Catholic Bishops. http://usccb.org/apa/vietnam.shtml (accessed October 10, 2007).

Maira, Sunaina. 2002. *Desis in the House: Indian American Youth Culture in New York City*. Philadelphia: Temple University Press.

———. 2009. *Missing: Youth, Citizenship, and Empire After 9/11*. Durham, NC: Duke University Press.

Malkki, Liisa. 1995. "Refugees and Exile: From 'Refugee Studies' to the National Order of Things." *Annual Review of Anthropology* 24: 495–523.

Maloney, William A., Graham Smith, and Gerry Stoker. 2000. "Social Capital and Associational Life." In *Social Capital: Critical Perspectives*, edited by Stephen Baron, John Field, and Tom Schuller, 212–225. Oxford, UK: Oxford University Press.

Markowitz, Fran. 1992. "Community Without Organizations." *City and Society* 6: 141–155.

Marquardt, Marie Friedmann. 2005. "From Shame to Confidence: Gender, Religious Conversion, and Civic Engagement of Mexicans in the U.S. South." *Latin American Perspectives* 32: 27–56.

Marshall, T. H. 1964. *Class, Citizenship, and Social Development*. Garden City, NY: Anchor Books.

Mazumdar, Sanjoy, Shampa Mazumdar, Faye Docuyanan, and Colette Marie McLaughlin. 2000. "Creating a Sense of Place: The Vietnamese-Americans and Little Saigon." *Journal of Environmental Psychology* 20: 319–333.

Mazumdar, Sucheta. 1989. "Race and Racism: South Asians in the United States." In *Frontiers of Asian American Studies*, edited by Gail M. Nomura, 25–38. Pullman: Washington State University Press.

McAlister, Elizabeth. 1998. "The Madonna of 115th Street Revisited: Vodou and Haitian Catholicism in the Age of Transnationalism." In *Gatherings in Diaspora: Religious*

Communities and the New Immigration, edited by R. Stephen Warner and Judith G. Wittner, 123–160. Philadelphia: Temple University Press.

McAloon, John J., ed. 1984. *Rite, Drama, Festival, Spectacle: Rehearsals Toward a Theory of Cultural Performance*. Philadelphia: Institute for the Study of Human Issues.

McLellan, Janet. 1999. *Many Petals of the Lotus: Five Asian Buddhist Communities in Toronto*. Toronto: University of Toronto Press.

Meagher, Timothy J. 1985. "Why Should We Care for a Little Trouble or a Walk Through the Mud? St. Patrick's and Columbus Day Parades in Worcester, Massachusetts, 1845–1915." *New England Quarterly* 58: 5–26.

Meyers, Jessica. 2006. "Pho and Apple Pie: Eden Center as a Representation of Vietnamese American Ethnic Identity in the Washington, D.C., Metropolitan Area, 1975–2005." *Journal of Asian American Studies* 9: 55–85.

———. 2009. "Refugees in Dallas Struggle to Find Their Place as Jobs Dry Up," *Dallas Morning News*, March 1. http://www.dentonrc.com/sharedcontent/dws/dn/latest news/stories/030109dnmetrecessionrefugees.3d4b64e.html (accessed February 1, 2011).

Min, Pyong Gap. 1992. "The Structure and Social Functions of Korean Churches in the United States." *International Migration Review* 26: 1370–1394.

———. 1998. *Changes and Conflicts: Korean Immigrant Families in New York*. Boston: Allyn and Bacon.

———, ed. 2002. *Second Generation: Ethnic Identity Among Asian Americans*. New York: AltaMira Press.

Min, Pyong Gap, and Jung Ha Kim, eds. 2002. *Religions in Asian America: Building Faith Communities*. Walnut Creek, CA: AltaMira Press.

Min, Pyong Gap, and Rose Kim, eds. 1999. *Struggle for Ethnic Identity: Narratives by Asian American Professionals*. Walnut Creek, CA: AltaMira Press.

Mintz, Sidney, and Christine M. Du Bois. 2002. "The Anthropology of Food and Eating." *Annual Review of Anthropology* 31: 99–119.

Miss India Georgia. 1998. Produced and directed by Daniel Friedman and Sharon Grimberg. Portland, OR: Urban Life Productions.

Mohapatra, Manindra K., Amiya Mohanty, Josna Mishra, Usha Rout, Primod Mishra, and Ruchi Tyagi. 2003. *Beyond September 11, 2001: Political Attitudes of the Indian Immigrants in America*. New Delhi, India: Authors Press.

Montero, David. 1979. *Vietnamese Americans: Patterns of Resettlement and Socioeconomic Adaptation in the United States*. Boulder, CO: Westview Press.

Moon, H. Jo. 1984. "The Putative Political Complacency of Asian Americans." *Political Psychology* 5: 583–605.

Morning, Ann. 2001. "The Racial Self-Identification of South Asians in the United States." *Journal of Ethnic and Migration Studies* 27: 61–79.

Moss, Kenneth. 1995. "St. Patrick's Day Celebrations and the Formation of Irish American Identity, 1845–1875." *Journal of Social History* 29: 125–148.

Mother Tongue, Fatherland: Stories of the Vietnamese Amerasians. 2005. Directed by Cuong Simon Phan. Collegeville, MN: Cuong Simon Phan.

Moya, José C. 2005. "Immigrants and Associations: A Global and Historical Perspective." *Journal of Ethnic and Migration Studies* 31: 833–865.

Mydans, Seth. 2009. "U.S. Officer Revisits His Past in Vietnam." *New York Times*, November 10: A8.

Narayan, Kirin. 2002. "Placing Lives Through Stories: Second-Generation South Asian Americans." In *Everyday Life in South Asia*, edited by Dian P. Mines and Sarah Lamb, 425–439. Bloomington: Indiana University Press.

National Conference of Catholic Bishops, Committee on Migration and Tourism. 1988. "Pastoral Care of Vietnamese Catholics in the United States." In *A Church of Many Cultures: Selected Historical Essays on Ethnic American Catholicism*, edited by Delores Liptak, 398–414. New York: Garland.

Neill, Stephen. 1984. *A History of Christianity in India: The Beginnings to 1707.* Cambridge, UK: Cambridge University Press.

Ngai, Mae M. 2004. *Impossible Subjects: Illegal Aliens and the Making of Modern America.* Princeton, NJ: Princeton University Press.

Nguyen, Cuong Tu, and A. W. Barber. 1998. "Vietnamese Buddhism in North America: Tradition and Acculturation." In *The Faces of Buddhism in America*, edited by Charles S. Prebish and Kenneth K. Tanaka, 129–146. Berkeley: University of California Press.

Nguyen, Kien. 2001. *The Unwanted: A Memoir of Childhood.* New York: Little, Brown.

Numrich, Paul David. 1996. *Old Wisdom in the New World: Americanization in Two Immigrant Theravada Buddhist Temples.* Knoxville: University of Tennessee Press.

Oboler, Suzanne. 1995. *Ethnic Labels, Latino Lives: Identity and the Politics of (Re)Presentation in the United States.* Minneapolis: University of Minnesota Press.

O'Brien, Eileen. 2008. *The Racial Middle: Latinos and Asian Americans Living Beyond the Racial Divide.* New York: New York University Press.

Office of Refugee Resettlement. 2007. *FY 2007 Report to Congress.* Washington: U.S. Department of Health and Human Services.

Okamoto, Dina G. 2006. "Institutional Panethnicity: Boundary Formation in Asian American Organizations." *Social Forces* 85: 1–25.

Okamura, Jonathan Y. 1983. "Filipino Hometown Associations in Hawaii." *Ethnology* 22: 341–353.

Ong, Aihwa. 1999. *Flexible Citizenship: The Cultural Logics of Transnationality.* Durham, NC: Duke University Press.

———. 2003. *Buddha Is Hiding: Rufugees, Citizenship, and the New America.* Berkeley: University of California Press.

Ong, Nhu-Ngoc T., and David S. Meyer. 2008 "Vietnamese-American Protests in Orange County: 1975–2001." *Journal of Vietnamese Studies* 3: 78–107.

Ong, Paul M., ed. 2008. *The State of Asian America: Trajectory of Civic and Political En-*

gagement. Los Angeles: LEAP Asian Pacific American Public Policy Institute. http:// www.leap.org/docs/PPI%20PDFs/PPI_Publication.pdf (accessed October 20, 2010).

Ong, Paul M., and David E. Lee. 2001. "Changing of the Guard? The Emerging Immigrant Majority in Asian American Politics." In *Asian Americans and Politics*, edited by Gordon H. Chang, 153–172. Washington, D.C.: Woodrow Wilson Center Press.

Orozco, Manuel. 2004. "Mexican Hometown Associations and Development Opportunities." *Journal of International Affairs* 57: 30–49.

Orsi, Robert Anthony. 1985. *The Madonna of 115th Street: Faith and Community in Italian Harlem, 1880–1950*. New Haven, CT: Yale University Press.

Otis, Eileen M. 2001. "The Reach and Limits of Asian Panethnic Identity: The Dynamics of Gender, Race, and Class in a Community-Based Organization." *Qualitative Sociology* 24: 349–379.

Pais, Arthur J. 2006. "Indians Fail to Win Spelling Bee." *Rediff India Abroad*. June 2.http:// www.rediff.com/news/2006/jun/02spec.htm (accessed September 30, 2008).

Panagakos, Anastasia N. 1998. "Citizens of the Trans-Nation: Political Mobilization, Multiculturalism, and Nationalism in the Greek Diaspora." *Diaspora* 7: 53–74.

Panchuk, Kerri. 2001. "Asian Trade District Boost for Harry Hines." *Dallas Business Journal*, November 16. http://www.bizjournals.com/dallas/stories/2001/11/19/focus2.html (accessed October 13, 2008).

Pantoja, Adrian D. 2005. "Transnational Ties and Immigrant Political Incorporation: The Case of Dominicans in Washington Heights, New York." *International Migration* 43: 123–146.

Park, Clara C., A. Lin Goodwin, and Stacey J. Lee. 2003. *Asian American Identities, Families, and Schooling*. Greenwich, CT: Information Age Publishing.

Parreñas, Rhacel S., and Lok C. D. Siu. 2007. *Asian Diasporas: New Formations, New Conceptions*. Stanford, CA: Stanford University Press.

Paxton, Pamela. 2002. "Social Capital and Democracy: An Interdependent Relationship." *American Sociological Review* 67: 254–277.

Payne, Darwin. 2000. *Big D: Triumphs and Troubles of an American Supercity in the 20th Century*. Dallas: Three Forks Press.

Peteet, Julie. 2005. *Landscape of Hope and Despair*. Philadelphia: University of Pennsylvania Press.

Pham, Andrew X. 1999. *Catfish and Mandala*. New York: Picador.

———. 2008. *The Eaves of Heaven: A Life in Three Wars*. New York: Harmony Books.

Phan, Peter C. 2005. *Vietnamese-American Catholics*. Mahwah, NJ: Paulist Press.

Phillips, Michael. 2006. *White Metropolis: Race, Ethnicity and Religion in Dallas, 1841–2001*. Austin: University of Texas Press.

Portes, Alejandro. 1998. "Social Capital: Its Origins and Applications in Modern Sociology." *Annual Review of Sociology* 24: 1–24.

———. 2000. "The Two Meanings of Social Capital." *Sociological Forum* 15: 1–12.

Portes, Alejandro, and Rubén G. Rumbaut. 2001. *Legacies: The Story of the Immigrant Second Generation*. Berkeley: University of California.

Prasad, Vijay. 2000. *The Karma of Brown Folk*. Minneapolis: University of Minnesota Press.

Prebish, Charles S. 1999. *Luminous Passage: The Practice and Study of Buddhism in America*. Berkeley: University of California Press.

Procter, David E. 2004. "Victorian Days: Performing Community Through Local Festival." In *We Are What We Celebrate: Understanding Holidays and Rituals*, edited by Amitai Etzioni and Jared Bloom, 131–148. New York: New York University Press.

Purkayastha, Bandana. 2005. *Negotiating Ethnicity: Second-Generation South Asian Americans Traverse a Transnational World*. New Brunswick, NJ: Rutgers University Press.

Putnam, Robert D. 2000. *Bowling Alone: The Collapse and Revival of American Community*. New York: Simon and Schuster.

———. 2007. "E Pluribus Unum: Diversity and Community in the Twenty-First Century." *Scandinavian Political Studies* 30: 137–174.

Putnam, Robert D., and Lewis M. Feldstein. 2003. *Better Together: Restoring the American Community*. New York: Simon and Schuster.

Rajagopal, Arvind. 2000. "Hindu Nationalism in the U.S.: Changing Configurations of Political Practice." *Ethnic and Racial Studies* 23: 467–496.

Ramakrishnan, S. Karthick, and Irene Bloemraad, eds. 2008a. *Civic Hopes and Political Realities: Immigrants, Community Organizations, and Political Engagement*. New York: Russell Sage Foundation.

———. 2008b. "Introduction: Civic and Political Inequalities." In *Civic Hopes and Political Realities: Immigrants, Community Organizations and Political Engagement*, edited by S. Karthick Ramakrishnan and Irene Bloemraad, 1–44. New York: Russell Sage Foundation.

———. 2008c. "Making Organizations Count: Immigrant Civic Engagement and California Cities." In *Civic Hopes and Political Realities: Immigrants, Community Organizations and Political Engagement*, edited by S. Karthick Ramakrishnan and Irene Bloemraad, 45–76. New York: Russell Sage Foundation.

Rangaswamy, Padma. 2000. *Namasté America: Indian Immigrants in an American Metropolis*. University Park: Pennsylvania State University Press.

Redden, Susan. 2008. "Carthage Preparing for Annual Marian Days Celebration." *Joplin Globe*, July 27. http://www.joplinglobe.com/carthage_jasper_county/x212145357/Carthage-preparing-for-annual-Marian-Days-celebration (accessed October 20, 2010).

Reed-Danahay, Deborah. 1991. "La production de l'identité régionale: L'Auvergnat dans le Puy-de-Dôme rural." *Ethnologie Française* 21: 42–47.

———. 1996. *Education and Identity in Rural France: The Politics of Schooling*. Cambridge, UK: Cambridge University Press.

———. 2005. "Desire, Migration, and Attachment to Place: Life Stories of Rural French

Women." In *Women on the Verge of Home: Narratives of Home and Transgressive Travel*, edited by Bilinda Straight, 129–148. Albany: SUNY Press.

———. 2008. "From the 'Imagined Community' to 'Communities of Practice': Immigrant Belonging Among Vietnamese Americans." In *Citizenship, Political Engagement, and Belonging: Immigrants in Europe and the United States*, by Deborah Reed-Danahay and Caroline B. Brettell. New Brunswick, NJ: Rutgers University Press.

———. 2010. "Citizenship, Immigration, and Embodiment: Vietnamese Americans in North-Central Texas." In *Contested Spaces: Citizenship and Belonging in Contemporary Times*, edited by Meenakshi Thapan, 101–119. New Dehli, India: Orient Blackswan.

Reed-Danahay, Deborah, and Caroline B. Brettell, eds. 2008a. *Citizenship, Political Engagement, and Belonging: Immigrants in Europe and the United States*. New Brunswick, NJ: Rutgers University Press.

———. 2008b. "Introduction." In *Citizenship, Political Engagement, and Belonging: Immigrants in Europe and the United States*, edited by Deborah Reed-Danahay and Caroline B. Brettell, 1–17. New Brunswick, NJ: Rutgers University Press.

Richmond, Anthony. 1988. "Sociological Theories of International Migration: The Case of Refugees." *Current Sociology* 36: 7–25.

Roark, Carol, ed. 2003. *Fort Worth and Tarrant County: An Historical Guide*. Fort Worth: Texas Christian University Press.

Rosaldo, Renato. 1994. "Social Justice and the Crisis of National Communities." In *Colonial Discourse/Postcolonial Theory*, edited by Francis Barker, Peter Hulme, and Margeret Iverson, 239–252. Manchester, UK: Manchester University Press.

———. 1997. "Cultural Citizenship, Inequality, and Multiculturalism." In *Latino Cultural Citizenship: Claiming Identity, Space, and Politics*, edited by William V. Flores and Rina Benmayor. Boston: Beacon Press.

Rosaldo, Renato, and William V. Flores. 1997. "Identity, Conflict, and Evolving Lation Communities: Cultural Citizenship in San Jose, California." In *Latino Cultural Citizenship: Claiming Identity, Space and Politics*, edited by William V. Flores and Rina Benmayor, 57–96. Boston: Beacon Press.

Rudrappa, Sharmila. 2004. *Ethnic Routes to Becoming American: Indian Immigrants and the Cultures of Citizenship*. New Brunswick, NJ: Rutgers University Press.

Rumbaut, Rubén G. 2006. "Vietnamese, Laotian, and Cambodian Americans." In *Asian Americans: Contemporary Trends and Issues*, edited by Pyong Gap Min, 262–289. Thousand Oaks, CA: Pine Forge Press.

Rumbaut, Rubén G., and Alejandro Portes. 2001. "Introduction." In *Ethnicities: Children of Immigrants in America*, edited by Rubén G. Rumbaut and Alejandro Portes, 1–19. Berkeley: University of California Press, and New York: Russell Sage Foundation.

Rutheiser, Charles. 1996. *Imagineering Atlanta: The Politics of Place in the City of Dreams*. New York: Verso.

————. 1999. "Making Place in the Nonplace Urban Realm: Notes on the Revitalization of Downtown Atlanta." In *Theorizing the City: The New Urban Anthropology Reader,* edited by Setha Low, 317–341. New Brunswick, NJ: Rutgers University Press.

Rutledge, Paul. 1985. *The Role of Religion in Ethnic Self-Identity: A Vietnamese Community.* Lanham, MD: University Press of America.

————. 1992. *The Vietnamese Experience in America.* Bloomington: Indiana University Press.

Ruttonji, Ardeshir. 1968. *History and Philosphy of Social Work in India.* Bombay, India: Allied Publishers.

Rydström, Helle. 2001. "'Like a White Piece of Paper': Embodiment and the Moral Upbringing of Vietnamese Children." *Ethnos* 66: 394–413.

————. 2003. *Embodying Morality: Growing Up in Rural Northern Vietnam.* Honolulu: University of Hawaii Press.

Sassen-Koob, Saskia. 1979. "Formal and Informal Associations: Dominicans and Colombians in New York." *International Migration Review* 13: 314–332.

Satyanarayana, M. C. 2008. *Concept of Sewa in Hinduism.* http://www.nhsf.org.uk/index.php?option=com_content&view=article&id=290:article-concept-of-sewa&catid=114:sewa&Itemid=186 (accessed July 15, 2009).

Schnapper, Dominique. 1998 [1994]. *The Community of Citizens: On the Modern Idea of Nationality,* translated by Séverine Rosée. New Brunswick, NY: Transaction Publishers.

Schneider, Jo-Anne. 1990. "Defining Boundaries, Creating Contacts: Puerto Rican and Polish Presentation of Group Identity Through Ethnic Parades." *Journal of Ethnic Studies* 18: 33–57.

Schrock, Susan. 2008. "Arlington Rejects Sign Toppers Honoring Minorities." *Fort Worth Star-Telegram,* December 3: B-1.

Sciorra, Joseph. 1999. "'We Go Where the Italians Live': Religious Processions as Ethnic and Territorial Markers in a Multi-ethnic Brooklyn Neighborhood." In *Gods of the City,* edited by Robert A. Orsi, 310–340. Bloomington: Indiana University Press.

Segura, Gary M., Harry Pachon, and Nathan D. Woods. 2003. "Hispanics, Social Capital, and Civic Engagement." *National Civic Review* 90: 85–96.

Shankar, Shalini. 2008. *Desi Land: Teen Culture, Class, and Success in Silicon Valley.* Durham, NC: Duke University Press.

Shelley, Mark. 2001. "Building Community from 'Scratch': Forces at Work Among Urban Vietnamese Refugees in Milwaukee." *Sociological Inquiry* 71: 473–492.

Sherrod, Lonnie R., Judith Torney-Purta, and Constance A. Flanagan. 2010. *Handbook of Research on Civic Engagement in Youth.* Hoboken, NJ: Wiley.

Silverstein, Paul. 2008. "Kabyle Immigrant Politics and Racialized Citizenship in France." In *Citizenship, Political Engagement, and Belonging: Immigrants in Europe and the United States,* edited by Deborah Reed-Danahay and Caroline B. Brettell, 23–42. New Brunswick, NJ: Rutgers University Press.

Singer, Audrey, Susan Hardwick, and Caroline B. Brettell. 2008. *Twenty-First Century Gateways: Immigrant Incorporation in Suburban America.* Washington, DC: Brookings Institution.

Siu, Lok C. D. 2005. *Memories of a Future Home: Diasporic Citizenship of Chinese in Panama.* Stanford, CA: Stanford University Press.

Skocpol, Theda, and Morris Fiorina. 1999. *Civic Engagement and American Democracy.* Washington, DC: Brookings Institution.

Skop, Emily. Forthcoming. *The Saffron Suburbs: Lessons Learned from an Asian Indian Community.* Chicago: Center for American Places, Columbia College.

Smith, Adam. 2006. "Casinos Aggressively Market to Asian Americans, but Few Services Help Addicts." *New American Media,* October 1. http://news.newamericamedia.org/news/view_article.html?article_id=c2e681fe5962fd168dfe1f3b92afa4af (accessed October 15, 2010).

Smith, M. K. 2003 *Communities of Practice.* http://www.infed.org/biblio/communities_of_practice.htm (accessed October 15, 2010).

Smith, Michael Peter, and Matt Bakker. 2008. *Citizenship Across Borders: The Political Transnationalism of El Migrante.* Ithaca, NY: Cornell University Press.

Sohrabji, Sunita, and Richard Springer. 2008. "Obama Wins! Largest Indian American Turnout Ever, Report Pollsters." http://www.indiawest.com/resultpage.aspx?s=0%20&str=Obama%20Wins%20%20&str1=Sohrabji%20&str3= (accessed Feb 20, 2011).

Somers, Margaret. 2008. *Genealogies of Citizenship: Markets, Statelessness, and the Right to Have Rights.* Cambridge, UK: Cambridge University Press.

Soyer, Daniel. 2001. *Jewish Immigrant Associations and Amerian Identity in New York, 1880–1939.* Detroit: Wayne State University Press.

———. 2006. "Mutual Aid Societies and Fraternal Orders." In *A Companion to American Immigration,* edited by Reed Ueda, 528–546. Oxford, UK: Blackwell.

Soysal, Yasemin Nuhoglu. 1994. *Limits of Citizenship: Migrants and Postnational Membership in Europe.* Chicago: University of Chicago Press.

Spellbound. 2002. Directed by Jeffrey Blitz. Los Angeles: ThinkFilm.

Spivak, Gayatri. 1987. *In Other Worlds.* London: Routledge.

Stepick, Alex. 2005. "God Is Apparently Not Dead: The Obvious, the Emergent, and the Still Unknown in Immigration and Religion." In *Immigrant Faiths: Transforming Religious Life in America,* edited by Karen I. Leonard, Alex Stepick, Manual A. Vasquez, and Jennifer Holdaway, 11–36. Walnut Creek, CA: AltaMira Press.

Stepick, Alex, Terry Rey, and Sarah J. Mahler. 2009. *Churches and Charity in the Immigrant City: Religion, Immigration, and Civic Engagement in Miami.* New Brunswick, NJ: Rutgers University Press.

Stepick, Alex, Carol Dutton Stepick, and Yves Labissiere. 2002. "Becoming American, Constructing Ethnicity: Immigrant Youth and Civic Engagement." *Applied Developmental Science* 6: 247–257.

————. 2008. "South Florida's Immigrant Youth and Civic Engagement: Major Engagement, Minor Differences." *Applied Developmental Science* 12: 57–65.

Sterne, Evelyn S. 2001. "Beyond the Boss: Immigration and American Political Culture from 1880–1940." In *E Pluribus Unum: Contemporary and Historical Perspectives of Immigrant Political Incorporation,* edited by Gary Gerstle and John Mollenkopf, 33–66. New York: Russell Sage Foundation.

————. 2004. *Ballots and Bibles: Ethnic Politics and the Catholic Church in Providence.* Ithaca, NY: Cornell University Press.

Subramanian, Ajantha. 2007. "Indians in North Carolina: Race, Class, and Culture in the Making of Immigrant Identity." In *Contemporary Asian America: A Multidisciplinary Reader,* edited by Min Zhou and J. V. Gatewood, 158–178. New York: New York University Press.

Tang, Irwin A., ed. 2007. *Asian Texas: Our Histories and Our Lives.* Austin: The It Works.

Taylor, Charles. 1992. "The Politics of Recognition." In *Multiculturalism and the Politics of Recognition,* edited by Amy Gutmann, 25–74. Princeton, NJ: Princeton University Press.

Terrazas, Aaron. 2008a. "Indian Immigrants in the United States." *Migration Information Source,* July. http://www.migrationinformation.org/USFocus/display.cfm?ID=687 (accessed August 15, 2008).

————. 2008b. "Vietnamese Immigrants in the United States." *Migration Information Source,* August. http://www.migrationinformation.org/USFocus/display.cfm?ID=691 (accessed August 15, 2008).

Texas Buddhist Council. 1998. "Texas Buddhist Council." http://www2.cs.uh.edu/tihuang/tbc/mission.htm (accessed October 20, 2010).

Thao, Nguyen Hong. 2000. "The China-Vietnam Border Delimitation Treaty of 30 December 1999." *International Boundaries Research Unit Boundary and Security Bulletin* 8: 87–90. http://www.dur.ac.uk/resources/ibru/publications/full/bsb8-1_thao.pdf

Thiess-Morse, Elizabeth, and John R. Hibbing. 2005. "Citizenship and Civic Engagement." *Annual Review of Political Science* 8: 227–249.

Thomson, Susan. 2007. "Along the Path to Nibbana: Civic Engagement, Community Partnerships, and Lowell's Southeast Asian Buddhist Temples." In *Southeast Asian Refugees and Immigrants in the Mill City: Changing Families, Communities, Institutions—Thirty Years Afterward,* edited by Tuyet-Lan Pho, Jeffrey N. Gerson, and Sylvia R. Cowan, 112–130. Lebanon, NH: University Press of New England.

Tillie, Jean. 2004. "Social Capital of Organizations and Their Members: Explaining the Political Integration of Immigrants in Amsterdam." *Journal of Ethnic and Migration Studies* 30: 529–541.

Tran, My-Thuan. 2008. "From Refugees to Political Players: Over 16 Years, O.C.'s Vietnamese Have Gained a Footing and Found Their Voice, at the Polls and in Office." *Los Angeles Times,* December 7: B-1.

Tran, Tini, and Peter M. Warren. 1999. "Store's Display of Communist Items Protested." *Los Angeles Times*, January 19: B1.

Trevino, Roberto R. 2006. *The Church in the Barrio: Mexican American Ethno-Catholicism in Houston.* Durham: University of North Carolina Press.

Tsai, Lisa S. 2000. "Emerging Power: A Study on Asian American Political Candidates." *Asian American Policy Review* 9: 76–98.

Tuan, Mia. 1998. *Forever Foreigner or Honorary Whites? The Asian Ethnic Experience Today.* New Brunswick, NJ: Rutgers University Press.

Um, Shin Ja. 1996. *Korean Immigrant Women in the Dallas-Area Apparel Industry.* Lanham, MD: University Press of America.

United States Census Bureau. 2000. *Census of Population and Housing, Summary Files.* http://factfinder.census.gov (accessed December 10, 2008).

———. 2005. *American Community Survey.* http://factfinder.census.gov (accessed December 10, 2008).

———. 2006. *American Community Survey.* http://factfinder.census.gov (accessed December 10, 2008).

———. 2006–2008. *American Community Survey, Three Year Estimates.* http://factfinder.census.gov (accessed July 15, 2010).

Verba, Sidney, Kay Lehman Schlozman, and Henry E. Brady. 1995. *Voice and Equality: Civic Voluntarism in American Politics.* Cambridge, MA: Harvard University Press.

Vermeulen, Floris, and Maria Berger. 2008. "Civic Networks and Political Behavior." In *Civic Hopes and Political Realities: Immigrants, Community Organizations, and Political Engagement,* edited by S. Karthick Ramakrishnan and Irene Bloemraad, 160–192. New York: Russell Sage Foundation.

Viswanath, K., and Karen Ka-man Lee. 2007. "Ethnic Media." In *The New Americans: A Guide to Immigration Since 1965,* edited by Mary C. Waters and Reed Ueda, 202–213. Cambridge, MA: Harvard University Press.

Visweswaran, Kamala. 1997. "Diaspora by Design: Flexible Citizenship and South Asians in U.S. Racial Formations." *Diaspora* 6: 5–29.

Vo, Linda Trinh. 1996. "Asian Immigrants, Asian-Americans, and the Politics of Mobilization in San Diego." *Amerasia Journal* 22: 89–100.

Volpp, Leti. 2001. "'Obnoxious to Their Very Nature': Asian Americans and Constitutional Citizenship." *Citizenship Studies* 5: 57–71.

Waghorne, Joanne Punzo. 1999. "The Hindu Gods in a Split-Level World: The Sri Siva Vishnu Temple in Suburban Washington, D.C." In *Gods of the City,* edited by Robert A. Orsi, 103–130. Bloomington: Indiana University Press.

Warner, R. Stephen. 1998. "Immigration and Religious Communities in the United States." In *Gatherings in Diaspora: Religious Communities and the New Immigration,* edited by R. Stephen Warner and Judith G. Wittner, 3–34. Philadelphia: Temple University Press.

Washington, Jesse. 2010. "Record Number of Indian-Americans Seeking Office." *Yahoo*

News, June 19. http://www.washingtontimes.com/news/2010/jun/19/record-number -indian-americans-seeking-office (accessed February 1, 2011).

Waters, Mary C. 1990. *Ethnic Options: Choosing Identities in America.* Berkeley: University of California Press.

———. 1996. "Ethnic and Racial Identities of Second-Generation Black Immigrants in New York City." In *The New Second Generation*, edited by Alejandro Portes, 171–196. New York: Russell Sage Foundation.

———. 2008. "The Challenges of Studying Political and Civic Incorporation." *Applied Developmental Science* 21: 105–107.

Wenger, Étienne. 1998. *Communities of Practice: Learning, Meaning, and Identity.* Cambridge: Cambridge University Press.

———. 2006. Communities of Practice: A Brief Introduction. http://www.ewenger. com/theory (accessed October 20, 2010).

Werbner, Pnina. 1985. "The Organization of Giving and Ethnic Elites: Voluntary Associations Amongst Manchester Pakistanis." *Ethnic and Racial Studies* 8: 368–388.

Wiessnert, Polly, and Wulf Schiefenhovel. 1996. *Food and the Status Quest: An Interdisciplinary Perspective.* Oxford, UK: Bergahn Books.

Williams, Raymond B. 1988. *Religions of Immigrants from India and Pakistan: New Threads in the American Tapestry.* New York: Cambridge University Press.

Wolfinger, Raymond E. 1965. "The Development and Persistence of Ethnic Voting." *American Political Science Review* 59: 896–908.

Wong, Bernard. 1998. *Ethnicity and Entrepreneurs: The New Chinese Immigrants in the San Francisco Bay Area.* Boston: Allyn and Bacon.

Wong, Janelle. 2006. *Democracy's Promise: Immigrants and American Institutions.* Ann Arbor: University of Michigan Press.

Wong, Janelle, and Adrian D. Pantoja. 2009. "In Pursuit of Inclusion: Citizenship Acquisition Among Asian Immigrants." In *Bringing Outsiders In: Transatlantic Perspectives on Immigrant Incorporation*, edited by Jennifer Hochschild and John Mollenkopf, 260–276. Ithaca, NY: Cornell University Press.

Wood, Joseph. 1997. "Vietnamese American Place Making in Northern Virginia." *Geographical Review* 87: 58–72.

Yang, Mayfair Mei-hu. 1994. *Gifts, Favors and Banquets: The Art of Social Relationships in China.* Ithaca, NY: Cornell University Press.

Zelinsky, Wilbur, and Barrett A. Lee. 1998. "Heterolocalism: An Alternative Model of the Sociospatial Behaviour of Immigrant Ethnic Communities." *International Journal of Population Geography* 4: 1–18.

———. 2004. "Are Asian Americans Becoming 'White'?" *Contexts* 3: 29–51.

Zhou, Min, and Carl L. Bankston, III. 1994. "Social Capital and the Adaptation of the Second Generation: The Case of Vietnamese Youth in New Orleans." *International Migration Review* 28: 821–845.

———. 1998. *Growing Up American: How Vietnamese Children Adapt to Life in the United States*. New York: Russell Sage Foundation.

Zhou, Min, and Jennifer Lee. 2004. "Introduction: The Making of Culture, Identity, and Ethnicity Among Asian American Youth." In *Asian American Youth: Culture, Identity, and Ethnicity*, edited by Jennifer Lee and Min Zhou, 1–32. New York: Routledge.

Zukin, Fliff, Scott Keeter, Molly Andolina, Krista Jenkins, and Michael X. Delli Carpini. 2006. *A New Engagement? Political Participation, Civic Life, and the Changing American Citizen*. New York: Oxford University Press.

Index

Italic page numbers refer to material in illustrations.